1974   Bonnie Bianca

Dorothy M. Johnson

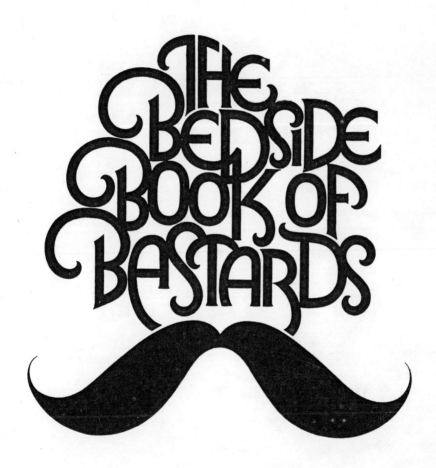

THE BEDSIDE BOOK OF BASTARDS

DOROTHY M. JOHNSON & R.T. TURNER

McGraw-Hill Book Company
New York   St. Louis   San Francisco
Düsseldorf   Mexico   Toronto

Designed by Elaine Gongora

123456789BPBP79876543

Library of Congress Cataloging in Publication Data
Johnson, Dorothy M
      The bedside book of bastards
      1.   Biography.   I. Turner, Robert Townley,
1917–1972, joint author.   II.   Title.
CT104.J64   920'.02   73-4615
ISBN 0-07-032585-5

We dedicate this book to
May

and to Lucius, Livius, and Polly, Nellie and Jerry, Ella and Jack, Fred and Van, Jo and Dorothy, Dick, Dixie, Billy and Bobby, Bill, Vicki, Kathy, and Karen, Gary, Betty Lou, and Terry, Jackie, Janet, and Johnny, Mike and R.T., Bill, Dale, Brian and Linda, Don, Betty, Sharon, Lois, and Leonard, George, Diane, and Fang, Bruce, Doug, Barry and Donna, Emma, Oscar and Barbara, Sande, Manny, Marcia, Felicia, Travis, Paul, and Maria, Joyce, Steve, Paula, Kenny, Jimmy, and Dawn, Jules, Joyce and Lewis, Walter and Jeanne, Betty and Les, Lois, Ken, Brian, and Randy, Don, Lucille, and Cuba, Wayne, Mark, Bob and Charlene, Bjarne, Rich, Keith and Judy, Scott, Jane, and Jamie, Sue, Lee, Royal, Aden, and Bob, Jim and Jane, Ellis and Phyllis, John and Maxine, Bob and Anne, Frank and Ann, Ross and Joan, Pete and Dorothy, Bob and Joyce, Roger, Tom, Bill and Rita, Vincent and Jean, Bud and Libba, Bunky and Elwood, Carle, Jerry and Mary Ann, Andrewa, Pat and Suzy, Rex and Trinda, Gary and Ann, Fran and Ed, Perry, Mary, and John, Thora, Ward, Agnes, Bob, Casey, Cathy, Kate, and Nan, Fergie, Gale, Larry and Edna, Don, Marguerite, Phil and Cynthia, Ron and Georgiana, Mary, Kirk, Torchy and Geoffrey, Al and Penny, Don and Karen, Gary and Diana, Dick, Kay, Clyde and Garnet, Mike and Joy, Elmo and Helen, Chuck and Lorretta, George and Lee, Warren and Genie, Alexandra, Ed and Lou, Bob and Dot, Todd and Kerry, Lillian, Jack and Frances, Charles and Julie, Oliver and Evelyn, Bob and Iz, Lucy, Johnnie and Virginia, Randi, Judy, Suzie and Andy, Stan and Sidne, Dorothy, Myron and Eleanor, Art and Mable, Verna and Bill, Doc and Gladys, John and Eleanore, Ray and Hannah, Fred and Dot, Doris and Bob, Marguerite and Albert, Bud and Carol, Steve, Grace and Cyrile, Ralph and Lillian, Carling and Arline, Laura, Jack and Mary, David and Frances, Rowena, Gordon and Maryann, Helen, Mel and Ruth, Becky, Frances, Stocky and Hope, Eva, Peter and Suzann, Bob and Virginia, Lloyd and Betty, Vi, Marion, Elizabeth, and Teena, none of whom (with the possible exception of some four-legged cats that are included) is a bastard.

Contents

Preface

What is a bastard? Technically, it's a person whose parents weren't married. But this kind of bastard can't help it. He's not responsible for what Mommy and Daddy did or didn't do. But there's another kind, defined in *The American Heritage Dictionary* as "an obnoxious or nasty person." That's the kind of bastards we're talking about—villains, murderers, plotters, stinkers, knaves, and assorted rascals.

History records the names and misdeeds of some perfectly awful people. The list, alas, is all too long. We present some of the worst of them, some famous and some obscure, chosen without malice toward race, color, creed, sex, or national origin. These were men and women of forceful personalities. They impressed their contemporaries and demolished a lot of them.

They are, we assume, sizzling in hell. The dead and damned guests at a dinner party cooked up by Sawney Beane, Liver-Eating Johnson, or a Borgia or two would have something to worry about.

There are lots of bastards in the Bible and in the twentieth century, but we decided to leave them out. The Bible bastards are too well known, or ought to be. And those who flourished in our lifetimes are too close to us to be even faintly funny.

In deference to Women's Liberation, we have included Parysatis, Fredegunda, Marozia, Nero's mother, and some other emancipated females. In their day they were the equals of any male. Given half a chance, women can be as bad as anybody.

We don't have a long list of people to thank. Those who helped us were mostly librarians and University of Montana faculty members. Our relatives weren't of much use; the sister of one of us fell asleep while reading a chapter in rough draft. She *said* she had taken a tranquilizer because the manuscript was so exciting. We are not ecstatically grateful to our typists. After all, we had to pay them. So there's really nobody but us without whom this book could not have been written.

D.M.J.
R.T.T.

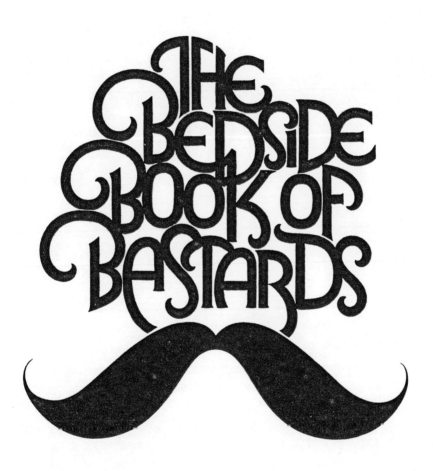

1
Parysatis

Fourth Century B.C.

Statira was a Persian queen with a problem: a really poisonous live-in mother-in-law right in the same palace.

This is a story of mother love. We don't know what Parysatis looked like or exactly when she was born or when she died. We do know she was living in Imperial Persia about 400 B.C. and was the mother of Artaxerxes II.

The Achaemenid family had been on the throne of Persia since the days of Cyrus the Great (who had died in 529 B.C.) and had twice tried and failed to conquer Greece. The sovereign was known as the Great King, or King of Kings, because he ruled such a large empire and had such an assortment of small-fry kings ruling under him.

Of royal lineage herself, Parysatis had lived through troubled times. Her father, Artaxerxes I, murdered his way to the throne. Her husband, Darius II, also murdered his way to the throne. He killed a rival, Terituchmes, then chopped his wife into little pieces and buried alive his mother and brothers and sisters. Parysatis was an apt pupil.

Her father, Artaxerxes I, is known as Longimanus, because his right hand was longer than his left. Her son, Artaxerxes II, was called Mnemon or the Mindful because he was thoughtful. What he thought of his mother we shall see.

Parysatis and Darius II had four sons, the oldest of whom was called Arsicas and became Artaxerxes II. He was a rather mild fellow and fairly gentle. His parents married him to a charming and lovely girl named Statira. Falling in love with her was one of the best things he ever did. Darius wanted to have her killed (because he didn't like her brother), so Arsicas went to his mother, Parysatis, groveled about at her feet, and persuaded her to talk to his father. Statira was saved. This untoward act of clemency Parysatis was to regret for years.

Parysatis didn't think much of her first-born, but she did love her second-born, a wild, headstrong youth named Cyrus. When Darius II lay dying, Parysatis sent out urgent messages to Cyrus to hurry back to the palace and become the next king. Cyrus was not quite quick enough. Arsicas got the job and changed his name to Artaxerxes II. His mother at once talked him into reappointing Cyrus as satrap, or governor, of Lydia— way off in Asia Minor. This was a mistake, as Artaxerxes soon found out.

Artaxerxes went to Persepolis, one of the Persian capitals, to be crowned. Cyrus returned for the occasion and made an attempt to kill Artaxerxes and take over the empire. He was arrested and trussed up like a chicken. As he was about to be beheaded, Parysatis threw herself on her son's body, pressed her neck against his, and entwined her long hair about him.

It was quite a scene, and Artaxerxes the Thoughtful was at a loss as to what to do. He just gave up, pardoned his brother, and sent him back to govern Lydia. He believed all his mother's pledges about Cyrus's future good conduct.

Cyrus behaved himself for a few months but finally decided to chance everything on armed rebellion. He gathered together his own army, including Xenophon and his ten thousand Greek mercenaries, and marched against his brother.

In the palace, there was a great to-do, and Statira went around saying nasty things about her mother-in-law. Parysatis decided that something would have to be done about her son's wife.

Meanwhile Artaxerxes bestirred himself, called out the Persian army, and headed for his brother. They met near Cunaxa in 401 B.C. Cyrus very nearly won, but somehow got killed in the mêlée, either by a blow from Artaxerxes (which was unlikely), or a bash on the head from a soldier named Mithradates, or from a cut on the behind from a Carian foot soldier.

The result was a dead Cyrus. As was the practice of the day, one of Artaxerxes' eunuchs, Masabates, cut off Cyrus' head and right hand and ceremoniously presented them to the Great King.

Artaxerxes was vastly pleased that he had won, but Parysatis was heart-broken and mad. She made up a list of those she would get even with: the Carian who had stabbed her beloved Cyrus in the behind, Mithradates who had wounded Cyrus in the head, Masabates who had cut off his hand, and—and then there was her demure daughter-in-law, Statira.

Number one on her list was the Carian soldier. Artaxerxes, believing himself to be his brother's slayer, was nevertheless generous to those who had helped him. He heaped wealth on the Carian foot soldier, a rather stupid man who loudly protested that he and he alone had killed Cyrus.

When this came to Artaxerxes' ears, he was furious and made it clear that he and no one else was to get credit for killing his brother. He ordered the Carian beheaded on the spot. Parysatis, pleased with this development, pleaded for the privilege of disposing of the luckless Carian herself. Parysatis had the Carian put on the rack for ten days and cruelly tortured. She then had his eyes gouged out, and finally had molten brass poured, drop by drop, into his ears until he died.

Next on the list was Mithradates. We don't know whether he saw what happened to the Carian, but it is likely that he did. Anyway, although richly rewarded by Artaxerxes for capturing Cyrus' horse and blood-stained saddle, Mithradates kept his mouth shut—at least for a while. One night at a palace banquet, however, Parysatis told her chief eunuch, a scoundrel named Sparamizes, to keep an eye on Mithradates, who was getting drunker by the minute. (All the Persians were great drinkers and believed that decisions made under the influence of wine were the wisest of all.) Mithradates soon began to blab about how he was the one who had killed Cyrus. Sparamizes listened carefully, noted the witnesses, and then went to Parysatis, who reported it all verbatim to Artaxerxes.

It was very annoying to Artaxerxes that people kept popping up who claimed that they, and not he, had slain his brother. Egging him on, Parysatis suggested to her son that Mithradates be put to death "by the boats." He agreed, and the now-sober Mithradates endured what surely must be one of the ghastliest tortures ever devised.

First of all, a shallow boat was made to fit Mithradates' body. He was put in it on his back. Then another boat, the same size, was laid on top so that only his head, feet, and hands stuck out. He was forced to eat as much as he could, and when he refused his eyes were pricked with needles. He was also made to drink a great amount of milk and honey. What was left over was smeared on his face, which was always kept facing the bright sun. A swarm of flies descended on his face and completely covered it. As time went on, Mithradates was forced to empty his bladder and bowels, and the mass of excretion attracted all sorts of loathsome things. His flesh was eaten away. Parysatis was delighted that it took Mithradates a full seventeen days to die.

With the Carian and Mithradates crossed off her list, the eunuch Masabates was the only one left who had a direct part in the death of Cyrus. Despite some grumbling on his part, Artaxerxes was once again reconciled to his mother and honored her, as in the past, with a seat at his table. Masabates was too clever to be trapped into any damaging word or action, so Parysatis had to rack her brains as to how to dispense with him.

She finally thought of a way. Fond of dice and gambling, she loved to play with Artaxerxes, if only because it kept him busy and away from the hated Statira. One day, she came across the Great King, who had nothing to do at the time, and suggested rolling the dice. Guilelessly she lost heavily.

When she had no more loose change on her, she suggested that she and her son play for different stakes. Each would stake a eunuch on the throw of the dice. Artaxerxes said he would play if she allowed him to except his five favorite eunuchs. Since Masabates was not among these, Parysatis agreed. They rolled the dice. Parysatis won, of course, and naturally selected Masabates as her trophy.

Artaxerxes was sorry to lose him but apparently had no idea of his mother's little schemes. It soon became all too apparent. Poor Masabates was skinned alive. His skinless body was then strapped slantwise on three stakes and his skin on another.

Having thought that Parysatis would merely give Masabates some menial job in her household, Artaxerxes was outraged when he heard about it. He ranted and raved, but his mother put him in his place by calling him a poor sport—and also one who had no sense of humor. As usual, Artaxerxes caved in, and Parysatis crossed Number Three off her list.

Statira didn't like her mother-in-law and was constantly nagging her husband about how she was ruining his reputation and interfering in running the palace, she suggested that Artaxerxes was too much a mamma's boy. Parysatis, who hadn't forgotten Statira's nasty remarks at the time of Cyrus' rebellion, now determined to settle affairs once and for all with her daughter-in-law.

By this time, both Parysatis and Statira had called a truce, at least on the surface. They even began to eat together, although each was careful to watch what the other did. With her code of morals, Parysatis was afraid of being poisoned by Statira, even though Statira didn't seem to be the type to go around poisoning people. Parysatis was. All that had to be done was to find some way to slip the poison into Statira's food.

Parysatis engaged the services of one of her trusted maids, a young girl named Gigis. She told Gigis that the rhyntaces would be the perfect instrument to eliminate Statira. The rhyntaces was a little bird that was said to feed off nothing but air and dew and thus had no excrement. It was a tasty delicacy. One night at dinner, Parysatis with great ceremony and charm served such a bird. She carefully took a knife, cut the bird in two, and popped one half into her mouth. Statira, thinking that the bird couldn't be poisoned, ate her half. What she didn't know was that the knife Parysatis used was poisoned—on one side only.

It wasn't long before Statira began groaning in agony. She immediately suspected Parysatis and told the grief-stricken Artaxerxes of her suspicions. Soon, suffering great convulsions, she died. Artaxerxes put most of his mother's household to the torture and finally got his hands on Gigis. For appearance's sake, she was named poisoner and suffered the fate decreed by the law for such a crime: her head was placed on a broad stone and with another was beaten to pulp.

Just this once, Parysatis didn't escape scot-free. Artaxerxes was very annoyed with his mother and exiled her to Babylon, which, he announced, he would never visit while she was alive.

Before long, Parysatis had wormed her way back into her son's favor and affection. He recalled her to his palace, where he installed her as one of his chief advisers and again treated her with great honor and respect. He even took her advice to marry his own daughter, Atossa, after whom he lusted. Parysatis thought it was an excellent match. It shocked the Greeks who heard about it, but to the Persians it was an old custom.

And so, after all her vicious crimes and perfidy, the old lady was restored to favor and lived happily until her death.

2
Shih Huang-Ti

Ca. 259–210 B.C.

Are you fed up with loud-mouthed
professors? So was Shih Huang-Ti.
He silenced a gaggle of scholars by
burying them alive.

Any ruler who goes around burning books and burying scholars alive is not apt to be popular with the literary crowd. And so it has been for over two millennia with China's great unifier and first emperor—Ch'in Shih Huang-ti. China's Confucian scholars have always hated Shih, although some Western historians list him among history's greats. In a sense, both are right. Shih was as outstanding in his villainies as he was in his achievements.

At Shih's birth in 259 B.C., China was a mess—nothing but scads of small, independent, and constantly warring states. What was needed was a strong-minded, dictatorial, brutal, and consequences-be-damned leader who could unify the country. The Mandate of Heaven fell on Cheng, a boy of twelve, probably a bastard son of the ruler of Ch'in.

One of China's smaller states, Ch'in was located where the present-day provinces of Kansu and Shensi are. Its neighbors considered it uncultured, crude, and dangerous. Even worse was Ch'in's penchant for making war a national sport—and a grim one at that. The other Chinese states conducted war in a civilized fashion, their soldiers obeying a complicated and rigorous code of knightly conduct on the battlefield. But not the soldiers of Ch'in. War was too serious to abide by the rules. And so they invented a kind of total war all their own. They prized efficiency and slaughter above all.

Ch'in officers held their commands by virtue of how well they killed. Promotions and pay depended on the number of heads the soldiers brought to their commanders at the end of the battle. It was fun to kill, of course, but the real thing about war was to win. Often in captured towns every man, woman, and child was slaughtered, and every now and then—in action that seemed strangely near to cannibalism—the bodies were tossed into a boiling cauldron. The victors would then drink this "human soup." Occasionally, any relatives of the victims left alive would have to drink too.

It was into this milieu of ruthless barbarism that young Cheng was born. He was an apt pupil and learned quickly. He ascended his father's throne at the age of twelve or thirteen and within a short time became master of Ch'in in fact as well as in name. Without so much as a murmur or a backward look, he set out to conquer everybody in sight. As one contemporary remarked, he "ate up his neighbors as a silkworm devours a leaf." Today, this would be termed a "great leap forward."

It is not clear from contemporary records whether the brilliance of strategy and tactics were Cheng's alone. We do know he was lucky in having a number of gifted generals under him. It took Cheng twenty years and a frightful cost in human life to achieve unification of the huge China land mass—the figure has been placed at 1,200,000 to 1,500,000 killed.

In the process, he managed to make his capital, Hsien Yang, the center of China's political, economic, and cultural life. As soon as he conquered another state, he deported any of its nobles left alive back to Hsien Yang. He also built in Hsien Yang a palace for every state conquered, so things got a bit crowded after a while.

By 221 B.C., Cheng had conquered China. His first act was to order all his victims' weapons melted down and fashioned into bells and twelve huge statues of himself, each weighing about twenty tons, which, in typical modesty, he placed in front of his royal palace in Hsien Yang. Then he took a new name. He called all his advisers to a big council and said: "Behold my Empire. What name shall the sovereign of such a land bear?" After numerous fanciful names had been advanced, Cheng decided on Huang-Ti or Great Emperor. "I will be called Shih Huang-Ti," the "First Great Emperor," he said. His son and successor was to be Great Emperor Number Two, and his grandson Great Emperor Number Three—and so on for 10,000 generations.

He was being too optimistic. The Ch'in dynasty (from which comes the word China) lasted just fifteen years and two generations—from 221 to 207 B.C.

In any event, China was now a united country for probably the first time in its history, and the new First Great Emperor was not one to hide his merits under a basket. All over the new empire he erected stelae to commemorate his rule. One reads: "For the first time, he has united the world."* On another we read:

> The inner ramparts have been cast down and destroyed. He has regulated and made equal the laws, measures, and standards for all men. . . . He has quelled the battles. . . . The black-haired people [the Chinese] enjoy calm and repose; arms are no longer necessary and each is tranquil in his dwelling. The Sovereign Emperor has pacified in turn the four ends of the earth.*

What manner of man was the new Shih Huang-Ti? Only one description (by one of his court officials) has come down to us. Shih was "a man with a very prominent nose, with large eyes, with the chest of a bird of prey, with the voice of a jackal, with beneficence, and with the heart of a tiger or a wolf."* Not an altogether flattering portrait.

But as great as his villainies were, Shih was not without virtue. Although he administered the empire with a heavy hand, he was tireless in his efficiency—he is said to have handled 120 pounds of reports every day. (And in Chinese, yet.) He also traveled constantly, possibly because of his pathological fear of assassination, but he kept a stern eye on his officials no matter where they were and he was. Everybody got to know personally who was boss.

He was as competent and avid an administrator as Napoleon. He standardized weights and measures, wagon wheels, and agricultural implements. Everywhere he built "royal roads," also called the "straight" or "racing" roads, so that "all the scenery of the rivers, the lakes, and the sea might unroll before his eyes." These roads were 250 feet broad and lined with shade trees.

* Quotations are from *The Tiger of Ch'in*, by Leonard Cottrell, used by permission of the publisher, Holt, Rinehart and Winston.

His mania to standardize things extended to the language itself, and Shih is credited with a system of writing on which modern Chinese script is based.

Shih tried to tame nature as he tamed the Chinese. He didn't always succeed, although he should have an "A" for effort. Once, while ascending a mountain, his progress was blocked by a strong wind. Enraged, he ordered 3000 slaves to cut down all the trees on the mountain and then paint it red—the color worn by criminals. What effect this had on the wind is not recorded.

The Great Emperor also interested himself in reorganizing the penal code. He made the punishment fit the crime. It was not a gentle code, but nobody ever accused Shih of being a gentle man. Some of the lesser punishments involved flogging, three years of hard labor cutting wood, branding, forced labor (on the Great Wall), enslavement, confiscation of all property, and deportation.

The harsher punishments show considerable ingenuity. A man condemned might be beheaded or cut in two at the waist or torn apart by chariots, or buried alive, or branded on the top of the head. Other serious crimes elicited the following: extracting ribs, boiling in a cauldron, decapitation (followed by impaling the head in a public place), extermination of a culprit's family to the third degree (that is, his parents, brothers and sisters, wife, and children), and the "five punishments." This variation involved branding on the forehead, cutting off the nose, severing the feet, death by flogging, and finally exposure of the corpse in the marketplace. (Grocery shopping must not have been much fun.)

Shih was a megalomaniac. He enjoyed doing things in the grand manner. He became the "Son of Heaven." He built 270 palaces for himself, on one of which he used 700,000 convicts for slave labor. And then he started on the Great Wall of China.

Various rulers before Shih had built bits and pieces of defensive wall on the barbarian frontier to the north. It took Shih about twelve years and maybe a million workers to join these sections together. Enlarged and completed, the Great Wall stretched for 2240 miles. When finished, it was about twenty-four feet high and wide enough for eight men to walk abreast. Every 100 to 500 yards was a watchtower forty feet high. Less frequently there were garrison towers capable of housing 100 to 200 soldiers. The Wall is considered one of the world's wonders.

Compared with it, as Voltaire said, "the pyramids of Egypt are only puerile and useless masses."

Probably 400,000 men and women died in the Wall's construction. Dead bodies were dumped into the rising Wall. The sick and injured were often buried alive. Even Shih seems to have been a bit taken aback at the human cost. Once a magician told him that the wall would never be finished until 10,000 bodies had been buried in it. This was a waste of good slaves, so Shih hunted around the empire until he found a man whose name included a reference to 10,000. Then he had the poor guy buried in the wall.

Shih was always consulting his sorcerers. Many of his superstitions related to death—of which Shih was pathologically afraid. Someone told him about "The Three Islands" that lay in the sea just over the horizon. There spirits drank from "the sweet-wine fountain of jade" and became immortal. Shih sent out an expedition under a rascal named Hsu Shih to find this elixir of life. Hsu Shih soon returned with empty hands but with the advice that a second expedition made up of "youths and maidens of good family" be sent out. Shih so ordered, but nothing was ever heard of them again.

Some of Shih's fear of death undoubtedly stemmed from the fact that people were always trying to kill him. After the first attempt, a chronicler noted that Shih "was not at ease for a long time." Other tries were made, and Shih never quite adjusted. He took to sleeping in a different room or palace every night.

After discovering one serious attempt to depose and kill him, he had everyone even remotely connected with the plot (from slaves on up) killed, exiled 4000 families just for the hell of it, and sent his mother away from court. He set a great cauldron of boiling water in the throne room and tossed into it people he didn't like. And he took to sitting on the throne with a naked sword on his lap as a hint to loose-tongued petitioners and advisers.

It took some time for him to get across that he meant business. He executed twenty-seven of his advisers before the word got around that the Great Emperor meant what he said. One incident, though, shows Shih in a different light. After Adviser Number Twenty-seven had been boiled alive, an elderly minister asked permission to speak to Shih. "Sure," said the Emperor, "go ahead." The minister was a brave man. He said something like this: "Your Majesty has a violent disposition. You banished your mother, and you don't listen to anybody's advice. This kind of thing can't be covered up, word will spread all over the country, and nobody will have much respect for you. I'm worried about you and your dynasty."

He then bowed to Shih, took off his robe, and walked over to the boiling vat expectantly. Surprisingly, Shih pardoned the man's insolence and asked him to be an adviser.

Of all Shih's misdeeds none has horrified Chinese intellectuals more than his burying of the scholars and the burning of the books. Fed up with Shih's cruelties, a number of eggheads at his court said and wrote some very nasty things about him and then took off for places unknown. Shih was fit to be tied. He set up a kangaroo court with himself as prosecutor and judge and summoned all the remaining literati. Everyone started blaming someone else until Shih was completely confused. Faced with this Gordian knot and showing a fine sense of justice, he declared all 460 guilty and had them buried alive. Shih has been a favorite whipping-boy of Chinese scholars ever since.

The background of the burning of the books is a little more complicated. On philosophical grounds, Shih hated the Confucians. Conversely they didn't like his authoritarian methods, they preferred the diversity of feudal rule, and they were always nagging Shih to do something he didn't want to do—like observing some obsolete rite. Tension built up over a number of years until Li Ssu, Shih's chief adviser, suggested the burning of all Confucian writings. The Great Emperor thought this was a dandy idea. Besides, if Chinese writings were to begin with Shih, it was obvious that history itself should begin with Shih.

Printing had not yet been discovered, and the Chinese books of Shih's time were made of rolls of bamboo. They were large, hard to hide, and heavy to lug around. Under Shih's decree, one copy of each book was to be kept in China's State Library. Certain types of technical works were exempted, but almost everything else was fed to the flames. The special targets were histories (of other than the Ch'in empire), poetry, and philosophical works. All over China, flames told the dismal story.

Actually, not all the books were burned. Many were hidden, although their owners (if caught) were hideously executed. Some Confucian scholars memorized the Master's teachings and saved them in that way. Unhappily, the single copies of each book saved in the State Library were destroyed in the fighting that overthrew the Ch'in Dynasty. In any event, the scholarly world for over twenty-two centuries has hated Shih. Their verdict was: "Fen shu k'en ju." ("He burned the books and he buried the scholars.")

Finally the time came for Shih Huang-Ti to die. He was only fifty years old. He had twenty sons from whom he might pick his successor. He caused his oldest and ablest son, Fu Su, to commit suicide and with uncharacteristic ineptitude picked his worst son to succeed him. Shih's dynasty, which he expected to last for 10,000 generations, lasted barely another ten years.

3
Lucius Cornelius Sulla

138–78 B.C.

*Bothered by the radical right? Read
about a real reactionary who was dictator of Rome.*

Wars between strangers are bad
enough, but civil wars are worse.
People hate more deeply, kill their neighbors and even their relatives with more zest, fight more cruelly, and generally sink to a
greater depth of savagery. And so it was with the first civil war
in Roman history.

It all started over politics. Some people (the Populares)
wanted change and some (the Optimates) didn't. The struggle
began when Lucius Cornelius Sulla was a boy. In 133 B.C. a
couple of brothers, Tiberius Sempronius Gracchus and Gaius
Sempronius Gracchus (known as the Gracchi), helped enact an
agrarian law limiting the size of citizens' landholdings. The great
patricians, or nobles, didn't like this and killed Tiberius and 300
of his followers. Some years later, Gaius advocated even more
radical plans for fair prices for grain, extending the suffrage and
limiting the powers of the Senate. The Senators didn't care for
these ideas. They put their bully-boys onto Gaius and killed him
(121 B.C.) when Sulla was seventeen.

This was bad enough, but when an old roughneck soldier
named Gaius Marius (he was the only Roman around not to
have three names) put himself at the head of the Populares,
things went from bad to worse. Lots of people were killed (the
good, the evil, and the innocent—depending on your politics).
One faction replaced another in control. All this indiscriminate
killing, though, finally led to more formalized warfare, with old
Marius heading the Populares and young Sulla the Optimates.
Although both were cruel, brutal, vengeful, blood-soaked psycho-

paths, there was something special about Sulla that continues to fascinate people to our own day.

By birth, Sulla was a patrician. It was a good beginning, but his family was poor and undistinguished, and poverty was no handmaiden of success in Roman politics. It took money, then as now, to buy votes. So Sulla entered the army to seek fame and fortune. Even as a youth, he was known as something of a fop, with tastes beyond his pocketbook, a young man of careless morals and questionable friends. When he died at sixty, he had come a long way, financially speaking. He was the richest man in Rome.

Of medium height and muscular build, Sulla had some impressive physical traits: his eyes, his hair, and his complexion. Everybody noted his blue eyes. They were bright, icy, and glaring, and he had an unnerving habit of staring at people without expression. His hair was golden.

Once, during an intermission in the political struggle, when he had left Rome on a campaign, the earth opened up to gush fire. This shook a lot of people, but soothsayers (Sulla always kept two or three around) said that it meant a man of great quality and "singular aspect" would take over the government. Sulla confided to his followers that he was that person.

As he grew older, his complexion began to attract a lot of attention, mostly unfavorable. He loved rich foods and couldn't leave the wine alone. His skin became white and blotchy, so much so that when he was besieging Athens in 86 B.C., a wit inside the city shouted from the walls that Sulla was "a mulberry sprinkled o'er with meal." It was not the sort of remark that endeared the Athenians to Sulla.

Once in the army, Sulla rose rapidly. Never did he allow anyone to outshine him in bravery, and he had that quality possessed by really first-rate generals of knowing how and when to appeal to both the base and the exalted in men. His soldiers worshiped him, and he never lost a battle. Although he attributed this partly to fortune (he called himself Sulla the Lucky), he was understandably proud of his achievements. He bored a lot of people by bragging about his battlefield success, but most of the time they were careful not to show it. For Sulla didn't have much of a sense of humor.

With Sulla, fortune was perhaps more important to success than merit. He saw many an able man ruined by bad luck, and indeed he did his share of ruin. The difference was fortune's smile. Although he wasn't very religious, he was always careful to observe the mumbo-jumbo of public prayers and sacrifices to the gods, more or less as window-dressing. As a public figure, he wanted to show everybody that he indeed followed the old conservative ways.

His favorite goddess was Fortuna, and he looked for her favor, as was the custom in his day, in all natural phenomena and in the entrails of chickens, birds, sheep, goats, cattle, and any other animals handy. Soothsayers interpreted these signs for him. He had his share of Roman "Chicken Littles" who foretold the worst, but these he reinterpreted to suit himself. Once, while campaigning in Greece and in need of money, he sent an emissary to the great shrine of Apollo at Delphi. He ordered the agent to confiscate the god's treasure, one of the wealthiest in Greece. Back came the poor man, however, with a cock-and-bull story that the signs were all wrong, that he had heard eerie lute music coming from the sanctuary. Pooh, said Sulla, that meant that the god wanted him to take the money. Besides, he was only borrowing it.

Everyone warned him of the god's wrath. But Lucky Lucius got away with it. Just to be sure, he sacked the city of Thebes some fifty miles away to repay Apollo's "loan." This piece of luck so pleased him that he adopted the name Epaphroditus—Greek for fortune. Sulla Epaphroditus! It sounded odd to Roman ears, a bit too foreign for this man who paraded as the noblest Roman of them all.

A soldier's life was fine, but Sulla was never one to turn down the sportin' life. His penchant for associating with "low companions" (actors, mimes, singers, and the like—this was long before stage people were accepted into the better homes) shocked those who knew about it. For Sulla was a hypocrite. The good life for him was no moral edifice built on sound ethical principles but an earthly one consisting of food, drink, bed, and power. And he enjoyed that life to the full. For others, of course, he preached (and killed many to prove his point) a return to the austere morals of early Rome's republican greats. The anomaly of it amused him, but politics is politics. He also had numerous love affairs and five wives, some of whom he loved.

His sense of humor was something else. He enjoyed the irony of being a profligate preaching virtue, a dictator ruling an oligarchy, and a skeptic forcing others to believe in the eternal gods. Once during the civil war, a slave betrayed to Sulla's vengeance his own master, Sulpicius by name, and Sulla killed Sulpicius. He rewarded the slave with freedom but then had the poor guy thrown from the Tarpeian Rock—a steep cliff in Rome from which criminals were tossed to their deaths.

Sulla never ceased to amaze people—even as he terrified them. In public he was cold, austere, merciless, and brutal, the epitome of the "wrinkled lip and sneer of cold command." But at the table, surrounded by low companions, he was the indulgent host; he laughed, jested, was easy-going and obliging, a real fun companion. He had a split personality, and the trick was to get him in the right mood.

Some people said he was half lion and half fox, but more dangerous as the latter. That wasn't quite true. With Sulla it was always mind over matter. Neither pity nor remorse touched him. He was a dispassionate butcher, methodical and systematic. He didn't care, even on those surprising occasions when he was merciful. He was the ultimate realist. He could forgive, but never with understanding as Caesar was to do. But then, unlike Caesar, Sulla died in his bed.

His coldness, his indifference, his horrible urbanity scared most people—the ones he left alive. But even here he was unpredictable. He was like a lion who licked his victim instead of chewing him. He once ordered young Julius Caesar (the odious Marius's nephew by marriage and obviously marked for death) to divorce his wife. Caesar surprised everybody by refusing. Sulla did nothing. Even so, Caesar thought it prudent to go into hiding.

This amazing man was no uneducated warhorse like Marius. He could speak Greek. He read literature, including poetry. He was even an author, writing twenty-two volumes of his *Memoirs* in good, sturdy Latin. He was also fond of art, and built one of the world's finest collections, almost all of it liberated from its legitimate owners in the course of the civil war, his campaigns in Greece and Asia, and his terrible proscriptions. He took time to bring Aristotle's works to Rome, among other things, after his sack of Athens.

As a young army officer, Sulla had been posted to North Africa where Marius was waging a war against Jugurtha, a local king who for years had been a real thorn in the flesh to Rome. In later years, Sulla was to appreciate the irony of having made

his debut as one of Marius's lieutenants. As chance would have
it, Sulla had been in the right place at the right time to receive,
personally, Jugurtha's surrender when he was betrayed into Roman hands. Actually, Sulla had little to do with it, but he took
most of the credit. Marius had been mad as hell, and from this
sprang the savage jealousy of the old Popular leader for the
young aristocrat.

The next few years found the two rivals winning magnificent
victories against Rome's foreign enemies as various barbarian
tribes kept invading Roman lands in northern Italy and southern
France. Finally it was safe enough for the Populares and Optimates to get down to the real business of killing each other.

The first round went to Marius. In success, the vengeful old
man had no plan except indiscriminate slaughter. In five days of
butchery, he smashed the Optimates in Rome, placed the heads
of distinguished political rivals in the forum, and ordered that
bodies lying in the streets be left there as dog food. Now, indeed, were the murders of the Gracchi avenged in full.

Round two went to the Optimates. Marius fled from Rome,
and the Senate re-established the old order—but on shaky foundations. Sulla didn't stay long enough to insure a complete destruction of the Populares. He induced the Senate to entrust him
with command of the armies being raised for an expedition to
Asia Minor where Mithridates of Pontus had ended Roman rule.
Sulla knew that victory in foreign wars (and he had no doubt
of his ability to crush the upstart Mithridates) was one way of
getting into Roman history books. And, as he well knew, there
was plenty of good gold lying around in the East. So off he went.

Sulla had little difficulty in defeating the Asiatic hordes under
Mithridates' command, but the campaign took longer than he
had expected. Meanwhile back in Rome, Marius told everybody
that any idiot could beat Mithridates. As the Optimates had
feared, with Sulla off in Asia, Marius reoccupied Rome and won
round three. Marius indulged in another orgy of murder and
looting, killing all those Sullan followers unlucky enough to fall
into his hands. He subsequently got the Senate to declare Sulla
a traitor and an outlaw, deprive him of his command, and confiscate all his wealth.

The Populares-controlled Senate sent one of its generals to
Asia to take Sulla's command away from him, but Lucky Lucius
had no trouble winning over the poor man's troops, and that was

the end of that. Sulla was still an outlaw in Roman law, but there were ways of changing that.

Of all his victories in the East, Sulla's siege, capture, and sack of Athens attracted the most attention. The famous city had capitalized on Mithridates' war to revolt against Roman control and join the enemy. It proved a tough nut for Sulla to crack.

When Sparta had beaten Athens back in the Peloponnesian War (431–404 B.C.), it had refrained from sacking the city out of deference to its high cultural reputation. Sulla disdained such nonsense. Athens had defied him, and it must pay. Why he exacted such a terrible accounting was not clear. Athenians were great blabbermouths, it was true, and some had gone so far as to shout obscenities from the walls about Sulla's current wife. Then, too, there was a little matter of his complexion being likened to flour and mulberry juice. And some had too loudly questioned Sulla's parentage. But historians have perhaps paid too little attention to another significant factor—the gout. This dread affliction visited Sulla during the siege and undoubtedly affected his famed equanimity and indifference.

In any event, Sulla gave Athens to his soldiers. Slaughter, rape, burning, and pillage were the order of the day. Finally, gagged by the blood-letting, some of his companions besought Sulla to stop. With a great show of magnanimity, he agreed. "I forgive the many," he said, "for the sake of the few." Actually, he couldn't have cared less. He had proved his point.

Sulla undoubtedly could have finished off Mithridates. But affairs back home were in a mess, and the Senate's proclamation of him as an outlaw rankled. The news that old Marius had died cheered him, but he was still anxious to get home and set things right. So he abruptly concluded a truce with Mithridates, tore from the old bandit all his winnings, and exacted a penalty of 20,000 talents (a sum in the millions today).

In 83 B.C., he headed for Rome, to be the first Roman in history to capture the Eternal City with a Roman army. He landed in southern Italy and observed the amenities by sacrificing to the gods. The omens were great. The liver of one animal revealed a crown of laurel with two fillets hanging from it. In a nearby field, two stately goats were seen fighting. Just to be sure, though, Sulla kissed a small golden image of Apollo (it had been a "gift" from Delphi) and asked the god to grace with victory the arms of "the fortunate Cornelius Sulla."

Sweeping all before him, he entered the capital undisputed master of the Roman world. He had 120,000 Roman veterans at his back. He destroyed the Popular forces, now led by Marius's young son (also called Marius), who was slain. Aides brought the latter's head to a contemptuous Sulla, who quoted Aristophanes: "You should have worked at the oar before trying to handle the helm." For good measure, he had the bones of old Marius dug up and tossed in the river. All Popular leaders within reach were murdered. In 82 B.C. the Senate (now Optimate) proclaimed Sulla the first Roman dictator in 120 years. A dictator's term was supposed to last for two years only; Sulla took the job for life.

At first the slaughter was haphazard, although Sulla was determined that his victory in what was now round four would be final. If he had his way, nobody—and he meant nobody—likely to restore the Popular party was to be left alive. (He was rather lax in letting young Caius Julius Caesar live, but how was he to know?) So day after day he marked men for death, confiscating their property and giving it to friends. He was nothing if not permissive. He indulged his companions' whims by having their enemies slain, too.

He had Rome—and the provinces—in a grip of an all-pervasive terror. No one knew who would be next. The lives and fortunes of literally all Romans were in the hands of this merciless and capricious tyrant. Some of his friends finally came to Sulla and screwed up their courage (it was no light thing to question the dictator's actions) to ask when he would end all this. Presumably, Sulla glared at them with his famous blue-eyed stare, but they hastened to tell him that they wouldn't think of asking him to pardon anybody he had decided to kill. But couldn't he just reassure those to be spared? No, said Sulla, that wasn't practicable because he didn't know yet whom he would slay and whom he would spare. Well, then, how about making public the names of the doomed? Sulla latched on to that. What a great idea! Thus began the great Sullan proscriptions.

Every day a roster of names was posted in the Forum. They were history's original S-lists. Sulla couldn't, or wouldn't, make one list and be done with it, so his friends' errand of mercy really hadn't helped. On the first day, Sulla listed eighty names and then took off a day to think things over. Sulla proclaimed these eighty as traitors and outlaws, put a price on their heads, confiscated their property, and attainted their sons and their sons' sons: they were proscribed. Anyone could legally kill them and collect the reward and, maybe, depending on Sulla's mood, get the property as well. Anyone succoring the proscribed was in turn proscribed. You got more for killing the VIPs than for the smaller fry. Marius's murders had been bad enough, but this systematic slaughter horrified people more by its cold-bloodedness.

List Number 2 contained 250 names, as did list Number 3. When would it end? Sulla finally decided that the proscriptions would last for six months, from December 1, 83 B.C., to July 1, 82 B.C., although he wouldn't hold too strictly to these limits. So the proscriptions continued, but now political affiliations took a back seat. Wealthy people were specially vulnerable, and one poor old Senator who found himself listed moaned: "Woe is me, my Alban farm has informed against me."

As the slaughter went on—and it is probable that 4700 noble Romans died as outlaws—Sulla turned to other problems. Indifferent as usual to bloodshed, pain, horror, and violence, he addressed himself to his triumph. He put on quite a show, appearing in a splendid cavalcade celebrating his eastern victories. He asked the Senate—and it was happy to oblige—to confer upon him the title "Felix," the Happy.

Lucky Lucius *was* happy. He had only one thing left to do. That was to rewrite the constitution and insure for all time the rule of the Optimates and the Senate. Sulla would—he thought—forever safeguard Rome against a revival of the Populares. But within ten years of his death the Sullan constitution was a scrap of paper. A few of his legal reforms remained, the rest were gone. And yet history tells us funny things. Maybe Sulla the dictator paved the way for Caesar, Augustus, Nero, and others to come.

And now Sulla did something that no tyrant had ever done before. He resigned. Even in our own time, history doesn't record many examples of dictators who have voluntarily given up supreme power to enjoy a peaceful old age. For one thing, it's dangerous. It gives enemies a chance for revenge. But Sulla didn't have any such trouble. The reason is not clear, but it's probable that none of his enemies was alive to trouble his twilight years. Why he resigned isn't clear either. It may have been that his life work was done. Maybe he was in ill health, as some said. It's probable that he was just bored.

In any event, Sulla now aged fifty-nine, became a private citizen. He appeared in the Forum without guards. He went hunting and fishing. He worked on his *Memoirs*, finishing volume twenty-two only two days before he died. He lived it up with wine, food, and women. Lucky Lucius was happy.

But by burning the candle day and night, he developed ulcerated bowels and soon "the corrupted flesh broke out into lice," as the old accounts would have us believe. In the midst of all this, servants brought him word that a neighbor was guilty of not having paid a public debt. Outraged, Sulla sent for the miscreant and had him strangled on the spot. Although a private citizen, Sulla couldn't entirely forget his past.

He died in 78 B.C. in his bed, a feat none of his enemies had managed to achieve. His body was cremated, after the Roman fashion, on a cloudy, disagreeable day. But the rain held off until Sulla was ashes. As some remarked, he was lucky to the last. Even the weather favored him.

Rome erected a monument to his memory, on which appeared the epitaph he himself had written: "No friend ever served me, and no enemy ever wronged me, whom I have not repaid in full."

4
Mithridates the Great

132–63 B.C.

*Faith in your fellow man may not pro-
vide protection when there are poisoners
around. Here's a case where suspicion
led to longevity.*

There was a king reigned in the East:
There, when kings will sit to feast,
They get their fill before they think
With poisoned meat and poisoned drink.
He gathered all that springs to birth
From the many-venomed earth;
First a little, thence to more,
He sampled all her killing store;
And easy, smiling, seasoned sound,
Sate the king when healths went round.
They put arsenic in his meat
And stared aghast to watch him eat;
They poured strychnine in his cup
And shook to see him drink it up:
They shook, they stared as white's their shirt:
Them it was their poison hurt.
—I tell the tale that I heard told.
Mithridates, he died old.

A. E. Housman, from *A Shropshire Lad*

He lived to be almost seventy. His
name was Mithridates. And every
day of his life, from the time he began to suspect something
was wrong, he took both antidote and poison, a little of each. He
took poison the way lesser people take aspirin.

It was when he reached puberty, or thereabouts, that strange
things started happening. Mithridates began to notice odd flavors

in his food. A groom would "inadvertently" saddle a wild horse for him to ride. While out hunting, stray arrows whizzed about his head. It was unnerving. From family table talk, he had heard of odd things, like mothers killing their sons. When his sister, Laodice the Elder, married young King Ariarathes VI of Cappadocia, she (and everyone else, for that matter) knew of the fate of her husband's five older brothers. One by one—as they approached majority—their mother, Queen-Regent Nysa, had killed them off. Laodice had the good sense to insist on their wedding night that her husband kill his mother. Which he did. He wasn't always so lucky, though, for Mithridates killed him a few years later.

During his minority, Mithridates' own mother was queen-regent for him. Could she really ...? He became very careful, especially about his food. He had heard tales of the poison normally used at court—it was slow acting, and the symptoms were those of a natural disease—so he had the court pharmacist prescribe both poison and antidote. These prescriptions served him well. He lived to become Mithridates VI, the Great, as well as Eupator (the Good Father).

When Alexander the Great died in 322 B.C., he left a huge empire, no heirs capable of ruling, and several greedy generals and underlings. Twenty years of chaos and fighting followed. The Alexandrine Empire fell apart, Egypt going to Ptolemy, most of Asia to Seleucus, Greece to Antigonus, and so on. Most of the new kings were Greeks, but here and there a "barbarian" ruler (anyone who wasn't a Greek) could be found.

One such, who claimed descent from the Imperial Persian Achaemenid family, established himself in Sinope (on the Black Sea Coast of what is now Turkey) and called his kingdom Pontus. He had been a Persian satrap loyal to Alexander. Now he became a Persian king with Greek manners and dress, but with family customs more Asian than Greek.

In all of these *nouveau* royal families, blood and other relationships became extremely confusing. Each king usually had one queen, whose sons were first in line to the throne, and a gaggle of concubines whose sons sometimes gained royal power through patricide, matricide, fratricide, infanticide, etc. One of the nice things about being a queen was that, after murdering your husband, you could become queen-regent until your oldest boy came of age to rule. And if, like Queen-Regent Nysa of Cappadocia, you weren't too squeamish about killing your sons, you could retain supreme power for some time. Very little of the moderation preached by some earlier Greeks had carried over into the Hellenistic world.

Seven Persian-blooded kings ruled Pontus between 302 and 132 B.C., when our Mithridates was born. Five of them were called Mithridates. Mithridates' father was called Mithridates, and so was his brother. To avoid confusion, each Mithridates added another name. Our Mithridates' father was Mithridates Euergates (the Benefactor), our Mithridates was Mithridates Eupator (the Good Father), and his brother was Mithridates Chrestus (the Virtuous). None of them bothered to live up to his title. It was only something to put on royal documents and coins.

These sovereigns of Pontus usually married daughters of the Greek royal families, so Mithridates was well over half Greek. Indeed, his own mother Laodice was a daughter of the Seleucid King of Kings in Antioch. Brought up as a Greek, Mithridates Eupator was the eldest son and second child (after his sister Laodice the Elder) of Mithridates Euergates V. His next sister was Laodice the Younger, and then there were three younger ones still, Nysa, Roxana, and Statira.

It was said that at his birth a strange comet appeared brighter than the sun and that lightning hit his cradle, touching his forehead and leaving a scar in the shape of a crown. Any nitwit who heard of these marvels knew that Mithridates was destined for greatness, although it is more likely that they were "remembered" after he became the Great. But descriptions of him by contemporaries and later historians cast him in a heroic mold.

A great one with the ladies, he kept a large harem and almost never slept alone. Not only was he the original tall-dark-and-handsome type, but he must have had a tremendous physique. His armor was so large that he sent a set to the Oracle at Delphi to impress everybody. He could ride a horse 120 miles a day (or so he said), outrun a deer (or so he said), out-drink and out-eat any of his court, and drive a sixteen-horse chariot with ease. Although he preferred to speak and make love in Greek, he knew twenty-two languages and never needed an interpreter.

Early on he developed one eccentricity that rather horrified the Greek world. He dressed like a "barbarian," that is, he wore

Persian dress—baggy trousers tied just above the ankles and a jewel-studded dagger at his waist.

He was only twelve when his father was murdered, leaving a probably bogus will naming both sons (Mithridates Eupator and Mithridates Chrestus) as co-sovereigns and their mother, Laodice, as Queen-Regent. Why father was murdered is not clear, but it apparently stemmed from his restlessness as a Roman client-king. By the time our Mithridates was born in 132, most of the lesser kingdoms in what is now Turkey had become associated in one way or another with Rome. Romans were involved politically, economically, and socially in all these petty Hellenistic kingdoms, including Mithridates' Pontus.

One day in 118 B.C. when he was fourteen, Mithridates set out on a hunting trip with a few teenage cronies. By this time, he suspected that every year brought him closer to the grave—not in the normal sense of human mortality, but because daily he became more of a threat to his mother. The mother–son relationship was rather strained, and Mithridates thought it might be a good idea to go hunting instead of hanging around the palace. The hunt lasted seven years. Although now and then he ate inside a house at the table of some trusted noble (he was taking the poison and the antidote), he slept outside, rode horses, and hunted for seven years. No wonder he became physically superb.

And so it was that in 111 B.C. a beautiful young man appeared in Sinope and announced that he was the king. Ever suckers for physical beauty, his urban Greek subjects welcomed him with joy and let themselves be led by Mithridates as a mob against his mother the queen-regent. Laodice gave up and was promptly put in durance vile. She lasted less than a year, but practically all sources agree that Mithridates didn't kill her. He just locked her up, and it was hardly his fault that his mother couldn't adjust to prison life.

Brother Chrestus was something else again. For the moment, Mithridates accepted him as co-king. But within a year, Mithridates accused Chrestus of treason, put him on trial, and publicly executed him. Chrestus was his brother, true, but Mithridates had not seen much of him during the past seven years.

So at twenty-one Mithridates was sole king, lord of the Kingdom of Pontus. And, like all kings everywhere, he had to insure the succession with legitimate sons. Somewhere along the line, he became enamored of the Egyptian custom of brother marrying sister. After all, if he was such a great guy, no mere woman of royal blood was worthy of him. Only a sister would do. So he married his sister Laodice the Younger. This peculiar reasoning worked in reverse. If only a sister was worthy of him, no other man was worthy of one of his sisters. And so his unmarried sisters, Nysa, Roxana, and Statira, were locked up for life.

While all this was going on Mithridates, as a sideline, began to meddle in Cappadocia where his big sister, Laodice the Elder, was married to Ariarathes VI. Through a wise use of Pontic gold, Mithridates raised a rebellion in Cappadocia that resulted in his brother-in-law's murder. His nephew Ariarathes VII came to the throne with sister Laodice the Elder as queen-regent.

Unhappy with the shrunken kingdom left by his mother's pro-Roman policy, Mithridates now embarked on a campaign in Armenia and along the north shore of the Black Sea. He didn't lead the army in person, but he was lucky to have good generals. The Crimea and the mainland of southern Russia (then called the Bosporus) readily accepted him as king. This was in 106 B.C.

In 100 B.C., Mithridates decided that, since travel was broadening, he ought to bat around for a while. Leaving his wife-sister as regent, he toured Asia Minor and got as far as the god Apollo's preserve on the island of Delos in the Aegean Sea. He loved the trip and got lots of good ideas for taking over the cities he had seen. Homecoming, though, was a bit of a shock. His beloved wife-sister tried to poison him. But since Mithridates had been using the old gray cells, the poison didn't kill him. Even so, he didn't like his wife's attitude, and he had her killed at once.

He could then have married another sister, but the dew had left the rose as it were. The one he had married had given him three legitimate sons and one daughter, and so for the rest of his life he contented himself with harem women.

It was now 99 B.C. And, having disposed of one brother and one wife, he now turned on his nephew, Ariarathes VII, the son of sister Laodice the Elder. He invaded Cappadocia, but this Laodice was too smart for him. She could pick as good a bunch of generals as her brother. Finally they arranged a truce. Both armies were camped around a large field, and Mithridates and Ariarathes arranged to meet in sight of the armed forces. It was to be a dramatic family reunion and reconciliation. As a matter of course in such family gatherings, both kings were searched for hidden weapons. None was found, the two kings met, and Mithridates had the forethought to strap a dagger (as to how long it was the authorities are silent) to his penis. His good old baggy Persian trousers came in handy for concealment. He used the dagger.

With Ariarathes dead, Mithridates expected to become king of Cappadocia, but once again that bitch of a sister outwitted him. She married the king of neighboring Bithynia and brought Cappadocia as her dower present.

Mithridates found this too humiliating. He began to meddle in Bithynian affairs and thus precipitated the first of what the Romans called the Mithridatic Wars. The First Mithridatic War lasted from 88 to 84 B.C. Mithridates was forty-three when the war started, at the height of his powers. It began with a Roman invasion of Pontus led by a Roman named Aquilius. Mithridates soon gained the upper hand. His 290,000 men cleared the Romans out of Asia Minor, and his 400 warships got the upper hand in the Black Sea.

Mithridates captured many Romans, two of them quite important. One was a general named Oppius, whom Mithridates dragged around Asia Minor to show everybody that Romans could be defeated. He later freed Oppius, at least part way, but kept him round his court like a pet animal. He also captured the unimpressive Aquilius. He had him tied to the back of an ass, and paraded around Asia Minor. Then, to show his contempt for Roman greed he poured molten gold in Aquilius' throat.

But the worst thing he did was to set a day for all Romans in the "liberated" dominions now under his thumb to be massacred. Historians differ, but apparently Mithridates' order led to the death of from 80,000 to 150,000 men, women, and children. He confiscated all their property and freed their slaves, 6000 of whom joined his army.

Mithridates went on with his conquests and soon drove the Romans out of Asia and Greece. Now it was Rome's turn to strike out. The redoubtable Sulla marched east with his legions and was victorious. He reconquered Greece, invaded Asia Minor, and had Mithridates on the run when the old civil war between Sulla and Marius broke out again back in Rome. Anxious to get home, Sulla arranged a peace (or was it a truce?) with Mithridates, demanding a large indemnity and eighty warships for his trouble, with Mithridates keeping Pontus but losing everything else.

No sooner had the war ended than Mithridates was up to his neck in plots against him. In Pergamum, four Greeks who were friends of his decided to kill him. One of them, a fellow by the name of Asclepiodotus of Lesbos, turned stoolie and told Mithridates all about it. With such friends Mithridates hardly needed enemies. His response was to kill some 6000 Greeks.

Then he had some family troubles, too. One son, a lad named Arcathius, had died naturally (of all things!) in 86 B.C. His only daughter, Cleopatra, married Tigranes the king of Armenia. It was our Mithridates' oldest son and heir, also named Mithridates, who was to cause Good Father some anguish. When news of Mithridates' defeat in the war with Rome reached his cities in Colchis, then a part of Pontus, they declared their independence. They thought they were leaving a sinking ship. But the truce with Sulla allowed Mithridates to send young Mithridates out to restore order. The young man showed great ability as viceroy of Colchis. He did exactly what his father ordered him to do; he did it too well, for his father's tastes. Mithridates didn't like the way his son was acting, called him home to Sinope for "consultations," arrested him, bound him with golden chains, and killed him.

Up in Bosporus around the Crimea, his loyal towns were fighting the barbarians of the steppes. To be viceroy of Bosporus, Mithridates sent his only surviving legitimate son, Machares.

Between wars Number 2 and 3 (81 to 74 B.C.), nothing much happened. Mithridates grew older and spent his time killing would-be poisoners and traitors, building up the army, and trying to cook up some alliances in preparation for war Number 3.

The last Mithridatic War broke out in 74 B.C. (and was to last until 64 B.C.) when Mithridates was fifty-eight. He had never before really led the army in person, but now he showed himself a capable field officer. He won some and lost some. But the losses were the ones that counted. Rome was inexorable in her determination to destroy him. After initial wins, Mithridates was forced back and back, until the Romans invaded Pontus itself. He was bested, but it took two of the greatest generals of his age to do it: Lucullus and Pompey the Great.

But before he fled to sanctuary with his brother-in-law Tigranes in Armenia, Mithridates had some last-minute chores to do. He didn't want any of his family or concubines to fall into Roman hands and be dragged away in chains to star in a Roman triumph. His sister Nysa was liberated by the Romans in 71 B.C., an aging and post-menopausal virgin who had been locked up all these years. We don't know anything more about what happened to her.

Two other sisters and some ex-concubines were locked up in Pharnacia, right on the Pontian border with the Caucasus region where Mithridates thought them safe from the Romans. But they weren't. As the Romans advanced, and just before Mithridates headed for Armenia, he sent a faithful eunuch named Baccides to talk to the ladies. Bacchides called all the ladies before him and told them the most important would have to kill themselves— orders from Mithridates. Mithridates' sister, Roxana, yelled and screamed for quite a while, cursing her brother all the while, but finally took a good dollop of Pontic poison and expired. Sister Statira was more of a lady. She thanked her brother for giving her this way out, drank the poison, and died.

In Pharnacia were two eminent ex-concubines. Berenice, whom Mithridates had once loved, was told to kill herself. She agreed and gave some poison to her mother. Too much, as it turned out. The old girl died at once from a real overdose, but there wasn't enough left for Berenice. She took what there was left and rolled around on the floor gasping and groaning until Bacchides, who seems to have been a rather kind-hearted old bastard, put her out of her misery by strangling her.

Next to go was the famous Monime, one of the most celebrated courtesans of her time. Years ago, when Mithridates had first laid eyes on her, he wanted to bed her down at once like any common whore. But Monime was high-class and coveted the position of chief whore in Mithridates' harem. She knew the risk she ran but opted for it anyway. As chief concubine, she wore a pretty band around her head, but she knew that keeping Mithridates' love was a must, for she could never return to her former profession. That's the way it turned out, and when Mithridates' attentions wandered elsewhere, Monime was locked up with Mithridates' ex's and sisters. Now she was asked to kill herself for Mithridates' sake, so she took off the linen band and tried to strangle herself with the cursed thing. Bacchides finally took pity on her and cut her throat.

While all this was going on, Mithridates was trying to put another army together. He invaded Pontus but was defeated by Pompey and fled back to Armenia. Brother-in-law Tigranes demonstrated his family loyalty by putting a reward of 1000 talents on Mithridates' head. Tigranes thought the Romans would win. He was right. They did. The only thing for Mithridates now was to fight his way around the Black Sea to Bosporus, which was being held for him by his son Machares. It was an epic journey and fight (in 65 B.C.) but Mithridates made it.

Machares had governed Bosporus for twenty-five years. But back in 70 B.C., when Mithridates had been really down and out, the son had decided to send his allegiance to Rome. Now, in 65 B.C., six years later, who should show up but Papa, and Machares knew Papa! Scared as hell, he burned all the ships he commanded, and fled to the Crimea. But he wasn't to get out of it so easily. Mithridates built some ships, crossed to his son's hide-away, and bullied him into taking poison. Mithridates also killed lots of others, including another of his illegitimate sons, Xiphares, and left the body to rot without a burial.

The war continued, and Mithridates now got the idea of collecting another army, marching through the Balkans to the Alps, and over the Alps and down to Italy to take Rome itself. At his age, he gave up the royal pleasures of the table, but he still kept the royal pleasures of the bed. Indeed, he lived in the harem and saw few but close associates.

Into this seclusion came yet another of Mithridates' sons, Pharnaces by name, a concubine's son whom Mithridates now thought of making his heir, all his legitimate sons having died or been killed by Good Father. Pharnaces thought that Papa had a screw loose for even thinking of invading Rome and decided to do away with him. And so, one day in 63 B.C., Pharnaces began a plot. It was betrayed, and Mithridates exacted his usual bloody vengeance by killing everyone in sight. But, entirely out of character, he was persuaded by an old friend to spare his son Pharnaces. It was the first time in his life he had pardoned a traitor.

After a touching reconciliation with his father, Pharnaces the very next day raised the standard of revolt and got the whole army to side with him. The army was not too happy about marching on Rome, anyway. On hearing this, Mithridates sent envoys asking his son to allow him to go into exile. The envoys went over to Pharnaces. To top all this, Pharnaces now appeared outside the walls of the fortress protecting Mithridates and was crowned king while Mithridates watched from the walls, grinding his teeth.

The old man, now seventy, realized that there was no way for him to avoid the supreme humiliation of surrendering to his own son except death. Hidden in his sword handle was a large cache of poison. This was the way out.

But before he died Mithridates rather gallantly looked out for the safety of his loyal soldiers and associates. He ordered them to join the enemy. But, when they marched out of the fortress, most were killed by the rebels before they could explain what they were up to. Two of Mithridates' daughters, Mithridatis and Nysa, stuck with their father and took poison.

Some poison was left—and Mithridates swallowed it. It didn't work and Mithridates ran around the room to increase his circulation. No effect. He then ordered a Gallic soldier who had stayed with him to cut him down, saying: "But, although I have been on my guard against all the poisons that a man might take with his food, I have neglected to provide against that most deadly poison to be found in every royal palace: the treason of soldiers, of sons, and of friends."

Mithridates, he died old.

5
Gaius, Called Caligula

August 31, A.D. 12–January 24, A.D. 41

Does your little boy pull the wings off butterflies? Then he's harmless compared with Caligula.

On March 16, A.D. 37, the Emperor Tiberius lay dying. He was a bitter old man of seventy-eight. He thought he had the imperial succession taken care of. His grandson Gemellus, seventeen, and his great-nephew Gaius, twenty-five, would rule Rome together. But it didn't work out that way.

Gaius, better known as Caligula, had been hanging around Tiberius' court on the Isle of Capri for years, toadying to the grouchy old Emperor, yet remembering how badly Tiberius had treated his parents and his two brothers and longing for a chance to show what *he* could do. Tiberius didn't die fast enough to suit Caligula. According to the Roman historian Tacitus, Caligula held a pillow over the dying man's face with one hand and strangled him with the other—and, realizing that a freedman had seen him do it, sent the fellow off to be crucified. In practically no time, Gaius persuaded the Roman Senate to shove Gemellus out of the way so he could be emperor all by himself.

Caligula was a nickname. Gaius's childhood had been spent in Roman army camps, because his father Germanicus, Tiberius' nephew, was a great general. The iron-hard legionnaires who followed the eagles were delighted and amused by the little boy, who wore high laced sandals like their own *caligae*. They called him "Little Boot," Caligula.

* Among the sources for this chapter: Cassius Dio Cocceianus, *Dio's Roman History*, translated by Earnest Cary. New York: G. P. Putnam's Sons, The Loeb Classical Library, 1924. (Harvard University Press.)

When he became emperor, his people called him other pet names for a while—he was their star, their chick, their pretty doll. He was a charming change from sour old Tiberius, who had been loafing around on the Isle of Capri for the last ten years of his life without even going near Rome. But Caligula's personality changed drastically after a severe illness that he suffered in his first year as emperor. He became mentally deranged.

Awful things had happened in Caligula's family. Germanicus, his father, died in Antioch in A.D. 19; Gnaeus Calpurnius Piso was said to have poisoned him at the suggestion of Tiberius. Caligula's mother, Agrippina the Elder (to distinguish her from a daughter of the same name), was banished by Tiberius and starved to death at forty-six, perhaps by order of Tiberius, or maybe it was her own idea.

Her oldest son Nero, also banished by Tiberius, starved to death voluntarily because he thought his jailer was going to kill him. He died in A.D. 31 at twenty-five. The next son, Drusus, was imprisoned in Rome for high treason and died of involuntary starvation. He even ate the stuffing in his mattress.

That left Caligula and three sisters, all named Julia. They had different middle names, however. Agrippina the Younger, the mother of Nero (the infamous Nero, not the one who starved) was exiled by her loving brother Caligula in A.D. 39 when she was twenty-four, but unfortunately she lived through it only to be killed eventually by her own son, *the* Nero. The two other sisters were Drusilla and Livilla. Caligula exiled Livilla, accused of conspiracy against him, the year after he became emperor.

But Drusilla he fell in love with. She was married to a man whom Tiberius had picked out for her, but Caligula had her divorced and wed to another fellow, named Lepidus. Then he took her away from Lepidus and let on that he was going to marry her himself. He probably had a wife of his own just then— he had four in all—but even a single man was not supposed to marry his sister. Such pairings had been usual in the royal house of Egypt, however, because the pharaohs were too divine to mix with common blood. Caligula figured he was just as divine as they were. He belonged to the Julian family, and everybody knew that a remote ancestress of theirs, way back in ancient Troy, was the goddess Venus. Anyway, Caligula was crazy about Egyptian customs. (Only a few decades before his birth a relative named Marcus Antonius had lost his head over the Serpent of the Nile,

Cleopatra. He also lost his life and the chance to rule Rome.)

Caligula planned to marry his Drusilla (there were those who said he had already taken her for his wife informally), but she did him wrong. She fell sick and died, perhaps of shame. He decreed an extravagant funeral for her, set up statues all over, and ordered that she be worshiped as a goddess. Meanwhile, his grandmother Antonia died. She was a virtuous Roman lady (they were scarce as hen's teeth), but he practically ignored her passing. She had scolded him about his attitude toward his sister, and he had replied contemptuously, "Everything is lawful to me, and I may do as I will to anyone."

Now Caligula took care of his unlucky young kinsman Gemellus, whom he had already done out of co-rulership of the empire. Gemellus was delicate, and he coughed. The emperor smelled cough medicine on his breath one day at dinner and accused him of having taken an antidote against poison. As if Caligula would poison anyone! Gemellus had to go, but the emperor hesitated to assign a man to stab him because it was unlawful to spill the blood of the Caesars. When worst came to worst in those days, if the emperor said "Commit suicide" it was wise to do so and not wait to find out what the alternative might be. When Gemellus got his suicide orders, he wanted to be agreeable, but he had never seen anyone killed and didn't know what to do with the sword an officer handed him. The officer had to show him where to aim it. The youth fell on it and died.

More mature people usually had some method figured out in advance. When Caligula's father-in-law got the word, he cut his throat with a razor.

Caligula's first wife, whom he married before he became emperor, was Junia Claudilla. She died young. In the first year of his reign he attended a wedding and ran off with the bride, Livia Orestilla, but he divorced her after a few days and then banished her. Next in the royal bed was Lollia Paulina, a great beauty with magnificent jewels. Caligula took her away from her husband but soon tired of her and divorced her.

His fourth wife was an older woman, Caesonia. He liked to make cute jokes about how he was going to stretch her on a rack to find out whether she had won his affection with a love potion, or he would touch her neck and chuckle ominously, "When I give the word, this beautiful throat will be hacked through." Caesonia got along with him pretty well, though. Very soon after they were married she gave birth to a daughter. Caligula named the child Julia Drusilla (after his deified sister). When the emperor saw her bite her nurse, he applauded. That was Daddy's girl, all right. Caligula laid the baby on the knees of a statue of Jupiter and announced fondly that both he and the god were her father and that it remained to be seen who was the greater.

Besides his interesting home life with ever-changing partners, the emperor took care, after his fashion, of his duties in government. Every ten days somebody brought him a list of prisoners to be executed. He was so casual that he stopped signing the list and simply motioned with his hand that the people named were to be killed. He liked to have executions prolonged, preferring not one stoke of the sword but many slight ones. He usually said, "Strike so that he may feel himself die."

His madness got no better. He built a temple to himself, with his own image made of solid gold, and worshiped himself there. Being a deity, he let on that he was in touch with Jupiter and held long conversations with the god while walking. Sometimes he wore a beard of gold thread and played he *was* Jupiter. Or he wore wings on his heels and his cap and expected to be recognized as Mercury; or he carried a bow and a quiver and wore a kind of halo: that was Apollo. Everybody played along, naturally. His uncle Claudius and a bunch of Roman Senators were priests of his self-worship.

Caligula liked shows in which gladiators fought to the death, but he liked mob scenes even better, with groups of men struggling in the arena. They didn't have to be tough, professional sword fighters or even condemned criminals. For one show he drafted twenty-six perfectly respectable citizens. He even condescended to take part in an occasional fight himself—with his opponent naturally being very careful not to hurt him. He fought one gladiator who tired him out without being wounded and then politely knelt to beg his forgiveness. Caligula took the opportunity to stab him while his head was bowed and then declared himself the victor.

It wasn't safe to sit in the front row at these affairs. On one occasion when there weren't enough condemned criminals to fight the tigers and lions provided, Caligula ordered a bunch of spectators to be dragged from the benches into the arena. They were not provided with weapons for self-defense. When the price of meat was high, he fed accused criminals to the wild beasts without bothering to find out whether they were guilty.

One thing Caligula loved was horse racing. His favorite horse was Incitatus, or "Go-ahead," which had its own retinue of slaves. The animal, which had a marble stall and an ivory manger, was sometimes official host at dinner parties for Caligula's friends. He made the horse a priest of his temple, and there is a story that he even nominated Incitatus as one of the two consuls of Rome, who ran the government.

It was made a capital crime for anyone to look down from a high place on the emperor as he passed by, because he was getting bald on top. But the rest of his body was very hairy, so it was all a man's life was worth to mention a goat in his presence. Baldness was one of his obsessions. When making a progress along the street he looked with insane jealousy on men who had plenty of hair and sometimes ordered them to the barber to have half their heads shaved.

Deeply involved in the plots and counterplots that surrounded Caligula like an angry swarm of wasps was a sometime friend named Marcus Aemilius Lepidus, who had been married for a while to the emperor's late sister, Drusilla. Caligula had indeed turned the tables on him, but, still, they were brothers-in-law. The future had once looked bright for Lepidus when Caligula fell very sick in the first year of his reign and bequeathed everything he had, including the Roman Empire, to Drusilla. If Caligula had only died, Lepidus might have become emperor. But it was Drusilla who died, cutting Lepidus off from succession to the throne.

The disappointed Lepidus entered into a plot with Caligula's surviving sisters, Agrippina the Younger and Livilla, and Gaetulicus, head of the Roman army in Germany. Lepidus would marry Agrippina and thus be in line for Emperor all over again. She was married to someone else, but what difference would that make? Her husband was old, while she was young and ambitious.

Caligula got wind of the plot and decided to go to Germany himself, taking his sisters and his good friend Lepidus along. There he had both Lepidus and Gaetulicus murdered. He charged his sisters with adultery and sentenced them to banishment. Everything they had was confiscated and sold, and he published their letters to their lovers. All the way back to Rome, he made

Agrippina carry in her arms the urn containing her late husband's ashes. She even had to sleep with it.

Caligula had been tyrannizing over his groaning empire for four years when another plot began to simmer. Tiberius had left the treasury full, but Caligula spent money furiously. He not only used up all the savings but also imposed dreadful taxes. It had long been customary for the army to be kept sweet with money gifts. Now there were no more gifts, and the legions began to grumble. Even worse, Caligula was downright insulting to the officers of the Praetorian Guard, his own protectors. He should have known better.

Cassius Chaerea, tribune of the Guard, had an especially onerous duty. The emperor assigned him to collect taxes and tributes, which had been doubled. Chaerea hated his job and the people hated him. When there were delays in collecting, the emperor railed at him and sneered that he was a mere woman.

The emperor added to Chaerea's hatred by making him administer torture to a beautiful actress named Quintilia, who was required to testify against her lover. She left the rack a pitiful, broken creature, but she hadn't told a thing. In a grand gesture, the emperor freed her and her lover and paid her off with a sum of money.

A conspiracy grew, with Chaerea helping it on. He had loved "Little Boot" as a child in Germany, but now he loathed him. The Palatine Games—an eight-day festival beginning January 17—looked like a good time for finishing off the emperor. But to kill him was an awesome undertaking. While a great many angry people agreed that the tyrant must be destroyed, and there was a lot of whispering in secret meetings, nobody had the nerve to offer to do the deed.

On the last day of the games, the conspirators were really alarmed. Nobody was *doing* anything. Caligula was leaving the great wooden theater to get a bite of supper before the evening performance when Chaerea asked him for the password to give the Guard. The emperor smirked and gave him an obscene one that applied only to women. That was the last time Caligula humiliated anybody. Chaerea slashed at him with his sword; the blade struck his collar bone. Caligula staggered, and another conspirator thrust at him and split his jaw. The emperor fell to the floor, drawing his limbs up to save his body, screaming, "I am alive! I am alive!"

Other angry plotters rushed at him, and when they had finished, his body was gashed with thirty wounds. Then his attackers ran. News and rumors sped through the milling crowds. Nobody dared cheer, because the news might not be true. The public crier came out on the stage and roared that the emperor was indeed dead. All hell broke loose, with everybody trying to get out of the place.

Chaerea sent an officer, Julius Lupus, to kill the emperor's widow, Caesonia. The man found her lamenting, drenched in blood, clasping Caligula's hacked body. When she saw the soldier coming, torch in one hand and naked sword in the other, she stumbled up to her knees, ordered him to hurry up with his job, and bent her head. Lupus killed her.

Thus the reign of the Emperor Gaius ended January 24, A.D. 41, after less than four years. He was twenty-eight years old. His body was buried in a garden, where apparitions disturbed the gardeners until his sisters, back from their banishment, had his remains properly burned and buried.

His successor was his uncle Claudius, who assumed that he was on the blacklist too and was cowering behind a curtain in the palace when he was dragged out only to be informed that the army wanted him to be emperor of Rome. Soon after Claudius took over, he was called upon to decide on punishment for the assassins of Caligula. Claudius asked his friends for advice. Chaerea had done a glorious deed, they agreed, but he'd better be executed to discourage other men who might get the idea that it was all right to kill emperors. Chaerea, Lupus, and many other conspirators were therefore executed. Another officer, Sabinus, who had helped with the regicide, was freed by Claudius and even allowed to keep his commission in the army. But Sabinus was an honorable man. If Chaerea deserved death, so did he. He fell on his sword, and the blade went through his body clear to the hilt.

6
Nero

December 15, A.D. 37–June 9, A.D. 68

Agrippina had raised her boy to be emperor of Rome. Then the ungrateful child turned out to be sharper than a serpent's tooth.

On October 13, A.D. 54, the emperor of Rome was delighted with his dinner. His fourth wife, Agrippina, had arranged to have him served with a tasty dish of mushrooms. They were delicious mushrooms, too, but the sauce in which they were served was concocted by a famous professional poisoner named Locusta.

After eating, the Emperor Claudius unaccountably dozed off. His wife (who was also his niece) was frantic. Apparently he wasn't going to die with decent dispatch. Then he spoiled her well-laid plans by vomiting up his dinner. Agrippina thereupon had him fed poisoned gruel, or else a fatal enema was administered, or perhaps the doctor tenderly helped him out of the world by tickling his throat with a poisoned feather, depending on which Roman historian's account you prefer.

Whatever was done to settle the emperor's stomach, it definitely settled his hash. Claudius spent a bad night and died the next morning. The grieving widow embraced her stepson, young Britannicus, Claudius' thirteen-year-old son, and wept all over him.

She had golden plans for her own son, Nero, a bouncing boy of seventeen, whose wife was Octavia, daughter of Claudius and

---

* Among the sources for this chapter: Cassius Dio Cocceianus, *Dio's Roman History*, translated by Earnest Cary. New York: G. P. Putnam's Sons, The Loeb Classical Library, 1924. (Harvard University Press.)

sister of Britannicus. Octavia was twelve years old, and Nero detested her.

At noon on the day of the emperor's death, the doors of the palace were thrown open and Nero appeared before the soldiers on guard there.

A few of them looked around and inquired cautiously, "Where's Britannicus? He's the real heir, isn't he?"

But nobody cared enough to protest very loudly when an officer suggested that they cheer Nero, the son-in-law and officially adopted son of the late Claudius. They dutifully raised a shout and carried the new emperor off to the camp of the Praetorian Guard, where he made a speech.

It was a beautiful speech, the guards felt—he promised them a lot of money, and that was a sure way to get on the good side of the army. At Claudius' funeral, the boy emperor made another impressive speech, which had been ghost-written for him by his tutor, Seneca. He gave each of the common citizens of Rome 400 sesterces, cut taxes, set up salaries for Senators who were broke, and arranged a free grain allowance for the Praetorian Guard.

During the first five years of Nero's reign, almost everyone thought he was a fine fellow. When he had to sign a death warrant, he moaned, "I wish I'd never learned to write!" Later he managed a great many deaths without the painful formality of writing anything down.

Agrippina, however, almost frothed at the mouth watching him rule Rome. She had capably managed the Emperor Claudius, and she had put Nero on the throne so that, as the power behind it, she could capably manage the empire. But the ungrateful whelp was doing it himself!

For a while, they got along outwardly very well. Once, when asked by an officer to set the password for the day, Nero gave it as *optima mater*—the best of mothers.

There was some nasty gossip to the effect that Nero and his best of mothers sometimes got along altogether too well, and not in decent privacy but in a curtained litter when they traveled together. The litter bearers talked about the goings-on behind those curtains.

Jealousy that was not strictly maternal burned in Agrippina's bosom when her son the emperor fell in love with a younger girl.

Her name was Acte, and she was absolutely nobody—a freed slave of no particular accomplishments. She was just a nice girl with no notions about murdering anybody.

Nero set her up in an establishment of her own and even talked about marrying her. Of course there was his wife, Octavia, and marrying Acte would have been illegal because she was only a freedwoman, but the royal family could usually find some way around inconvenient laws. Agrippina's own marriage to her uncle Claudius had been incestuous under Roman law.

Agrippina raged and railed at her lovesick, stubborn boy. She went so far as to remind him that there was still a potential emperor around the palace, young Britannicus, and that she still had influence. The boy was a nuisance to his never-loving stepbrother and brother-in-law anyway. At a celebration, Nero tried to embarrass him by asking him to sing in public. Britannicus stepped right out and sang some appropriate verses about a youth who had been deprived of his rights and his father's throne. Everybody applauded, and there were snide remarks about "How true!"

From Nero's point of view, Britannicus had to go. The celebrated poison-brewer, Locusta, wasn't hard to find. She was in prison. But a supposedly fatal dose administered to Britannicus by his own tutors didn't work. Nero threatened Locusta and the army officer in charge of the poisoning detail with sudden death if they didn't hurry things up.

"Yes, *sir!*" said the officer. "Quick like a dagger."

The royal prince normally ate with young noblemen of his own age, in full view of the grown folks at court, so a public murder had to be arranged. It went off very well, on the day after his fourteenth birthday.

Britannicus had an official taster who was supposed to save him from just such a fate as Nero planned. If the taster fell dead, the prince would be warned. So the taster was by-passed by a neat stratagem.

Somebody handed him a cup of harmless hot liquid, which he dutifully sipped and passed on.

"Ouch!" complained Britannicus. "Burned my mouth! Cool the stuff off."

Someone kindly cooled it with cold water into which a fast-acting poison had been thoughtfully introduced in advance. The taster had already done his duty, so the cup went directly to

Britannicus, who drank, lost consciousness, and died then and there.

"Oh, never mind him," Nero remarked. "He has fits." This was true. But when it became obvious that the boy wasn't going to recover, a funeral was held. Poor little Octavia showed no emotion as her brother died. Young as she was, she had learned to mind her own business.

The empress-mother was scared out of her wits. She knew an assassination when she saw one. If Nero could so neatly abolish his stepbrother, without even consulting her, would he hesitate about abolishing his best of mothers, too?

Agrippina had reason to worry. Nero took away the guard to which she was entitled and moved her into her own house. He made duty visits now and then, surrounded by plenty of friends and guards to keep her from trying to lure him into the bedroom, kissed her hastily, and then departed.

Nero worked hard at governing Rome. In his spare time, he took up the serious study of music. He relaxed with a gay group of young blades, notably Marcus Salvius Otho, Claudius Senecio, and Petronius, known as the Arbiter, a languid young authority on elegance. They helped him along the primrose path, which he was eager to explore. For instance, he raped one of the Vestal Virgins.

By the time the emperor turned twenty, Acte was beginning to seem tiresome. She adored him, but she couldn't compete with the attractions of society women. There was, for example, Poppaea Sabina, a divorcée who had recently married Nero's friend Otho. Poppaea was a raving beauty with amber-colored hair and a skin so white that people said she took her daily bath in the milk of five hundred asses. She was determined to get the utmost out of her beauty. Once she cried, "Ah, let me die before it fades!"

Here, Nero discovered, was just the girl for him. He suggested to Otho that thereafter Poppaea should be his wife in name only.

"It's a little embarrassing," Otho protested. "Maybe I should leave Rome."

"I have just the job for you," Nero told him. "How would you like to be governor of Lusitania?"

So off went Otho to what is now Portugal, and someone made up a verse that convulsed high society:

Why is it Otho lives an exile's life?
Because he dared to sleep with his own wife.

Now the empress-mother had additional cause for jealousy and
rage. She wasn't ruling Rome, and she wasn't even ruling her
boy Nero. Agrippina and Poppaea heartily hated each other.

This time Agrippina had to go. Three attempts to poison her
failed, because Agrippina—no fool she—had immunized herself
with antidotes. One of Nero's admirals, Anicetus, suggested,
"How about a collapsible boat?"

Nero invited his mother to a fine banquet at Baiae on the Bay
of Naples, bade her farewell afterward with affectionate kisses,
and saw her off on the boat. While she rested with some friends
around her, the lead-lined ceiling fell in, as planned. It killed
one of her friends but only scared the empress. The boat did not
fall apart, as it was supposed to (some days nothing goes right),
but in the excitement the crew managed to overturn it. Agrippina
swam to shore with only a slight shoulder wound and sent her
loving son word of her fortunate escape.

Admiral Anicetus took a few men to finish off Agrippina. One
of them hit her over the head with a club, and she got the idea of
what was about to happen. As a centurion bared his sword, she
tore her clothing apart and exclaimed, "Smite the womb that
bore Nero!"

Just before the hurried funeral that night, Nero took a long
look at her and sighed, "I did not know that she was so beautiful."

Nero's tutor, Seneca, helped him draw up a letter of explanation to the Senate, laying forth Agrippina's crimes. The Senate
answered with congratulations and decreed that the day of her
death should be celebrated thereafter with thanksgiving ceremonies.

Now Poppaea whimpered that it was time Nero made an
honest woman of her, but he was in no hurry. He had his empire
to govern, with no unwelcome advice from the late Agrippina,
and he had become fanatically devoted to the stage. (On his
twenty-second birthday, December 15, A.D. 59, he celebrated his
maturity by shaving off his beard for the first time. He had murdered his mother in the spring of that year.)

The following summer he instituted a series of contests, the
Neronian Games, similar to the Olympian Games, which had
been celebrated in Greece ever since 776 B.C. The games included

music, poetry, wrestling, various athletic competitions, and chariot racing. Nero took part in the musical events himself.

By the end of A.D. 61, Poppaea was still the emperor's mistress but not yet his wife, and at thirty-one she felt that she was getting long in the tooth. Nero still wouldn't divorce his wife Octavia, but in the year 62 he did pack her off to a house of her own where she was out of the way. He also rid himself of his long-time playmate, Acte, shipping her off to a villa. Where she lived to survive him.

In May A.D. 62, Poppaea jubilantly announced that it was time to start knitting little garments. Nero had never had news like this before. He was delirious with joy. He divorced Octavia (on the grounds that she was sterile) with speed approaching that of light and made her a handsome settlement. Twelve days later, Poppaea got her wedding, and who's to say she hadn't earned it?

But the Roman people were furious at the banishment of Octavia. They held mass meetings and parades, and in a riot in the imperial gardens they furiously overthrew some statues of Poppaea.

Nero had had enough. Octavia would have to go. On June 9, messengers arrived at her house with the news that the emperor wanted her to commit suicide. Screaming protests, she refused, so she had some unwanted help. A doctor opened her veins while other attendants held her down. The blood didn't flow freely, so they carried her, bound hand and foot and still screaming, into a steamroom where she suffocated. Her severed head was taken back to Rome. Poppaea looked it over carefully, to make sure.

Nero was twenty-five, and Poppaea nearly thirty-two, when their daughter Claudia was born, January 21, A.D. 63. Two weeks later there occurred some disasters that made it look as if the gods didn't favor the royal house. A violent earthquake struck several towns. In Rome, the amphitheater built for the Neronian Games was struck by lightning and burned to the ground. A metal statue of Nero was melted to a blob.

In the middle of May, the baby Claudia died. Nero turned to his music lessons. He wrote poetry, played the harp, and cultivated his voice. He did breathing exercises for hours while lying on his back with a heavy weight on his chest, and he ate lots of onions and oil, for the good of his voice. Every time someone suggested a new idea for improving his singing, he adopted it.

He gave the Roman people every opportunity to enjoy the musical talents of their inspired emperor. At Naples in A.D. 64, he put on a performance that lasted for days. Then the theater roof fell in, literally. Fortunately, the audience had all escaped. Unfortunately for Rome, the emperor had too.

The talented Nero went all out as an entertainer. Singing was not, in his day, simply a matter of getting up before an audience with an accompanist in the background. The standard numbers were more like grand opera.

One of Nero's best parts was the title role in *Canace in Childbirth*. While he was groaning in labor before an admiring audience, an astonished soldier asked an officer, "Ye gods, what's the emperor doing?" and was told, "Shut up. He's having a baby."

The ambitious singer found, as time passed, that it was getting harder to hold his audiences. He fixed that by having the doors locked. People couldn't get out even to heed the call of nature, unless they sneaked over the wall. One man played dead and had his friends carry him out on a stretcher. Occasionally a pregnant woman, unable to get home, had a baby right in the theater, though not on the stage as the emperor did.

In A.D. 64, the imperial city of Rome burned, with terrible loss of life and treasure. Nero probably didn't set the fire; one of his biographers, Tacitus, says he was at Antium when it started. The city was ablaze for a week. Only four of its fourteen districts were untouched. Three were completely destroyed, and only a few shells of houses remained in the other seven. The emperor arranged for emergency food supplies to be rushed in for the survivors, but a disturbing rumor spread through the city faster than the fire. It was said that Nero, on a private stage, had sung of the destruction of Troy while the destruction of Rome was taking place. (He did not, however, play the fiddle. It hadn't been invented yet.)

The emperor planned an improved city, offered bonuses to builders who really produced, and at his own expense constructed colonnades so that water could be poured on future fires. While the Romans were crawling out of their ruins and starting to rebuild, he began his famous palace, the Golden House.

The nasty rumor that Nero himself had set the fire as an excuse for urban renewal annoyed him so much that he had to find someone else to blame. There was a small but disturbing religious sect handy, called Christians. "They did it!" said Nero and set out to abolish them. He had them sewed up in animal skins and thrown to the dogs; some were crucified; others were burned to light the streets. The Romans enjoyed cruelty—they liked the gladiator contests better than their emperor's singing—but what Nero did to the Christians turned even their stomachs.

One Saul of Tarsus, known as Paul after his conversion to the new faith, was executed at this time. So was Simon, called Peter, the Rock on which the Christian Church was founded. St. Peter's Basilica is built over his tomb.

The year after the Great Fire, Nero lost his wife. Poppaea nagged at him for coming home late from the races, and he kicked her in the abdomen. She was pregnant at the time, and the kick brought on a miscarriage that was fatal.

In the same year, the emperor disposed of his old tutor, Seneca. Accused of complicity in a treason plot, Seneca remarked—as was suitable for a philosopher—that he'd been living every day as if it were his last anyway. He wasn't permitted to make out a will, but he told his friends that he bequeathed to them his noblest possession, the pattern of his life. Seneca found death not easy to invite. He opened the veins of his arms with a dagger, then took poison, and finally had himself carried to a steamroom, where he suffocated.

A noblewoman who was accused in the same plot wouldn't name names even when she was broken on a rack. The next day, carried in a litter toward the torture chamber for more of the same, she managed to hang herself inside the closed litter although her limbs had been dislocated. There were funerals all over the city. Several lucky people were only banished.

In A.D. 66, Nero had his old friend, the elegant Petronius, arrested. Rather than wait for execution, Petronius opened his veins. He took a long time dying and enjoyed it as much as possible. While he was bleeding, he had someone read cheerful poetry aloud, and now and then he had a tourniquet applied to stop the bleeding for a while. He made a list of Nero's vices and sins and sent it off to the emperor by messenger before he died, quite calmly, at his own dining table.

In the same year, Nero married twice. One bride was a widow named Messalina, about whom not much is known except that she survived him. The other bride was a boy named Sporos, who was either a eunuch or a hermaphrodite. After a scandalous mock marriage ceremony, friends of the emperor congratulated the

happy couple and expressed the hope that their union would be
blessed by children. Someone remarked sourly that it was too bad
Nero's father hadn't had a wife like Sporos.

On the eighth anniversary of his mother's murder, Nero was
in Naples. There he received bad news: the Roman legions in
Gaul had rebelled against him. He rushed back to Rome, and more
bad news came: Spain had joined the revolt. Nero fainted. A
Roman emperor who didn't have the Roman army on his side
was a gone goose.

Nero made frantic plans for his future. So magnificent a musical performer might as well turn pro, he thought. He could escape to Egypt and earn a living on the stage. He would take along
a theatrical troupe, with his concubines as Amazons, carrying
shields and axes.

Once the long-enduring citizens of Rome discovered that they
loathed their emperor, they let him know it. But he clung to hope;
the Oracle at Delphi had once warned him, "Beware of the
seventy-third year," and he was only in his thirty-second. He
overlooked the known fact that the Delphic Oracle commonly
spoke in doubletalk, and he ignored another point: leading the
revolt out in the provinces was a grim old general named Galba,
seventy-two years old.

On a night in June A.D. 68, Nero awoke to find himself alone in
his palace. Not one of his bodyguards or friends was in sight.
While he ran around looking for them, somebody stole his bed
linen and even the box of poison (prepared by Locusta) that he
always kept handy. Then he shouted for an executioner whom
he kept around the place. Nobody answered.

"What!" shouted the Emperor of Rome. "Have I neither
friends nor enemies any more?"

Nero, who had easily made up his mind about ways of disposing of thousands of other people, went into a panic about what
to do with himself. He ran down to the Tiber, then changed his
mind about drowning.

He had one friend, a freedman named Phaon, who offered to
hide him in a nearby villa. In undershirt and slippers, wearing an
old cloak, Nero mounted a horse and fled. With him went his
boy-wife, Sporos, and four servants. He crept into Phaon's house
through a dirty tunnel, arriving in a slave's bedroom, and ordered
his companions to start digging his grave.

A note came from Phaon: the Senate had declared him Public

Enemy Number 1 and had decreed that he be punished "in the ancient style."

"What's that?" Nero demanded, and was told, "Well, sir, they strip you naked, hold your head with a wooden fork, and whip you to death." This didn't sound exactly dignified to Nero.

Nero hopefully suggested that the servants show him how to commit suicide by doing it themselves. They declined. He remarked to himself, "This is no credit to Nero, no credit at all!"

There was no more time to delay. When the galloping horses of a troop of cavalry were heard, Nero stabbed himself in the throat—with some help from one of his attendants. His last words were, "Jupiter, what an artist is lost in me!" He died June 9, A.D. 68, on the sixth anniversary of his first wife's death.

His two old nurses and Acte, the faithful mistress whom he had discarded, prepared his body for the funeral. His successor was General Galba, who ruled only eight months before he was murdered at the instigation of Otho, Poppaea's former husband. Otho lasted only three months as emperor before he committed suicide to escape a nastier death.

7
Commodus

A.D. 161–192

*Some boys seem to be just plain bad.
It's a good thing they can no longer
grow up to be Roman emperors.*

Most of the Caesars had no sons to
succeed them, so the best way
for an ambitious young aristocrat to become emperor of Rome was
to get himself adopted by the incumbent of that office. It is too bad
that the great and good Marcus Aurelius wasn't one of the son-
less. Alas, he fathered Commodus, who even as a boy was a
catastrophe. Marcus Aurelius was almost too good to be true, but
Commodus was almost too bad.

One day, at age twelve, the good emperor's bad son found his
bath water not hot enough, so he commanded that the slave in
charge be thrown into the furnace. But the slave in charge of
throwing people into the furnace tossed in a sheepskin instead.
Young Commodus sniffed something burning and was content;
it smelled like scorched bath attendant to him.

Commodus was nineteen when his father died, and Dio Cassius,
a Roman historian (who wrote in Greek), says that Marcus
Aurelius didn't die of an infection but with the help of his doctors. They wanted to be in good with the next administration. As
a contemporary of Commodus, Dio Cassius was in a position to
pick up most of the dirt.

The empire was at war, as usual, with some Germanic tribes
along the Danube, and Emperor Commodus only needed to finish

---

* Among the sources for this chapter: Cassius Dio Cocceianus, *Dio's
Roman History*, translated by Earnest Cary. New York: G. P. Put-
nam's Sons, The Loeb Classical Library, 1924. (Harvard University
Press.)

the pacification job his father had begun. Did he? Of course not. He gave the Germanic tribes a peace treaty on very good terms (for them) and let some new provinces his father had fought for go back to the barbarians. But Commodus staged a triumph anyway on his return to Rome, as if he had won a war. In the parade he rode with a friend named Saoterus, whom he kept kissing with enthusiasm. This would have been unseemly enough if Saoterus had been female, but he wasn't.

Commodus wasn't dead set on male companions. He associated with women, too. He had a wife, Crispina (chosen for him by his father), and a girl named Marcia was on hand enough to be known as his mistress. Marcia could wind Commodus around her finger, so it was a good thing that she favored the bumptious sect known as Christians. She protected them from a lot of trouble.

The emperor also had a sister, Lucilla, who in A.D. 183 persuaded her husband, Pompeianus, to block Commodus's way into a theater and show him a sword, announcing, "See what the Senate has sent you!" Pompeianus was supposed to kill him with this sword, but he bungled it.

The natural reaction of Commodus was to have his brother-in-law executed. While he was at it, he banished sister Lucilla and wife Crispina (charged with adultery) to Capri where they were executed.

The Praetorian Guard slaughtered the kissable Saoterus. The Emperor thereupon executed the prefect, or commander, of the guard and appointed a friend named Perennis to the job. Commodus was an expert at delegating authority. He did practically nothing that he should have been doing as emperor but instead let Perennis handle everything, including military affairs. The troops way up north in Britain became annoyed about the way things were going back home and voted to depose Commodus. They informed a lieutenant named Priscus that he was about to become emperor, but Priscus was too smart to want the job. He told them with a sneer, "I am no more an emperor than you are soldiers."

Those troops were reprimanded for insubordination, so they sent 1500 javelin men from their own ranks back to Italy. They were near Rome when Commodus, after pulling himself together, went out to meet them and inquire what they had in mind. Their spokesman spun a story about how they had come to protect the dear emperor from Perennis, who they said was plotting to make his own son emperor. Commodus handed over Perennis to the soldiers, who killed him, his wife, his sister, and two sons.

Commodus went back, not noticeably grieving, to his chariot racing and other amusements. He was drunk much of the time in company of his choosing: three hundred girls selected from among Rome's most notorious prostitutes and three hundred pretty young boys. Letting other men run the empire, Commodus found ample time to spend in the arena. With his own hands, in two days he dispatched five hippopotami and two elephants. This wasn't as dangerous as it might have been: he shot his arrows from a high platform, and those big targets in a relatively small space didn't even require a very good bowman. One day he killed a hundred bears.

Privately, he contended as a gladiator with real weapons and, said Dio Cassius with a sniff of disdain, "managed to kill a man now and then," or cut off a nose or an ear. For a gentleman, not to speak of an emperor, to fight with gladiators was to stoop very low. Gladiators were either slaves, trained and bought in job lots by rich men as an investment, or criminals condemned to death. In public contests, Commodus played at fighting, using a shield and a wooden sword against opponents armed only with a wand. Naturally, he always won. After he was back to his safe seat, the really bloody battles began down in the amphitheater.

Commodus got his jollies in peculiar ways. Once he gathered all the men in the city who had lost their feet by disease or accident. He had their knees bound and costumed them so they looked like snakes. For weapons, he gave them sponges. Then he beat the cripples to death with a club.

Some of Commodus's extravagances only made him look silly, but when he took a notion that various people were out to get him he was very dangerous indeed. He lopped off heads. When a great pestilence spread through Rome, so bad that two thousand people a day were dying, our reporter, Dio Cassius, commented that the emperor was "a greater curse to the Romans than any pestilence."

Commodus's good opinion of himself became more and more inflated. He had his name put on long-established statues and monuments as the builder of them, he arranged to set up statues of himself as Hercules, and he even ordered that the Eternal City should be named Commodiana. This idea didn't catch on, however. Rome is still Rome.

Money was always in short supply, no matter how much he wrung out of the available sources. He spent wildly, on one occasion suddenly sponsoring thirty horse races in two hours. He brought charges against rich men and women and let them buy their lives with their money. One pretty nice source of funds was the Roman Senate, to which Dio Cassius belonged. That plainspoken historian wrote:

> And finally he ordered us, our wives, and our children each to contribute two gold pieces every year on his birthday as a kind of first fruits, and commanded the Senators in all the other cities to give five denarii apiece. Of this, too, he saved nothing, but spent it all disgracefully on his wild beasts and his gladiators.

Commodus gave the months of the year new names—his various names and titles. This idea didn't quite catch on. July and August are named for two of his illustrious predecessors, but there's no Commodus on the calendar. When he sent a written message to the Senate, he pulled out all the stops with this salutation:

"The Emperor Caesar Lucius Aelius Aurelius Commodus Augustus Pius Felix Sarmaticus Germanicus Maximus Britannicus, Pacifier of the Whole Earth, Invincible, the Roman Hercules, Pontifex Maximus, Holder of the Tribunician Authority for the eighteenth time, Father of his Country, to consuls, praetors, tribunes, and the fortunate Commodian Senate: Greetings."

Like everybody else, the Senators of Rome were afraid of him. Once they reached a state of hysterical panic and almost burst out laughing—which would have been disastrous. On this occasion Commodus had killed an ostrich and cut its head off in the amphitheater. He climbed up to where the Senators were sitting, wearing laurel garlands as was customary at such ceremonies. Holding the bird's head in one hand and in the other, upraised, a bloody sword, he grinned and wagged his head, getting the idea across very nicely that he was thinking about lopping the Senators' heads. Dio Cassius wrote:

Many would indeed have perished by the sword on the spot, for laughing at him (for it was laughter rather than indignation that overcame us), if I had not chewed some laurel leaves, which I got from my garland, and persuaded the others who were sitting near me to do the same, so that in the steady movement of our jaws we might conceal the fact that we were laughing.

The Romans began to suspect that something big was going to happen. There were portents: eagles (birds of ill omen) circled over the Capitol, screaming, and an owl hooted there. A fire that began in a house spread to the Temple of Peace and then to some warehouses. Not all the efforts of civilians and soldiers could extinguish the flames, even when the godlike Commodus arrived to cheer the firefighters. When everything in the area was burned, the fire stopped.

The omens were right. Something did happen to Commodus shortly after that. A slave dropped a tablet from a palace window, not by accident, and on it was found written a long list of names: the people Commodus could do without. Included were Laetus, currently prefect of the Praetorian Guard, Eclectus, the imperial chamberlain, and Marcia, the Emperor's mistress.

The three nominees conferred. Marcia fed her lover some poisoned beef, but he vomited it up (because, Dio Cassius said, of his "immoderate use of wine and baths") and became nastily suspicious. So the three plotters called in one Narcissus, Commodus' wrestling partner, who obligingly strangled him while he was indulging in one of those immoderate baths.

When Commodus died, December 31, A.D. 192, an old soldier named Pertinax was elevated to the throne, protesting every step of the way. He tried to pattern himself after Marcus Aurelius, of revered memory. He hustled to reform the government (thus turning all the hogs at the public trough against him) and held a rummage sale of the treasures of the late Commodus to raise badly needed money. But he was a dull fellow; the people just didn't like him. He reigned for two months and twenty-five days; then the Praetorian Guard murdered him. (The grim veterans of the far-flung legions sometimes schemed, but the local guard were the effective king makers, being closer to the political action.)

So the empire was up for grabs. In fact it was auctioned off. The guards who had assassinated Pertinax started bidding against each other. One named Julian promised each guardsman more money than the other candidates did and was proclaimed emperor. The citizens rioted, and a couple of provincial governors marched on Rome with their legions. Julian was assassinated after a reign even shorter than that of Pertinax—two months and five days.

The year A.D. 193 was a bumper one for Roman emperors. The third one, Septimus Severus, one of the rebellious governors, was a tough soldier who was proclaimed emperor by the legions in the woods near Vienna. He was smart. He banished the Praetorian Guard, which had thrown its weight around in previous administrations, and kept his job for eighteen years.

8
Attila the Hun

Died A.D. 453

*If you yearn for power and glory, re-
member that Attila gained them but is
still hated after fifteen centuries.*

In World War I, the English-speaking
Allied peoples applied the ultimate
epithet to their enemies. Every German was a "Hun." For fifteen
centuries, the name Hun had stood for the worst kind of barbarism. He revelled in indiscriminate slaughter, rape, looting, burning, unrestrained avarice, and vicious duplicity—crimes which
had earned for the formidable Hun leader Attila the title of
"Scourge of God."

It was widely believed in Attila's day—the fifth century A.D.—
that the Huns were offsprings of devils fornicating with humans.
And it may have been this supposed ancestry which helped account
for the fear they roused wherever they went. Actually, the Huns
came from the plains of east or central Asia, and Attila claimed
descent from a 1000 years of ancestral marriages with Chinese
and Indo-Scythian princesses. He had no reason to be impressed
by Roman emperors whose families had been commoners a gen-
eration or so before.

We don't know when Attila was born, but in 434 his uncle
Ruas—then king of the Huns—died leaving the throne to the
brothers Bleda and Attila. Bleda apparently was the older, but
Attila killed him in 445 and ruled as sole king until his death in
453. Fratricide thus launched a career notable for its violence
and cunning.

Most of what we know about Attila—his looks, personality,
living habits—comes from two more or less contemporary historians, the Byzantine historian Priscus, who actually met Attila,
and Jordanes the Gothic historian, who lived some years after

Attila's death. Oddly enough, considering their subject, both painted Attila in relatively favorable terms.

Jordanes described him as "a man marvelous for his glorious fame among all nations," a man who "was born into the world to shake the nations, the scourge of all lands." His walk was haughty and arrogant, and he had an unpleasant habit of rolling his eyes like a toad in a hailstorm. Physically, Attila was "short of stature, with a broad chest and a large head; his eyes were small, his beard thin and sprinkled with gray; and he had a flat nose and a swarthy complexion, showing the evidences of his origins." Although Huns had a custom of flattening the heads of their children, no mention is made of this as far as Attila is concerned.

In 448, the government of the Eastern Roman (or Byzantine) empire in Constantinople sent its ambassador, Maximin, on a special mission to Attila. The historian Priscus went along for the ride. And he was impressed by what he saw.

Attila apparently had the same quality so much noted in Napoleon: simplicity of dress, manners, and actions in a sea of garish vulgarity. Priscus found Attila living in a wooden house, sitting on a wooden chair, eating meat from a wooden trencher, all this surrounded by a wooden fence. In everything, says Priscus, Attila showed himself temperate. His clothes were clean and plain. He didn't have his sword or his shoes or his horse's bridle duded up with gold and gems as other Scythians did.

Attila threw a great party for the Romans, with lots of wine, naked slave girls, and jesters. In the midst of it all, Attila made a "dignified" entry, and while his guests were living it up Attila remained aloof and of "unchanging countenance." Only when his young son, Ernas, showed up did Attila smile. Priscus learned that some seer had told Attila that his empire would crumble at his death, only to be restored by this boy. This seer proved fallible, for it never happened.

All available sources indicate that Attila was no mere slob of a barbarian. He could be courteous; the great historian Edward Gibbon comments favorably on the way Attila treated guests. He occasionally showed pity to fallen foes, almost alone in this respect among the hordes of barbarian leaders who attacked Rome. And, again almost unique among barbarian leaders, Attila used guile, cunning, and deception as a prelude to naked force. He was as much at home with the dagger of treachery as with the battle ax of war. In this he matched the Romans, and indeed outplayed them at their own game.

But Attila was not to be used by anyone. Under his rule, the Huns became "the terrors of the world," conquering, looting, and overcoming. And of Attila it was said that "grass never grew on the spot where his horse had trod." He sent chills up and down Priscus' spine when he noted: "For what fortress, what city, in the wide extent of the Roman empire, can hope to exist, secure and impregnable, if it is our pleasure that it should be erased from the earth?" It was no idle boast. In his lifetime, Attila literally destroyed dozens of cities, putting their inhabitants to the sword and the flame.

Attila loved war. For him, it was the only way to get ahead in the world. But he excelled his followers not so much in courage as in brains. War was fun, of course, but it was a means to an end rather than an end in itself. Terror was a calculated objective. It pleased him when his Thuringian allies followed the ways of the Huns. It amused him when they massacred hostages, slaughtered prisoners, and killed some 200 young girls who fell into their hands, their bodies torn apart by horses or crushed under heavy wagons and left by the wayside for vultures and dogs.

From about 445 to his death, Attila was the most powerful man in the known world. The two Roman empires—both East and West—cringed before him. Attila took this as a matter of course. After all, he had the "Sword of Mars" (sometimes called the "Sword of God") in his hands. Priscus reported the curious circumstances of its discovery: A herdsman noticed that a heifer was limping because of a cut foot but he couldn't understand how she had been wounded. He backtracked along the trail of blood left by the injured animal—and found a sharp sword, partly buried. He dug it up and took it right to Attila, who accepted it as a gift of the gods and a token that he was to be ruler of the world. He named the weapon the "Sword of Mars" and believed it would give him victory in all his battles.

Soon after murdering his brother Bleda in 445, Attila consolidated his rule over the Hunnish world. It stretched from the Don to the Rhine, a vast amalgam of peoples rather than of territories. Included in his empire were present-day Austria, Hungary, Rumania, part of the Balkans, and southern Russia. How far north it extended is uncertain, but clearly all the major Germanic tribes were his vassals. These had influenced the Huns mightily,

as even Attila is a Germanic name meaning "Little Father."
From this enormous position of power, he set out to contest
Rome's rule of the world.

The Rome of Trajan (at its greatest extent) had long since
disappeared. From the days of Diocletian and Constantine the
Great, the empire had been divided into two parts, the Eastern
empire with its capital at Constantinople, and the Western empire with its capital at Rome—and then (the ultimate indignity)
at Ravenna. Theoretically, it was still one empire; in fact it was
not. The augustus (emperor) in Constantinople was completely
free of the augustus in Rome—and vice versa.

At the beginning of his reign, Attila demanded—and got—
tribute from both Theodosius II in Constantinople and Valentinian III in Ravenna. There was something to his boast that both
emperors, by paying tribute, became his slaves, but neither
Roman emperor recognized such status. In 441, when Attila invaded the Eastern empire, he routed the armies sent against him
by Theodosius II. The upshot was an increase in the yearly tribute from the Eastern empire from 700 to 1200 pounds of gold.

Not content with that, Attila again attacked the Eastern empire in 447. He sacked over seventy cities in Thrace, Thessaly, and
southern Russia. After killing most of the men, the Huns hauled
thousands of women into captivity. The resulting blood mix-
tures account for Mongol features today as far west as Rhine-
land Germany.

Although Attila couldn't read or write (he had to hire a secretary who knew Latin), he had an awful lot of correspondence in
the year 450. Theodosius II died in Constantinople, and Marcian
I, who succeeded him, flatly refused to pay further tribute. This
led to a great many letters and threats, and Attila was sorely
tempted to strike again. But he had ravaged the Balkans enough,
and greener pastures lay to the west. Besides, he was involved
in a very peculiar affair with Valentinian III's sister (whom he
never met, by the way).

Valentinian was an oaf, and a stupid one at that. He didn't know
the first thing about running an empire, although he had done
fairly well under the guidance of his famous mother, the Empress
Galla Placidia, until her death in 450. All the brains, ambition,
and character were to be found in his sister, Justa Grata Honoria.
As a young girl, she had been elevated to the rank of augusta
(empress), probably about the time Valentinian became augus-

tus, and she had been an important pawn in her mother's and brother's politics until brother Val had produced heirs of his own.

Honoria was tough-minded and not about to play second fiddle to anyone. And she didn't like her brother's plan to marry her to some old dotard who wouldn't think of plotting to become emperor himself. At age thirty, she was still unmarried and at long last decided to do something about it. In 449, she had an affair with her steward Eugenius. Maybe she was in love, but her main aim was to talk Eugenius into killing her brother. Unfortunately for Honoria, the plot was discovered. Eugenius was executed, and Honoria barely escaped the same fate. Instead she was betrothed to a dull old man, Flavius Bassus Herculanus, whom she couldn't abide.

Something had to be done at once. Why she latched on to Attila we don't know, but she sent a trusty slave, Hyacinthus, to Attila with a goodly amount of cash (to buy his assistance to stop the marriage with Flavius) and her ring (to show Attila that the whole deal had lovely possibilities).

When the money and ring reached Attila, together with the plea to be Honoria's champion in her fight with her brother, the "Scourge of God" revealed a puckish sense of humor. Obviously, said Attila, Honoria wanted to marry him (why else send her ring?), and he was happy to oblige. And he thought that just about half of the Western Empire ought to be turned over to him for his new fiancée.

So Attila wrote to Valentinian demanding his bride and half the empire. Valentinian was fit to be tied. He thoroughly tortured Hyacinthus and then beheaded the wretch. His mother talked him out of killing Honoria, but he sent her into exile to Constantinople. But, even worse, he refused to pay any more gold to the Huns.

Attila needed no more excuses to stop harassing the Eastern empire and turn to the west. With 500,000 horsemen under his command, early in 451 he wheeled out of Hungary through Germany and into France. On the way, he sacked Trier and Metz and liquidated the entire population of the two towns.

At this point, a curious Christian tradition enters the story. A princess of Cornwall, Ursula by name, was sailing across the English Channel with 11,000 virgins in her train. (This is the first questionable part of the story—that as many as 11,000 virgins existed in the whole of Europe!) In any event, a storm blew up and carried Ursula and her gaggle of virgins all the way up the Rhine to Cologne. There they had the misfortune to run into Attila and his crowd who massacred them all.

Centuries later, lots of bones were discovered in Cologne (they are still on view), along with an inscription which read: "Ursula et Undecimilla Virgines." This can be translated as either "the virgins Ursula and Undecimilla" or "Ursula and the 11,000 Virgins." Take your pick. In any event, Ursula is now a saint.

After presumably meeting with Ursula, Attila launched a full-scale invasion of France. So frightened were the Romans and Visigoths (who had conquered Spain by this time) that they joined forces under Aetius, the last of the great Roman generals. In 451 near present-day Troyes (although the battle is traditionally called the Battle of Châlons), the contending forces met in a crunching and bloody mayhem. Over 165,000 men were killed, including the king of the Goths. Actually, the battle was a kind of draw, although Attila was first to retire. As a result, the Battle of Châlons has for centuries been on everybody's list of the ten or twenty "greatest battles of history." Significantly, for the first time Attila the "Scourge of God" was in retreat.

Undaunted by his "defeat" at Châlons, Attila again demanded Honoria as his bride and invaded Italy in 452. He first laid siege to Aquileia, the major city of what is now Venetia. It was a hard nut to crack, and things didn't go at all well. Attila's soldiers became discouraged (after all, they were nomads attacking a walled city). Another retreat seemed in order, until one day Attila was out for a stroll. He noticed that the storks in Aquileia were carrying their young out of the city. To Attila, who was always superstitious, this was a good sign. He assembled his troops and informed them that the storks were leaving because they foresaw the future of the city: it was doomed to fall.

Taking heart from the signs and his words, Attila's troops soon captured the city and it was literally destroyed, never to rise again. A few of its citizens managed to escape to some islands in the Adriatic and there founded the city of Venice.

Attila then swung into Italy proper. On the way to Rome, he reduced to ashes and rubble Vicenza, Verona, Padua, and some other cities. Both Milan and Pavia, by now scared out of their wits, bought mercy with all their portable wealth. A curious incident occurred in Milan. Attila came across a picture showing a Roman emperor seated on his throne with the princes of

Scythia prostrate at his feet. This wouldn't do, said Attila, and he called in a painter to reverse the characters in the painting.

With this affront to his ego settled, Attila now set out for Rome. Attempting to stave off another sack of Rome (Alaric the Visigoth had taken the city in 410), Valentinian sent out an embassy headed by Pope Leo.

The meeting between Pope Leo and Attila was memorable. The Apostles Peter and Paul appeared with swords above the pontiff's head and threatened Attila with all kinds of horrible things. Raphael's version of this may still be seen in the Vatican. Attila at once ordered his hordes to retreat. Why is not clear, but plague had broken out among his troops, and food was in short supply. Besides, a number of his friends pointed out to Attila that Alaric in 410 had died almost at once after sacking the Holy City.

Attila returned to his capital at what is now Budapest. (In the Niebelungen legends, Attila was called Etzel, and as late as the nineteenth century some Hungarians called Budapest Etzelnburg or Attila's City.) Once home, Attila apparently gave up all hope of marrying Honoria. Instead, he took as his last wife a beautiful maiden named Ildico in 453.

The marriage banquet must have been a knockout, and, contrary to habit, Attila drank himself almost literally to death. Or else the pleasures of the bed were too much for even him. He died during the night of a massive throat hemorrhage. As Jordanes described it: "Thus did drunkenness put a disgraceful end to a king renowned in war." And Priscus reports that the Emperor Marcian in Constantinople dreamed of Attila's bow broken asunder.

Oddly enough, Attila conquered through death what had eluded him in life. Valentinian the Stupid slew Aetius with his own hands, once the Hunnish danger was averted, and never again did the Western Roman empire produce a man of such quality. In twenty-three years the Western empire was gone too, although the Eastern empire was to last for another 1000 years.

9
Fredegunda and Brunechildis

Died A.D. 597 and 613 respectively

*Have you any female in-laws who don't
get along very well? Thank your lucky
stars they aren't as bitchy as
Fredegunda and Brunechildis.*

In the early decades of the fourth
century A.D., numerous barbarian
tribes swept into and through Roman Gaul and formed the basis of
what we now speak of as France. The Franks were the last of
these barbarians to settle in the area, and in 481 Clovis became
their king.

The first thing Clovis did was to unite—forcibly—all the
Franks under his rule to create the Merovingian dynasty. (A lot
of the Franks lived in what is now West Germany, and the
French and the Germans haven't been very good neighbors ever
since.) Now that he was king, Clovis was persuaded by his wife,
Clotilda, to become a Christian. This was in 496, and Clovis then
made everybody become Christian. The conversion of Clovis and
his family was less than skin-deep. They may have made it into
the main tent, but all their little pagan sideshows went merrily
on.

Clovis made Paris his capital on the Seine. In 511 he died, king
of the united Franks and nominally a Roman consul. Essentially
more barbarian in his ways than Roman, he followed the stupid
barbarian custom of dividing his estate among his four sons.
Each got a part of the empire, with capitals at Metz, Soissons,
Orléans, and Paris.

After a lot of in-fighting among the boys, only Chlothar survived, and once again (558–561) the Frankish empire was united.
But Chlothar hadn't learned a thing, and he divided the empire
among *his* four sons.

Sibling rivalry was just as intense this time, and there was a lot more fighting. Finally, three more or less definable kingdoms emerged. In the east was Austrasia, with its capital at Metz. This became the bailiwick of a certain lady named Brunechildis. In what is now mostly France was the kingdom of Neustria ("new land"), and it was as queen of Neustria that Fredegunda made her mark. Gallo-Roman influence was strong here. And then there was Burgundy, which often recognized the king of Neustria as ruler.

Keeping all these lands and peoples in mind is very confusing. This period is called the Dark Ages because we don't know as much about them as we should like. A lot of our knowledge of the vendetta between the two royal rivals Fredegunda and Brunechildis comes from just two men. One was an eminent churchman, Bishop Gregory of Tours. Like everybody else, he thought Fredegunda was a bitch—and a murderess. But to Gregory Brunechildis was virtue and beauty incarnate. He never wrote a nasty thing about her. Fredegar was the other writer who left us descriptions of Fredegunda and Brunechildis. Like Gregory, he thought Fredegunda was a bitch—and a murderess. As a matter of fact, nobody ever said anything nice about her. As for Brunechildis, Fredegar was equally frank. She too was a bitch—and a murderess. But Gregory and Fredegar agreed on one thing. Both Fredegunda and Brunechildis were exceptionally beautiful and willful ladies.

Our story begins in 561. Chlothar I, who had reunited his father's realm by disposing of his brothers and their sons, died and in his turn divided the empire among his four sons. The same old mess all over again. But this time sibling rivalry among the four was accentuated by the fight-to-the-death between Brunechildis and Fredegunda.

Chlothar's eldest, Caribert, soon disappeared (probably at the hands of his brothers), and the other three sons divided up the empire. Chilperic—soon to be Fredegunda's husband—got Neustria. Sigibert—shortly to marry Brunechildis—got Austrasia. And Gontran got Burgundy. To add to the confusion, each brother got a slice of the others' lands. Most of the hard cash and serfs were in the northern part of the empire, and each wanted some of that. The south was graced with vines that produced good red and white wine. And ever since they had become civilized, the Franks had discarded their old fermented barley drink and

had taken to wine. In short, almost all of them became winos.
Between eating with their fingers and swilling down the vino,
their dinners were rather messy.

The three brothers were not nice people. They broke their
solemn oaths, slaughtered persons to whom they owed gratitude,
robbed everybody (dead or alive), murdered their relatives, and
tortured their enemies. They'd had good training at home. Their
father, Chlothar, killed one of their brothers by locking him with
his wife and children in a wooden house and setting fire to it.

Merovingian royalty had something else in common. They were
royal hippies. At one time, every Frank wore long hair, but the
style had changed—except among the royal family—and now
long hair distinguished the rulers from the subjects. They took
this long-hair business very seriously. Any prince who got a
haircut couldn't become king.

Being good Merovingians (which means being bad people), the
three boys had all kinds of things to fight about. This was normal
Merovingian family life. Gontran of Burgundy wasn't a king,
and he stayed out of the fighting between Chilperic and Sigibert
most of the time. Somebody even called him "the good Gontran."
It was different with Chilperic and Sigibert, who had the added
spark of rivalry between their wives.

It all started with the marriage of Brunechildis to Sigibert.
At this time, another barbarian tribe, the Visigoths, controlled
Spain. Their king, Athanagild, had two beautiful daughters,
Brunechildis and Galswintha. Stories of their loveliness were told
all over Europe, and Sigibert became interested. In 567, he sent
an embassy bearing rich gifts to Athanagild and asked for the
hand of Brunechildis. After some haggling, the Visigoth king
accepted the deal, and off to Metz went Brunechildis to marry
Sigibert with great pomp and luxury. The wedding was the talk
of the age.

We don't know much about Sigibert, except that he wore long
hair and was a first-rate stinker. He wasn't exceptional in his
villainies in any way. His only memorable act was to marry
Brunechildis. And he did not last long.

A lot is known about Brunechildis, but trying to assess her
character is not easy, as the evidence is contradictory. Everybody
agreed that she was beautiful, intelligent, ambitious, strong-
willed, and full of energy. But to what purpose did she put her

ambition and will power? Bishop Gregory of Tours thought she
was tops. He found her prudent, restrained in counsel, virtuous,
a devout churchwoman, and pleasant to be around.

Her detractors found her less than perfect. They attributed
all kinds of minor atrocities to her, like ordering people to be
stoned, debauching her grandsons, and hiring assassins. Fredegar thought she was "a second Jezebel." She was very likely
guilty on all scores, but her mini-crimes were so insignificant
compared to those of Fredegunda that Brunechildis seems almost
saintly. After all, she only did what everybody was doing.

The marriage was celebrated, and Sigibert soon got his new
wife with child. The newlyweds seemed very happy. Not at all
pleased with the coup his brother had pulled off, Chilperic was
jealous as hell. For one thing, he didn't like to hear that Brunechildis was the most beautiful woman in France, which meant
more beautiful than his assorted wives and concubines.

Nothing would do but for Chilperic to send off to Spain and
ask for the hand of Galswintha, Brunechildis' beautiful younger
sister. King Athanagild turned him down cold. Chilperic's reputation was already so bad that the Visigothic king had no desire
to have him as a son-in-law. Chilperic already had some wives,
and tales of his infatuation with a palace servant named Fredegunda had reached the Spanish court.

But Chilperic kept on trying. In the process, he backed himself
into a corner. On a stack of holy relics, he swore that he would
put away all his other women and love only Galswintha. He convinced Athanagild, despite the weeping and yelling of Galswintha
and her mother. So Galswintha became Chilperic's bride.

Nobody had anything nice to say about Chilperic—and with
good reason. When Bishop Gregory called him "the Nero and
Herod" of his age, he wasn't kidding. Chilperic was brutal and
cruel, cunning and superstitious, a man whose love for hunting
carried over to his passion for vendettas and atrocities. He was
given to fits of temper, and once in a fury he had one poor wretch
burned with red-hot irons in the armpits, the elbows, behind the
knees, and in the crotch—and then had him torn limb from limb.

Chilperic was a terrible man and also a strange one. He loved
rare ornaments, meddled in theological arguments (to the extent
of heresy, thought Bishop Gregory), and wrote some pretty good
poetry. Once he even got involved in reforming the alphabet for

the Frankish speech and ordered everybody to write the new way—or have their eyes put out, hardly the best method of teaching people to read and write.

Such a man as Chilperic was not apt to find much marital bliss with his new wife. Galswintha was pretty, cloyingly sweet, and reticent, a regular sixth-century Elsie Dinsmore. Chilperic stood her as long as he could—about three months—and then had her strangled in bed. He probably was put up to the job by Fredegunda, although he obviously didn't take much persuading.

Ever since Chilperic could remember, Fredegunda had been hanging around the palace doing odd jobs, a servant by day and a whore by night. Lowborn but with vaulting ambition—and the talent to go with it—she had set her cap at Chilperic. She slept with him whenever she could, but that didn't mean much to Chilperic, who slept with anyone. Somehow she had to insinuate herself into the heart and guts of this terrible man.

She used every dirty trick in the book. One of Chilperic's early wives (chroniclers of the day gave up hope of trying to count how many he had) was a girl named Audovera. While Chilperic was away at war, Audovera gave birth to a girl. When the question of baptism came up, poor dumb Audovera asked Fredegunda's advice. She followed it and Audovera became her own daughter's godmother—but canon law forbade such a relationship. Chilperic occasionally followed church law, and this was such an occasion. He shut Audovera into a nunnery where the duped innocent lived for fifteen years before Fredegunda had her murdered.

Fredegunda had a beautiful face and a great figure. Chilperic was a sucker for both. He found her intelligent, cunning (almost all accounts of Fredegunda's life use this word repeatedly), and as cruel, unscrupulous, and vicious as he was. Theirs was a union made in hell. Following Galswintha's murder Chilperic married Fredegunda, and the serving wench became queen of Neustria. Both body and brains aided her to the top.

It was Galswintha's murder and the instigator's marriage to the murderer that began the lifelong feud between Brunechildis and Fredegunda. Brunechildis, outraged at her sister's murder, demanded that her husband Sigibert wreak vengeance on his brother. Open warfare started and it was not to end for forty years. Husbands, sons, and grandsons—not to mention odds and ends of nephews, nieces, cousins—engaged in a bloodbath.

At first, Brunechildis's forces (nominally Sigibert's) success-
fully invaded Neustria, and things got tight for Fredegunda and
Chilperic. But in 575, Fredegunda hired an assassin who managed to kill Sigibert in Paris. Paid killers flourished at this time,
and Fredegunda often employed them. She once hired a fellow
to stab Brunechildis. He failed, poor lad. Fredegunda was a
stickler for success, and things had to be done right. To show
her displeasure, she had his hands and feet cut off.

With Sigibert dead, Brunechildis was really in hot water. She
had accompanied Sigibert and her oldest son, Childebert, to Paris.
Sigibert's allies sensibly went over to Chilperic, and Brunechildis
found herself about to become the prisoner of her sister's murderer. Her first worry was Childebert, now king of Austrasia.
Her son wouldn't stand a chance if Chilperic got his hands on
him. With the aid of faithful friends and servants, she got him
to safety by hiding the boy in a market basket and smuggling
him out of the palace. He reached Metz, where the nobles crowned
him Childebert II.

Brunechildis wasn't so lucky. Chilperic got hold of her and her
treasure. Strangely enough—maybe it was because she was so
beautiful and so unhappy—she came to no harm. All Chilperic
did was to send her under guard, as a prisoner, to Rouen, while
he kept her jewels.

With Brunechildis under lock and key, it looked as though
Fredegunda had won hands down. But apparently Brunechildis
had that same fascination that Mary Queen of Scots later used
to make men do stupid things. While Chilperic's prisoner in
Paris, the tragic—but still young and beautiful—queen had won
the heart of Merovech, Chilperic's son (by Audovera) and heir.

The young fool went completely gaga over Brunechildis. When
his father ordered him on a military raid, he rushed to Rouen
instead. He proposed marriage. Brunechildis—who had nothing
to lose—said yes, and the two found a bishop named Praetextatus
to marry them, although it was against canon law for a nephew
to marry his uncle's widow. And she became Fredegunda's step-
daughter!

It was a lucky break for Brunechildis. She was free and soon
found herself safe in Metz. Things didn't go so well for young
Merovech. Chilperic was furious when he heard the news and
condemned his son to death. After many adventures, flitting from
hiding place to hiding place, Merovech induced a faithful vassal,

Galen, to kill him lest he fall into his father's hands. Cheated of the joy of torturing his son to death, Chilperic took due pleasure in killing his son's friends. Praetextatus was killed at the foot of the altar. Galen had his feet, hands, ears, and nose cut off before being butchered. One friend was tortured and beheaded, another broken on the wheel.

Meanwhile back in Neustria, Fredegunda was bearing children and getting rid of people who annoyed her. An official in the government, a fellow named Leudast, particularly irritated her. She talked Chilperic into having him killed, but Leudast managed to stay one step ahead of the posse sent out to grab him. Finally his luck ran out. While crossing a bridge, he broke his leg and suffered severe head wounds from his pursuers. Always one to lend a flavor to murder, Chilperic ordered physicians to tend Leudast's wounds so that he could be subjected to prolonged tortures when well. As luck would have it, Leudast's wounds began to putrefy, and it was clear that his end was near. It was too bad, of course, but Fredegunda rose to the occasion. Leudast was laid flat on the ground. She had a large iron bar placed under his neck. Then her servants hit his throat with another. It was the best she could do under the circumstances.

One of Fredegunda's problems was that Chilperic had had several wives and legitimate children before she appeared on the scene. One way or another, she would have to dispose of them. But first she had to have sons of her own. As a brood mare, Fredegunda was no slouch. One after another, Samson, Clodebert, and Dagobert were born. But all three died of the plague within days of each other.

Fredegunda was convinced that witchcraft had caused her little princes to die. And it just so happened (conveniently) that the court lady Fredegunda figured as the witch had a beautiful daughter who was in love with Chlodovech, the last living son of Chilperic and Audovera. Fredegunda said they were all guilty, and Chilperic believed her.

Fredegunda had the girl stripped naked and flogged before her mother and her lover. The mother was put to the torture and confessed herself a witch. With a touching show of paternal feeling, Chilperic threw Chlodovech into a dungeon. A few days later, he was found stabbed to death. Only one of Audovera's daughters was left alive. Fredegunda "gave her to the soldiers" (which means that she was raped several hundred times) and then locked her up in a nunnery.

While continuing to bear sons by Chilperic, Fredegunda eventually liquidated all her husband's other sons. Her next oldest son, a boy named Theodoric, died, and Fredegunda again convinced herself that witches had done the foul deed. She decided to use the incident to rid Neustria of a few witches and her favorite enemy at the time. She had run out of Chilperic's children to kill and could devote her attention to people around Chilperic whom she didn't like. One such was the prefect of the palace, Mummolus.

It took some doing, but Fredegunda persuaded Chilperic that Mummolus was somehow behind the death of her beloved Theodoric. She found a gaggle of old crones in the Paris slums and accused them of witchcraft. They all confessed that Mummolus' was the cause. "We gave your son, O Queen," they said, "in exchange for Mummolus the prefect's life."

With that handy confession, she finished off the Parisian ladies. Some were drowned, a few burned, and some were tied to wheels which broke all their bones. Mummolus was next. With his hands tied behind his back, he was strung up to a beam like a trussed chicken. That hurt, but Mummolus didn't confess a word. Fredegunda then had him stretched on a wheel until his bones came out of their sockets. She then had him beaten with leather thongs until, as Bishop Gregory relates, "the torturers were wearied out." Then, to add a little finesse to the scene, Fredegunda had splinters of wood driven under his finger- and toenails. By this time, Mummolus was in pretty sad shape. For some unexplained reason, Fredegunda said enough was enough and sent him home, where he promptly—and understandably—died.

Having done in Chilperic's other children, Fredegunda ended up with two of her own. Her boy was to succeed his father as Chlothar II, and very quickly showed that he had inherited father's cruelty and mother's viciousness. The girl's name was Ridegunda, and she was another chip off the old block. She and her mother didn't get along, and they were always slapping and kicking each other. One day, after Ridegunda had been particularly abusive by ridiculing Fredegunda's serving-wench background, Fredegunda decided she'd had enough. She lured Ridegunda to an old chest by promising the girl the jewels under the layer of clothes. Ridegunda poked her head in the chest, and Fredegunda slammed down the lid on her daughter's neck.

In 584, it was Chilperic's turn. He and Fredegunda hadn't been getting along too well for some time. She charmed one of the guards officers, a rogue named Landeric, and often bedded down with him. In time, Fredegunda feared that Chilperic knew something was going on, so she decided to kill him. One day, after an arduous hunt, Chilperic returned home and dismounted. Up ran a man who stabbed the king in one armpit and then in the belly. Old Chilperic never had a chance. He died within minutes.

Nobody knew for sure who killed Chilperic, but the assassin was certainly one of Fredegunda's servants. It didn't take long for most people to put two and two together. Fredegunda grabbed her boy, Chlothar, and headed for the Burgundian court of Chilperic's brother, Gontran. With three brothers murdered, Gontran vowed to get to the bottom of Chilperic's assassination "to put an end to the wicked custom of killing kings."

In a complicated series of maneuvers, Fredegunda convinced Gontran of her innocence (was he ever gullible!) and under her brother-in-law's protection established her son Chlothar II on the throne of Neustria. For a time, Gontran questioned little Chlothar's legitimacy, but Fredegunda's old charm still had its magic. She got three bishops and 200 nobles to swear on holy relics that the boy's father was Chilperic.

Fredegunda tried to spread it around that Brunechildis was really Chilperic's murderess, but she couldn't make it stick. Nobody believed her, with the possible exception of young Chlothar.

And so the war between the two queens went on and on. Fredegunda ruled Neustria as regent for Chlothar, and Brunechildis ran Austrasia for her son Childebert II and his two sons, Theudebert II and Theuderich II.

At last—it was 597—Fredegunda took to her bed and died. She was as serene in conscience as an angel and apparently looked forward to a life in paradise. She died a happy and successful woman.

Brunechildis lived another sixteen years, meddling like mad in the affairs of Austrasia and Burgundy. The years were chaotic, but finally Brunechildis decided it was time to settle accounts with the late Fredegunda by disposing of her hateful son, Chlothar II. The contending armies of Austrasia and Neustria met in 613, and Brunechildis's men ran away. Those left surrendered the aging queen to Chlothar.

Her rival's son showed Brunechildis no mercy. Chlothar accused her of the murder of ten kings, history's record for regicide: Sigibert, Merovech, his father Chilperic, Theudebert and his son Chlothar, Chlothar's son (another Merovech), Theuderic and his three sons. It is almost certain that Brunechildis was blameless on all counts, but Fredegunda's son cared as little for truth as she had.

For three days, Brunechildis was subjected to "nameless tortures." Finally Chlothar ordered her mounted naked on a camel and exposed to the catcalls of the troops. She was then tied by the hair, one leg, and one arm to the tail of a wild horse which dragged her to her death. Fredegunda would have loved the whole ghastly scene.

10
Marozia
the Pope-Maker

*A thousand years ago one woman
proved supremely able in running
church and secular affairs and set an
unequaled record.*

For centuries women have been trying to get equal rights. Now and then one succeeds. There is a legend that in the ninth century a woman even became pope. Her name was Joan, and several hundred years later, from 1400 to 1600, a bust of "Johannes VIII, *femina ex Anglia*," is said to have been displayed among the busts of popes in Sienna Cathedral.

Passing as a man, Joan of England became a very learned monk and a teacher in a college in Rome. The story goes that, on the death of Leo IV in 855 she became pope, but after a reign of two years, one month, and four days her sex was discovered when, during a solemn procession, she gave birth to a baby and died. (Obviously somebody had discovered her sex several months earlier.) She was buried on the spot where this remarkable event took place, between the Colosseum and St. Clemente. A statue was erected there of Joan with the child in her arms and the papal miter on her head. After her, candidates for the papacy had to undergo a physical examination so that no such embarrassment would occur again.

Believing all this requires some imagination, of course. Joan is supposed to have reigned between Leo IV (who became a saint) and Benedict III, but Leo died July 17, 855, and Benedict was consecrated immediately thereafter, so how Joan reigned as *la Papessa Giovanna* for more than two years between them is something you will have to figure out for yourself.

A few decades later the ambitious wife and the daughter of an Italian noble named Theophylact came close to equaling the record of the legendary Pope Joan. Neither of them actually became pope or even wanted to, but they made popes, ruled them, and murdered them. Theophylact and his wife Theodora had daughters named Marozia and Theodora. Theodora the younger didn't do anything historically spectacular.

The elder Theodora and her daughter Marozia were pretty successful in using all their God-given advantages—good looks, no scruples, and great talent for public (and private) affairs. Their era became known as the pornocracy, government by dissolute women.

Theophylact presided over the papal treasury. He was a sort of Prime Minister and Commander-in-Chief. As his womenfolk's meddling became more and more successful, he assumed the titles of Duke, Consul, and Senator of Rome. He was not just *a* Senator, but *the* Senator, *dominus urbis*, lord of the city. Theodora the elder and her daughter Marozia, unwilling to be ignored, also assumed the title of Senator.

Those were turbulent times in Italy, which was united only by religion. Scandals at the ecclesiastical as well as the secular level were the order of the day. There was usually a power struggle in the church and in the various secular governments, and in addition the church claimed temporal as well as spiritual sovereignty. A few years before Theodora and Marozia came to the fore (and certainly while they were in power), there were wild goings-on. In the years between 896 and 904, known as "the dark age of the papacy," there were ten popes, most of whom gained or lost the office by murder and intrigue. In those days popes were not elected in the solemn ceremony that now prevails. It was more like a dogfight.

Pope Formosus (891–896) made a fatal error: he crowned one of Charlemagne's numerous illegitimate descendants Emperor of the West. But he had already crowned another candidate for this rather empty honor, and to this candidate a papal aspirant named Stephen was partial. There couldn't be two Emperors of the West.

Formosus died and was succeeded by Boniface VI, who reigned only fifteen days. Then Stephen became Stephen VII and got even with the late Formosus. He dug up the rotting corpse and held a trial over the stinking remains, which had been eight months buried. In this trial, known as the *synod horrenda*, he found the late Formosus guilty as charged, had the three benediction fingers of the right hand hacked off, and threw the naked corpse to a yelling mob in the street.

Right after this there was a disastrous collapse of the Lateran basilica, where the *synod horrenda* had taken place. Some people attributed the collapse to the nasty trial; others said it was caused by an earthquake. Anyway, admirers of the late Formosus caught Stephen VII, stripped him, and strangled him in prison. His immediate successors were Romanus, who reigned for four months, and Theodore II, who lasted for only twenty days. Then *two* popes were elected, Sergius III and John IX, but of course this wouldn't do at all. In the ensuing scramble, John won out— he had more political punch—and excommunicated Sergius, who escaped into Tuscany.

John lasted until 900; Benedict IV followed, holding office until 903. Leo V took office for one month, until a Cardinal named Christopher led an uprising and had him thrown into prison. Christopher usurped the papal throne from September 903 until the following January. He is not, however, named in the church's official list of popes; he was an interloper, an anti-pope. Now the exiled Sergius, who had been plotting with the French, came back and threw Christopher into prison. One story has it that Sergius strangled both Leo and Christopher. Sergius has been described as "malignant, ferocious, and unclean." The one good thing he is remembered for is that he rebuilt the Lateran basilica, which had collapsed after the *synod horrenda*.

With Sergius III in power, Theophylact's family came into its own. Theodora the elder was one of Sergius's supporters, and Marozia, an ambitious teenager, was his paramour. A son was born to Marozia and Sergius. This infant was destined to become John XI. But Sergius died after a reign of seven years and somebody had to fill the papal throne while John was growing up.

Anastasius III reigned uneventfully for the next two years. Landus succeeded him in July 913, and nothing much is known about him except that he took his orders from Theodora the elder. He appointed as archbishop of Ravenna a lover of Theodora's, who succeeded him in March 914 as John X.

For a while this John did as he was told by the ladies of the pornocracy. In a political horse-trade he even appointed a five-year-old child as archbishop of Rheims. And at the behest of these powerful female ward bosses he crowned Berengar, a grandson of Charlemagne, as Emperor of the West in 915. This was an empty title but much in demand.

But John X showed a fatal tendency to branch out and take action without permission. He crowned Rudolf of Burgundy as king of Italy in 922, although the Emperor Berengar had been king for years and thought he still was. Marozia thought he was, too, and Berengar was one of her favorites. She began to take a long, hard look at John X for challenging her authority.

About 924 Marozia's father, mother, and husband—Theophylact, Theodora, and Alberich—disappeared from the pages of history without a trace. Now Marozia was all-powerful, and she had every intention of maintaining that position. She was rich, beautiful, ambitious, and about thirty-four years old. Needing a nice place to live, suitable for a lady of her standing, she seized Hadrian's Tomb and moved in. This roomy mausoleum even had convenient dungeons, and the late Emperor Hadrian wasn't really using it any more, because he had been dead for almost eight hundred years. (The Borgia pope, Alexander VI, fortified it in the fifteenth century, and now it is called the Castle of St. Angelo.) Marozia was senator; she ruled Rome. And she began to look around for another husband. We don't know what had happened to Alberich, but no doubt his widow did.

In 926 the ungrateful John X crowned Hugo of Provence as the next king of Italy (Berengar had been assassinated); and Marozia was fretting because her advice hadn't been asked. But she found a suitable candidate as successor to her missing-presumed-dead husband Alberich. This was Guido, duke of Tuscany, who had political connections and a potential future that appealed to her. She let it be known that she wouldn't mind marrying him.

John X made another awful mistake. He put his foot down. The union of Marozia with Duke Guido was not his idea of sound politics. He had on his side of the argument his brother Peter, Count of Orte, but Marozia was more powerful than both of them combined. At her command, the brothers were seized. Peter was killed before the pope's very eyes, and John X himself was thrown into prison and smothered. The triumphant Marozia married Guido of Tuscany. Her next candidate for the papacy reigned as Leo VI for a few months. There is no record of what became of him. His successor, also put forward by Marozia, ruled for two years as Stephen VIII. He was assassinated, probably by her orders.

The year was now 931, and Marozia's boy John had been growing up. Her younger son Alberich, by her first marriage, had been growing too; she should have kept a closer watch on him, because he turned out to be a menace. Son John became Pope John XI in March 931. He was under age, but that was a small matter. Marozia intended to run things anyway.

While he was in office she became a widow again. The facts are not clear; anyway her second husband disappeared. She had always wanted to be a queen, and the chances looked good. Hugo of Provence, whom John X had crowned king of Italy in 926, had just lost his official wife. Marozia offered him her hand and heart. Hugo was willing. True, he was her brother-in-law by her second husband, so they were related within the prohibited degrees of kinship for marriage, but Marozia told her son the pope to relax the rule. He married the happy couple in the bride's home, Hadrian's tomb.

The obvious next step was to revive the vacant title of emperor for Hugo so that his bride could become empress. The stage was now set for the entry of the other son, Alberich, about eighteen. He had political ambitions, and his mother's shenanigans could wreck them. Furthermore, he didn't like his new stepfather, Hugo, in whose court he was required to act as a page. Alberich spilled a cup of wine on Hugo, who rewarded him by boxing his ears. Alberich rushed out in a rage and began yelling to the people outside the castle. He was a fiery orator and the people of Rome were always open to suggestions. Besides, they considered Marozia's latest marriage incestuous. They assaulted the castle with enthusiasm and damage in mind. The terrified King Hugo had himself let down from a window with a rope and fled from Rome. Alberich threw his mother into prison, and nothing more was ever heard of Marozia.

Alberich governed Rome for twenty years, keeping a tight rein on his half-brother, Pope John XI, who died of natural causes about 935. Alberich was a severe ruler but a good one. This statement is based on the fact that after he died conditions in Rome became far worse. He brought about several needed reforms. He saw to it that the popes who held office during his regime were responsible for spiritual but not temporal affairs. And three times, when King Hugo came clamoring at the city gates with conquest in mind, Alberich repulsed him. Alberich married Hugo's daughter, who was his stepsister, during a lull in the hostilities.

Alberich's ambitions stretched longer than his life. When he was near death from a fever, at about age forty, he assembled the nobles of Rome and made them swear that they would elect his young son Octavian to succeed him as ruler and, when the next vacancy occurred in the papacy, to that high office. Thus he overruled his own decision that spiritual and temporal affairs should be kept separate—but the fact that Octavian was his own son made the difference. Alberich died in 954. Octavian became prince, and, a year later when Pope Agapitus II died, he was crowned Pope John XII. He established the custom, which popes still adhere to, of changing his name.

John XII, sixteen when he began his reign, was a *real* hell-raiser. Grandmother Marozia would have been proud of him. In 963 he was deposed, and a year later he was killed by an outraged husband who came home unexpectedly.

Marozia's descendants were remarkably lucky in attaining the papal throne many decades after she had gone to her eternal reward. Two of her great-grandsons became pope: Benedict VIII (who wasn't even a priest when elected but became a strong and effective pontiff), 1012–1024; and his brother John XIX, 1024–1032. The successor of John XIX was his nephew Theophylact, who became Benedict IX at age twenty. During his lifetime there were so many fights for supremacy that he resigned once and was deposed twice. He was pope for three periods: 1032–1044; 1045; and 1047–1048.

Marozia was a tyrant and a murderess. She was mistress of a pope (Sergius III), mother of a pope (John XI), grandmother of a pope (John XII), great-grandmother of two popes (John XIX and Benedict VIII), and great-great-grandmother of another (Benedict IX). Nobody has beaten that record.

11
Basil II Bulgaroctonus

You may be tired of reminders that adults should set a good example for kids, but go on setting a good one. This is the horror story of an emperor who had only bad examples to follow.

Basil II was emperor of the Eastern Roman or Byzantine empire from 976 to 1025. His boyhood was a weird combination of sheer hell and luxurious profligacy. Despite his undoubted genius, he grew into manhood with a warped personality. And no wonder. It's surprising that he was allowed to live at all, and even more so that he didn't turn into a complete psychotic.

Basil's grandfather, the Emperor Constantine VII, had six kids, a boy (Basil's father, who became Romanus II) and five girls. The girls in the family ended up with all the brains. Romanus was tall, dark, and handsome—and a boob.

In 957, when he was eighteen, Romanus married one of the most beautiful women of her time. Her name was Theophano. The future Basil II was born the following year. In October 959, Constantine died, so Romanus and Theophano ascended the throne as Basileus and Basilissa (emperor and empress) of the Eastern Roman empire.

Basil's mother was a real bitch. One historian quaintly notes that Theophano "was certainly the wife of two emperors and the mistress of a third; but whether she killed one monarch or four cannot be accurately determined." She had great beauty, and she used it shamelessly to become empress—and to stay empress, as succeeding emperor-husbands or paramours died.

Theophano didn't like other women, especially if they were pretty. So her first act on becoming empress was to dispose of her husband's five sisters. All were beautiful, intelligent, well educated. There was no need to kill them. It would be just as effective to make them nuns.

The sisters were appalled at the news of their religious intentions. They screamed and yelled at Romanus, who was completely under his wife's thumb. Even at the altar, as they took their holy vows, they violently objected to the cutting of their hair. And once in the nunnery, they tore off their habits and ate meat on fast days. But Theophano won out, and all five were at least in their youth lost to the world. The Basilissa had no female rivals at court. She alone among women wore the purple.

Then quite unexpectedly, at age twenty-five, Romanus up and died—as one historian noted, probably from "sportive and other excesses." Another delicately put it that "his energies were prematurely spent." Anyway, he was dead, most probably at Theophano's hand. He was succeeded by his two sons as co-emperors (Basil II, aged seven, and Constantine VIII, aged two). Theophano became empress-dowager and regent for her boys. Eleven years were to pass before Basil became emperor in his own right.

But Theophano's hold on power was pretty shaky. Everyday Bringas, the Imperial Chamberlain and Theophano's enemy, took more power into his own hands. What she needed was a man, a hero to the army and the people, to overthrow Bringas and make himself emperor. Her choice fell on Nichephorus Phocas, the greatest general of the age, the man who had recovered Crete, Mesopotamia, and Syria for the empire.

He was a strange one. Something of a religious nut, he wore a hair-shirt under his armor, slept on the floor, ate no meat, and went around in clothes that nobody else would be caught dead in. He founded the first monasteries on Mount Athos and picked out a dismal cell in one of them—there to retire at the end of his military career.

Nor was he much to look at. A monk from western Europe described him as a pygmy in size, with tiny eyes, a disfiguring broad beard, hair like a pig's, and very dark skin. He also had a big belly and huge feet. Obviously Theophano didn't pick him for his looks!

Ever since his wife and son had tragically died years before, Nichephorus had foresworn women and booze. He avoided the palace like the plague. Then he met Theophano and went completely gaga over her. He wanted her—and nothing else.

After a complicated intrigue in which Theophano promised to marry Nichephorus, the latter struck down Bringas and proclaimed himself emperor. Theophano married him and once more became a reigning empress. Actually, he was Emperor Number 3, because little Basil and Constantine were still nominally on the throne. He was their guardian.

At first, Nichephorus was a changed man. He dressed in silks, made mad love to his wife, and capered around like a teenager. But it wasn't too long before the tug of the old ways was felt. Theophano realized something was wrong when he took to wearing his old hair-shirt and sleeping on the floor. Well, thought she, I'll have to get rid of this idiot and find somebody else to be emperor.

She latched onto her husband's good-looking nephew, John Tzimisces. John had elegant manners and lots of ability and knew how to please the ladies. At first, he became Theophano's lover, but she soon persuaded him to kill her husband, marry her, and become emperor.

The palace was no stranger to family rows. Years before the Empress Irene had blinded her son Constantine VI. In St. Stephen's Chapel, murderers chopped up Leo V while—as was his custom—he was directing the choir. There, too, Basil the Macedonian (Basil II's forebear and namesake) assassinated Michael III. But none of these could match in cold-blooded horror what Theophano and John did to poor old Nichephorus.

The deed was set for a December night in 969. A few days before, Theophano smuggled some conspirators into the women's quarters. Nichephorus at the time was full of gloomy thoughts, and, on his way into church, someone he didn't know thrust into his hands a note which read: "I am only a worm, but I know that you will die within the next few days."

The more Nichephorus thought it over, the more worried he became. He had the entire palace searched, including the women's quarters—but the conspirators were not found. He was still anxious. On the evening chosen for the murder, the emperor wrote to his brother, Leo—the head of the guards—to bring a force of men at once to the imperial apartments. Leo received his brother's note, but he was involved in a chess game. He put the note aside unopened and then forgot all about it.

Meanwhile back in Theophano's rooms, the conspirators were getting antsy. It was snowing and blowing outside, and where in hell was John? They heard that Nichephorus had moved into a different room and were worried he might lock himself in.

Theophano thought of a way. As cool as you please, she visited her husband and sat chatting pleasantly for some time. Then, with the excuse that she had to leave for a few minutes to attend to some Bulgarian princesses who were her guests, she told Nichephorus to leave the door unlocked. She'd be right back, she said.

Nichephorus waited for about half an hour. Then he threw himself on a panther skin in a corner of the bedroom and went sound asleep.

At just this moment, John showed up. He'd had a devil of a time rowing across the Bosphorus in the snowstorm. He signaled to his fellow conspirators in Theophano's room, and they let down a basket. He got in, and they hauled him up.

The whole bunch, Theophano included, then headed for Nichephorus's room. The door was unlocked, and in they went. To their consternation, the bed was empty. But an obliging servant pointed out the sleeping form in the corner. As they rushed him, Nichephorus awakened and had just time enough to say "Help me, Blessed Virgin" before he reeled under a ghastly blow on the head. The assassins dragged the half-dead emperor to his nephew's feet, where this gentleman pulled out the emperor's beard and spat in his face. He then sliced off the blood-soaked head.

At just that moment, Nichephorus's loyal guards arrived. Theophano was a quick thinker. She proclaimed John the new emperor, and, loyalty being what it was at that time, the troops joined in acclaiming "ten thousand years to John Augustus."

Nichephorus was given a decent burial. Later, when it was safe to do so, someone inscribed on his sarcophagus: "He overcame all, save one woman."

It was now time for Emperor John to be crowned, but this time Theophano didn't get her way. The Patriarch of Constantinople refused to marry John and Theophano. Never, he announced, would he marry the infamous murderess to John. Too bad, said John, and allowed the Patriarch to banish Theophano to Armenia. The two ex-lovers saw each other just once before Theophano started on her travels. Young Basil, now twelve, was brought in to see his mother's humiliation.

It was a memorable scene for the young emperor. Theophano raged and wept. What she said about John was not fit for any young boy's ears. She lost control completely and rushed at little Basil, beating him on the face with her fists. No one knows exactly why.

When, six years later, in 976, John died a mysterious death, Theophano was accused of having a hand in it. In any event, Basil became emperor in fact and allowed his mother to return home. But never again was she of any importance, and not even the date of her death is known.

Basil was eighteen when John died, and he and his little brother became sole co-emperors. It had been a trying childhood for both boys. Everybody said their mother had killed their father, Romanus II, and that she had done the same to their step-father, Nichephorus, and that she had had a hand in John's death. Stories like these are apt to unsettle a boy's mind, and Basil and Constantine grew into manhood with some rather peculiar boyhood memories.

Little brother, Constantine VIII, sought relief in pleasure. He spent the rest of his life dancing, drinking, eating, singing, and fornicating. Life became one grand party. And although he out-lived Basil II by a few years, he was nothing but a cipher during the forty-nine years of Basil's personal rule.

Basil was cut from a different mold. His memories—perhaps because they were more vivid and personal than his brother's—only accentuated his indomitable will, his spasmodic and cold cruelty. His senses were already heightened by undoubted genius. But the Emperor Basil II was only eighteen, and Basil the man had yet to be shaped.

So far he had been dominated all his life by his mother and by his co-emperor Nichephorus, and then by his "guardian" John. At John's death in 976, it seemed as though the whole dreary thing would have to be lived through again. Bardas Sclerus, a great nobleman and general, donned the purple and proclaimed himself co-emperor with Basil and Constantine.

Numerous battles were fought, with Basil getting a first-hand military education. He picked an able general named Bardas Phocas to defeat Sclerus. But then Phocas proclaimed himself co-emperor, and for a while there were four. Everybody was fighting everybody else. Phocas defeated Sclerus, who escaped into exile, and then took out after Basil.

The wars dragged on for thirteen years before Basil emerged victorious. The climax was dramatic. The armies of Basil and

Phocas met at last in a final confrontation. From his vantage point, Phocas could see the young emperors Basil and Constantine inspecting their troops. Unable to hold still, he called for a horse and a body of warriors to ride with him.

It was an ill-fated charge. First of all, his horse stumbled, and he had to mount another. Then as he rode across the plain toward Basil, he began to sway in his saddle. And finally, in front of both armies, he fell to the ground and died almost at once. Some said he was poisoned, but it was probably a stroke.

Whatever caused Phocas's death, it was certainly a lucky break for Basil. In due time, Sclerus—who by now had reappeared with his own army—asked for pardon. To put an end to the whole bloody mess, Basil agreed. At long last he was master of the empire he had inherited twenty-six years before.

All these rebellions, with their concurrent fighting, intrigue, and treachery, put the capstone on Basil's character. Before he was thirty, Basil changed from a pleasure-loving youth into the grim, indomitable tyrant he was to be for the rest of his life. In this, he resembled his stepfather Nichephorus more than he did his own blood relatives, even in looks.

His father and grandfather had been tall men, with elegant faces and small beards. Basil was short, pudgy, and red in the face, "with little beard but abundantly bushy whiskers." All his family gloried in sex; Basil had nothing to do with women and never married. His relatives were great clotheshorses and reveled in purple and gold finery. Basil went around in dull, dirty garments that a well-to-do tradesman wouldn't have been caught dead in.

Unlike his immediate ancestors who never knew a thing about warfare, Basil was the greatest military genius of the time—and one of the best in history. Whereas his relatives were voluptuaries, Basil was grim, ascetic, and physically hard as a rock. He was also a religious bigot and wore a monk's robe under his armor. Unlike his grandfather, Constantine VII, and his great-grandfather, Leo the Wise, both of whom had been devoted to the arts and scholarship, Basil couldn't have cared less. He despised painting, literature, and music as effeminate pastimes.

But as an administrator, Basil was superb. He paid great attention to details and still could formulate the larger areas of policy. Sometimes his administration of justice was a bit hard to take—he often had declared rebels impaled and crucified. Certainly he never shrank from shedding blood, and although he always thought of himself as "prudent, just, and devout," others called him "severe, rapacious, cruel, and bigoted." But he did have a certain grim sense of humor.

By the time of Phocas' death, Basil had learned most of all that an emperor's main job was to head the army in person. His ancestors who had spent their time writing sermons, studying Greek grammar, and having parties had almost lost the empire. Nichephorus and John had taught him a useful lesson. They had been able to shove him and his brother aside because they commanded the troops.

By leading the army in person, Basil could do almost anything. He became the ultimate pantocrat. As such, the stage was now set for the battle of his life—the great duel with Samuel of Bulgaria.

At the time of Basil's birth, most of the Balkan territories in the empire had fallen to the Bulgarians. At one time, the latter invaded Greece and approached Constantinople itself. At their head was the great hero, Samuel Cometopoulis, a crafty and energetic foe. Samuel traveled widely, usually at the head of his army, and he had studied Byzantine military strategy. At first, he beat Basil at his own game.

The duel between Basil and Samuel lasted for thirty-four years. Although Basil occasionally took time out from fighting Samuel to put down rebels and recover Syria for the empire, his mind always seemed to be on the Bulgarians. We don't know why he hated them so much, although when he was eleven Nichephorus had betrothed him—for political reasons—to a Bulgarian princess. At that time, for an emperor to marry a Bulgarian barbarian was unthinkable, and Basil was always proud. He never forgot nor forgave an injury. Maybe the insult had been too much.

Even before besting Phocas, Basil had mounted his first campaign against Samuel. In June 986, he jauntily set out for Bulgaria at the head of a large army. Everything went wrong. Samuel was no pushover. Here, at the very beginning of his remarkable military career, Basil sustained a dreadful defeat. Of the legions he took into Bulgaria not one escaped. Basil and a couple of generals were lucky to get away. Round one went to Samuel.

In 990, with Phocas dead, Basil mounted his second invasion

of Bulgaria. Things went rather well, although in five years of campaigning he was unable to smash Samuel once and for all. Round two was his, but it was inconclusive.

Despite his campaigns and victories in Asia, Basil always had his mind on Samuel. The war went on year after dreary year, until finally it rose to a climax in 1014. The Byzantines collided with the Bulgars near Prilep. Basil won hands down, although Samuel managed to get away. Over 14,000 prisoners fell into Basil's hands.

It is Basil's treatment of these Bulgarian prisoners that has added infamy to his name. He divided them into groups of 100. He completely blinded 99 men in each group and put out one eye of the other. He did this with all 14,000. He then set them free. Yes, he said, go on home, if you can make it; one eye for each 100 men should suffice. And so began the long trek to Samuel's camp. When Samuel first heard that his men were coming, he was overjoyed. He went out to meet them. Horrified at the sight of his blinded veterans, he was overcome with both sorrow and shock. He fell to the ground with a stroke and died two days later. Basil was henceforward called "Bulgaroctonus"—the "Bulgar-Slayer."

In such a way, the Bulgarian wars ended. Basil had won. But he had not beaten Samuel in a fair fight, and the ultimate atrocity has forever stained Basil's fame.

Basil continued campaigning, and in 1025 he decided to drive the Moslems out of Sicily. He never made it. At age sixty-eight he died, the last of the great Byzantine emperors:

> There was to be no one after him who could boast that he had fought thirty campaigns in the open field with harness on his back, and had never turned aside from any enterprise that he had ever taken in hand.

12
King William Rufus

An early king of England paid his dues to the Devil and look what happened.

The life of William II of England—known as William Rufus because of his red face—was not especially admirable, but he is chiefly remembered for the mysteries that surrounded his death. He was grasping and rapacious, always wanting more money to toss around; but then most rulers of his time were no better in that respect. He was not notably cruel. But he had absolutely no use for the Christian religion, although his father, William I, the Conqueror, had a healthy respect for the religion. Rufus turned the Christian church against him, and thus he turned history against him, because all the men who kept records were churchmen. It was normal to be illiterate. Rufus himself couldn't read; his brother Henry was known as Beauclerc because he could.

William Rufus was the third son and chosen successor of the Conqueror. The other boys were Robert, who inherited the duchy of Normandy, whence the family came; and Henry, who received only his mother's property but later ruled England.

The Conqueror had been a harsh king, especially in the way he treated the defeated English barons. He kept them miserable while the Norman foreigners he had brought with him ran just about everything, including the church. The archbishop of Canterbury was an Italian from Normandy named Lanfranc. But even the powerful Norman barons didn't *own* the revenue-producing lands they occupied. The Conqueror owned all of England's green land and granted great estates to his supporters, who paid rent by supplying armed knights and other services.

The conquered country was under pretty good control when William Rufus was crowned king on September 26, 1087, twenty-one years after his father arrived at Hastings. Strange to say, during Rufus's reign the defeated English lords favored him more than his Norman henchmen did. The reason for this, and for the wicked reputation that history has given him, may have been that Rufus belonged to a religion that was still deeply entrenched in the British Isles. The pagan worship of a horned deity that Christians equated with the Devil had been going on long before the first missionaries sailed for England.

Rufus, while he detested the church, did pay attention to the sound advice of Archbishop Lanfranc, whom he respected. When Lanfranc died, Rufus went hog-wild. As bishops and abbots died off, he delayed in nominating their successors but used the revenues of church properties for his own purposes. Not until four years after Lanfranc's death did the king get around to finding a new archbishop of Canterbury. The appointee was Anselm, a good and learned man who didn't want the job at all. As he had foreseen, the requirements of the king collided with Anselm's allegiance to the Holy See, so as soon as possible the archbishop set off for Rome. He didn't return to England until the king was safely dead.

The court of William Rufus became a scandal. Unlike most powerful men of this time, the king was no womanizer. He had neither wife nor mistress. He didn't *like* women. Effeminacy became stylish among his courtiers. Before his time, men wore practical clothing so they could jump on a horse and fight a battle at a moment's notice; they cut their hair and shaved their beards. But the king's close friends let their hair grow, wore long gowns, and minced around in elegant shoes with long, pointed toes. Some let their beards grow so their after-shave bristles wouldn't scratch their friends when they kissed—and these friends were not women. One historian says, "Vices before unknown, the vices of the East . . . were rife among them," and then retreats behind a smokescreen of Latin.

William had long blond curls; although he was called Rufus because of his fiery complexion, there was probably another reason for calling him the Red King. Blood color was witch color, and there is reason to believe that he was not only an adherent of the old religion that worshiped Lucifer, ruler of Hell, but the actual head of it in England.

William Rufus didn't die in bed. In the thirteenth year of his reign while he was out hunting, he was shot with an arrow by a man who was his friend and hunting companion. This may have been ritual murder and quite intentional.

There had been all sorts of portents. Rufus was killed August 2, 1100. Two nights before, the abbot of Cluny, in France, had a dream: he saw Rufus brought before the throne of God, who condemned him to eternal damnation. On August 1, Archbishop Anselm himself received a strange message. A young man came to his door in Lyons and told the clerk who answered that the strife between the king and archbishop was over.

Signs and wonders had been noted before that. In 1098, and again in 1100, blood welled up in a pool in Berkshire. In both those years at Michaelmas, a church festival celebrated on September 29, the sky was so bright all night that it seemed to be burning. In November 1099, a tremendous, destructive tide swept up the Thames beyond London, wiping out people, cattle, and even villages. Such awesome events were believed to be prophecies of something terrible. Or, in the case of the tide up the Thames, was it punishment for somebody's sin?

Just before the king's peculiar death, a monk at Gloucester had a dream which he reported to his abbot. He saw a fair lady (the church) kneeling before the throne of God, praying for pity on the people who were ground down by the king. (The people of the church, that is. The common people, the peasants, were ground down by everybody.) The abbot was so concerned when he heard about this dream that he sent a monk to deliver a note of warning to the king. The abbot must have been a very brave man.

At Shrewsbury, on the very day of William's death, another abbot preached a resounding sermon, promising that the Lord was coming to judge the enemies of the church. "Lo, the bow of wrath from on high is bent against the wicked," he intoned, "and the arrow swift to wound is drawn from the quiver." He was right—but how did he know?

Another monk dreamed he saw the king, looking scornful, enter a richly decked church. Suddenly its glory faded, and a naked man lay on the altar dead. The king approached and tried to eat the body, whereupon the dead man demanded, "Is it not enough that thou hast thus far grieved me with so many wrongs? Wilt thou gnaw my very flesh and bones?"

On August 1 the king was with his hunting companions in the New Forest, an immense tract in the South of England that his father had turned into a private hunting preserve. William Rufus talked with his good friend Walter Tyrell and others about plans for defending the duchy of Normandy (which brother Robert had mortgaged to him in order to go off on the First Crusade) and for buying Aquitaine. That night the king had bad dreams, so distressing that he called for lighted torches and asked his attendants to stay with him. In the morning he wasn't sure he would go hunting. He spent some hours taking care of serious business and, after a good dinner at noon, resolved to go hunting after all.

He was putting on his boots when a smith came in and offered him six new arrows for a crossbow. The king was delighted with them and gave two to Wat Tyrell, remarking, "It is right that the sharpest arrows should be given to him who knows how to deal deadly strokes with them." Later this was understood to have meant that he knew Tyrell was supposed to kill him.

Then came the monk-messenger from Gloucester with the abbot's note of warning. William sneered; monks dreamed for the sake of money, he said, and told somebody to give the fellow a hundred shillings—a very large tip indeed, but Rufus had a reputation as a generous fellow. Then he mounted his horse, and his party divided into small groups for hunting. The king and Wat Tyrell rode together. One story is that the sun was sinking when Rufus dismounted to take better aim at a herd of deer, while Tyrell got behind a tree. As a stag bounded by, Wat's arrow pierced the king. Tyrell fled. He galloped to the coast and as soon as possible took ship across the Channel, out of range of the English.

Another version of the homicide is that the king's bowstring broke and he cried to Tyrell, "Shoot, in the Devil's name! Shoot, or it will be the worse for you!" When the arrow pierced the king's chest he broke off the shaft and fell.

There is more than one version of what happened next. According to one account, the king's noble companions gathered around the body, wailing and mourning, and carried the corpse on a bier to the minster of St. Swithun, where it was buried with great religious pomp.

More likely is the tale that leaves the king's body deserted in the forest while all his friends galloped off to look out for their own interests, suddenly endangered by the ruler's demise. The low-born peasants gathered, mourning, put the body on a farm cart, and took it to Winchester. Blood dripped all the way. There was no splendor about the funeral—no mass, no prayers. The body was hustled into a grave under the pavement of St. Swithun, where William, as a consecrated king, had a right to be buried. A few years later the tower under which his body lay crumbled and collapsed. The wickedness of the king was said to be responsible.

One hunter who didn't weep and wail over the bleeding body of the king was his brother Henry, who was hunting in another part of the New Forest. His bowstring broke, so he and his companions stopped at a peasant's hut where he had it mended. An old woman there, when she found out that Henry was the king's brother, announced that he was soon going to be king himself. This might have been the flattering nonsense of a peasant currying favor, but as Henry and his friends rode on they met a man who told them William was really dead.

Henry spurred his horse toward Winchester, where the royal treasury was, and demanded the keys. He had an argument about that, for his brother Robert, equally eligible for the throne, was older than he, and Robert was on his way home from the First Crusade. But Henry got the keys. By sunset of the day after Rufus's death, everybody who mattered agreed that Henry was their rightful liege lord. One argument strongly in his favor was that he had been born in England. On August 5 he was crowned Henry I.

The twelfth century was rife with superstitions, but superstition and scary stories told almost nine hundred years ago cannot account for the apparent fact that news of William's death spread faster than was physically possible by any means of communication then known to man—unless the death was expected and an involved, far-reaching system of signals had been prearranged to speed the message. Within a few hours the news was known as far away as Italy. On the very day of death, one of Anselm's clerks, who was singing at matins, felt a paper thrust into his hand and heard a voice urging him to read it. There was no messenger in sight, but the words he read were "King William is dead."

The only explanation that fits the case is that William Rufus belonged to, and was head of, the "old religion" of the British Isles, Devil worship, the witch cult. It was widespread in Europe then, and witches were still being searched out and executed five hundred years later. Witches congregated in covens of thirteen for Esbats, weekly meetings. Very large meetings, Sabbats, took place quarterly at festival times that Christians called Roodmass (the eve of May 1), Lammas (August 1), Allhallows (the eve of November 1, Hallowe'en, which still features witches), and Candlemas, February 2. William Rufus died "on the morrow of Lammas."

The priest in each coven was known as the Devil, and the whole organization was headed by a Supreme Devil, who faced the fact that he was liable to be sacrificed for his people. In England this sacrifice took place at one of the Sabbats every seventh year. Sometimes a substitute could die for him, but Lammas in A.D. 1100 may have been a time when the Supreme Devil himself had to die.

If Rufus died as a required royal sacrifice, a "divine victim" in the witch cult, several mysteries are explained. The news was no shocking surprise to adherents of the old religion. They expected it, because the king had to die. They knew it must happen in that year, at the time of one of the great Sabbats. It happened on the morrow of Lammas. And William Rufus knew. He worked on the business of kingship until noon, after nightmares that had distressed him, and he left his affairs in better order than would be expected of a man who thought he would return from a hunt. His admonition to Tyrrel to shoot suggests that he wanted to get the ordeal over with and knew that Tyrrel was the man who would kill him. The peasants, the pagans, sincerely mourned for the king who had died for them. His body could not have dripped blood all the way to Winchester, but part of the ancient ritual was that the victim's blood must soak into the earth to make the land fertile.

The Devil was believed to be Rufus's great-grandfather. The story was that the wife of Duke Richard II of Normandy was walking in a forest one day when she met her husband—or so she thought—and they made love. The result was a baby. But Duke Richard hadn't been in the forest that day, so it was assumed that the man she met was really the Devil. Therefore the offspring of this forest idyl, who grew up to be Duke Robert I, was always known as Robert the Devil. He had an affair with a tanner's daughter, and their enterprising little bastard became not only duke of Normandy but, by virtue of the Conquest, King William I of England. He married a cousin, so their children were descended from the Devil through both parents.

William Rufus detested the Holy Church and made no bones about it. But it was churchmen, who were naturally prejudiced, who chronicled his reign and his death. Hundreds of years passed before the ancient witch cult, worship of the god with horns, was obliterated—if it ever was.

13
King John of England

December 24, 1167–October 18, 1216

Some days nothing goes right for you?
For years and years nothing went right
for King John of England, but he de-
served his bad luck.

England has had eight kings named
Henry and eight named Edward,
but only one John. And he was a born loser. He even lost England,
by handing it over to the pope as his feudal overlord. He lost many
of the privileges that he thought were his rights when he signed
Magna Charta almost a century and a half after his great-great-
grandfather conquered England.

John's father, Henry II, had eight children by Eleanor of
Aquitaine. The first son, William, died in infancy. The second
Henry, was Daddy's pet. King Henry even had him crowned as a
junior king at age fifteen, but this Henry does not appear in the
line-up of English kings because he never reigned in his own
right. He would have to be considered Henry 2½.

The third son, a big, handsome fellow who became Richard I
and known to history as Coeur de Lion, was Mamma's favorite.
The fourth, Geoffrey, married the heiress of Brittany and was
Duke. The fifth son and last child was John, born on Christmas
Eve, 1167. His mother was forty-four; his father was twelve
years younger than the beautiful and formidable Eleanor.

When John came along, Henry II had provided for his other
sons by handing over, or making them heir to, great portions of
his domain. The king remarked that there wasn't much left for
the new baby and spoke of him as Jean Sans Terre, John
Lackland.

All Henry's sons were a greedy, feisty lot who fought one

another and their father, sometimes siding with the king of France, who also fought him.

In 1173 the family feuding reached a peak. Henry Junior and Richard and Geoffrey were all fighting their father on the Continent. Their mother sided with them, but while in flight from their father she was captured. King Henry shut her up in a castle in England and kept her prisoner. This situation displeased her no end. She had, after all, been queen of France before she was divorced from Louis VII; she was queen of the English by virtue of her marriage to Henry; and she was duchess of Aquitaine in her own right. But she stayed locked up for something like sixteen years.

Henry Junior, his father's darling, died in 1183. The elder Henry then took on young John as his pet. Now Richard would succeed as ruler of England and Normandy, so the king had the idea of taking care of landless John by giving him the duchy of Aquitaine, which Richard was to inherit through his mother Eleanor. Richard naturally refused to part with it. So John, now seventeen, and brother Geoffrey fought Richard, which was exciting fun for them but got quite a lot of innocent people killed. Henry finally calmed his boys down. Geoffrey was killed in August 1186. He left a son, Arthur, whose tragic story will be told a little later.

Richard and Philip Augustus, king of France, ganged up and fought poor old Henry, who was stricken with fever and disheartened by defeat. He died July 6, 1189. One of the last things he said was, "Shame, shame on a beaten king!"

About the first thing Richard did on succeeding to his father's throne was to release his mother from her long imprisonment. He reigned for ten years, squeezing money out of his subjects even when they didn't have any. He needed it to pay for the Third Crusade, which interested him much more than his vast holdings in the British Isles and about a third of modern France. Richard died of a wound incurred while besieging a castle in Normandy.

Now it was John's turn to rule—or was it? The boy Arthur, son of the late Geoffrey, had as good a right as John, or maybe better.

With his brother Richard dead, and with himself in line to become king of the English and to succeed also to Richard's fiefs on the continent, John reformed mightily from his normal swaggering ways. For a few days he was a model of piety and humility. If a beggar wished him luck, John bowed his head and thanked the ragged fellow. But this couldn't last. When Hugh of Avalon, bishop of Lincoln, went to Fontevrault for Richard's funeral, on Palm Sunday, April 11, 1199, John gushed all over him. But on Easter Sunday John was himself again. He smarted off about putting money in the collection. The bishop was so mad that he wouldn't touch the coins but made John put them in the silver dish himself. Then he preached a long sermon directly at John, who became bored and three times sent one of his attendants up front to demand that the bishop hurry up and finish. John did not receive Holy Communion then or, apparently, ever.

He went on being irreverent later that month when he was officially made duke of Normandy in the Cathedral of Rouen. He had with him a bunch of friends who laughed and gabbled all during the ceremony, and when the archbishop gave him the lance bearing the banner of Normandy, John turned to crack a joke and dropped the lance. This was taken by the gasping congregation as a prophecy that if he couldn't hold a lance he couldn't hold his duchy either.

In England, most of the nobles didn't object to having John as king, but on the other side of the Channel most of the nobles preferred his young nephew, Arthur. The king of France was one of them. He could boss Arthur around. Just the same, John was anointed and crowned in Westminster Abbey on May 27, 1199. Soon thereafter John crossed the Channel again to fight Philip II of France about who owned what. They made peace the middle of the following January. For a while, all John's territories were at peace, including Ireland.

This couldn't go on. John alienated many of his vassals on both sides of the Channel by divorcing his wife, Isabel of Gloucester, after ten years of marriage and no children. He had upset everybody when he married her, too, with a dispensation from the pope, which John's bishops now obligingly ignored. John was on the lookout for a new wife—and he fell head over heels in love with Isabel of Angoulême, who was all of twelve years old. John was thirty-three. The entrancing new Isabel was, of course, betrothed to someone else, so when John married her on August 26, 1200, he made several important families simply furious. And nobody could get the king to do anything much about the business of reigning because he spent so much of his time in bed.

In 1202 Queen Eleanor, John's mother and Arthur's grandmother, was stranded in the castle of Mirebeau when Arthur
attacked it. His army even broke through the outer walls. The
aged queen got word to her boy John, who dashed over to rescue
her and captured Arthur along with more than two hundred
knights. He loaded his prisoners with shackles and dispatched
them to various castles. Most of the twenty-five who were imprisoned at Corfe died of starvation.

John had his bold young nephew hauled up before him. Arthur
answered in an insolent—that is, a knightly—manner. John
sent him to be imprisoned at Rouen. And there Arthur simply
disappeared. One chronicler said that John killed the youth
himself and threw his body in the Seine. Another said John
ordered that Arthur be blinded with a white-hot iron bar and
otherwise mutilated. Whatever really happened, Arthur was out
of the way of his loving uncle from that time on.

John refused to explain Arthur's disappearance to Philip of
France, who had been backing Arthur and was John's feudal
overlord on the Continent. This gave Philip an excuse to attack
and conquer Normandy, Maine, Anjou, and Touraine, shattering
John's extensive empire. He recovered some of it later, at the
cost of much blood and grinding taxes.

A man named William de Braose was in charge of the castle
at Rouen where Arthur of Brittany disappeared. De Braose had
been in favor with John for so long that there was talk; he must
have something on the king or this amity couldn't have lasted.
He must know what had become of Arthur. De Braose talked
back as nobody else dared to do. Now John ordered him to send
one of his sons as a hostage. This was nothing new. In order to
keep his unruly and increasingly angry barons under control,
John had been requiring them to deliver a child from each family
to serve as a page to the queen at Winchester and Windsor. But
until this time he had not asked for a de Braose hostage.
William's wife, Maude, a haughty Amazonian type, remarked in
the hearing of some of the king's officers that she wouldn't deliver
her children to a king who had murdered his own nephew.

The cat was out of the bag, and Maude de Braose heartily regretted it. She hastened to send the queen a herd of four hundred beautiful matched cattle. She didn't even get a thank-you
note. John began to persecute de Braose in earnest, seizing his
castles. His men captured Maude and her oldest son, William,

while they were trying to escape from Ireland to the Scottish coast. And John got even with his former friend in a particularly nasty way. He had Maude and her son thrown into a cell in the prison keep at Windsor Castle with a side of uncooked bacon and a sheaf of wheat for provisions.

When the dungeon door was opened eleven days later, both were dead. (They must have been deprived of water; even a very thin person does not die of starvation that quickly.) The son was lying propped against a wall. He had died first. His mother was seated between his knees, and one of his cheeks had been gnawed, not by rats.

In July 1205 word came to John of the death of Hubert Walter, archbishop of Canterbury, and he cried triumphantly, "Now for the first time I am king of England!" Real trouble came to England as a result of John's disagreement with Pope Innocent III about a successor to Hubert. Some young monks at Canterbury elected their sub-prior, Reginald, and sent him off to get the pope's approval. But John had a candidate, John de Grey. The pope had one, too, an English cardinal then in Rome, Stephen Langton. The pope won, and the king was furious. He swore that Langton should never set foot in England. The pope threatened to lay the realm under an interdict. John threatened to throw every priest and monk out of England. He swore he would burn out eyes and slit noses.

There was no Easter rejoicing in England in the year 1208, for on Monday of Passion Week the pope's interdict was pronounced by three bishops. There could be no masses, no proper weddings or burials in sacred ground. As was usual, the common people, the faceless villeins without rights, suffered the most. The rites and celebrations of the church were about all they had to brighten their bleak lives. And how could they dare even to live when the Devil lurked everywhere and God had been removed from them?

The quarrel between irascible John and implacable Innocent went on. The pope loosed another weapon from his arsenal. He excommunicated the king, pronouncing him accursed. John didn't mind that; he was scarcely the religious type. But the faithful— except family members and servants—cannot pray, talk, or eat with an excommunicate. A great number of persons connected with the government rated as servants of the king—or did they?

Geoffrey, archdeacon of Norwich, told his fellow workers at the Exchequer that they must not serve the excommunicated king.

John, in a rage, summoned a rough knight to throw Geoffrey into prison, fettered and with a cope of lead soldered over his shoulders. Geoffrey's bones broke under the weight, thus hastening a little his death by starvation.

In 1212, almost everything was going against John. The pope and the rulers of Europe were lined up against him. Early in 1213 the pontiff ordered Philip Augustus of France, for his soul's health, to expel John from England and to take over the sovereignty himself. In short, the pope undertook to depose the king of England and Ireland.

That jarred John into submission. He couldn't fight the whole of Europe. On May 15, 1213, he gave up. John surrendered England and Ireland to a stand-in for Innocent III and in proper feudal fashion swore fealty to the pontiff as his liege lord. Thus he retained his realms for all practical purposes and, with the pope now protecting him, he could thumb his nose at the monarchs who coveted his kingdom. John promised to make restitution to the bishops and monasteries for the lands and revenues he had seized, but this created no particular hardship for him. His subjects, already ground down by taxes, were simply taxed some more.

But Stephen Langton, archbishop of Canterbury, with the best of motives and what he considered plain logic, got himself and England into trouble. Assuming that all was well now that John had accepted Innocent as his feudal lord, Langton absolved John of his sins and performed the Holy Eucharist. *No!* thundered the Pope. When he saw fit, *he* would raise the interdict. Almost a year passed before Innocent saw fit to do so—in the summer of 1214, after six years.

The following year, while John was warring again in France (and being badly beaten, so that he earned the derisive nickname of Soft Sword), Stephen Langton brewed up more trouble for the king that developed into a great blessing for his subjects. Stephen preached a sermon at St. Paul's in London, reminding the congregation of a great promise that had been made to restore human rights and constitutional government. This was the Charter of Henry I, John's great-grandfather. One hundred copies had been made long ago. Only one was known to exist in

1215, and Stephen Langton had it. It was the first written safeguard of constitutional liberties. This document, little remembered now, became the basis of Magna Charta, which John was forced to sign before the assembled barons at Runnymede on June 15, 1215.

Magna Charta, the Great Charter, is vaguely remembered by most people as a ringing statement of the rights of the common man. The fact is that the common man, the villein, is mentioned only once in it. Nobody in the seats of power gave a hang about the common man. Villeins couldn't even move to another estate for a better job. They were property, inherited or sold along with the land. The only mention of villeins is in this provision:

> A freeman shall not be amerced [arbitrarily fined] for a little offence, but according to the manner of his offence; and for a great offence he shall be amerced according to the greatness of his offence, saving his contenement [means of supporting his family]; and so a merchant saving his merchandize; and a villein in like manner shall be amerced saving his wainage, if he fall into our mercy: and none of the said amercements shall be affeered, but by oath of good and lawful men of the vicinage.

This was a fine idea, to make the punishment fit the crime without ruining the defendant, but we have moved away from it. A man can still be ruined by taxes or a damage suit.

A great guarantee was this provision: "To no one will we sell, to no one will we deny or delay right or justice." Delay of trials has become an important part of legal shenanigans, usually delay prayed for by the defendant.

Magna Charta did not set forth the philosophy of *habeas corpus,* as some of us fondly and vaguely recall. It did not guarantee trial by jury. Juries in John's day were fact-finding commissions that settled such matters as land ownership. Juries decided whether a case was strong enough to require the accused to prove his innocence by ordeal—fire or water or trial by combat. Accused women were usually put to the ordeal by fire. The defendant carried a hot iron for a specified distance, and naturally she suffered a painful burn. If after three days the burn was healing cleanly under its bandage, the accused was innocent. Ordeal by water was for men. The defendant was tossed in; if he sank, he was innocent; if he floated, he was guilty. (It must have been very difficult for a good swimmer to keep from struggling to the surface.)

Many of the provisions of Magna Charta are difficult to understand now because they are out of date. Feudalism, which was implicit in the Charter, is as dead as King John and the barons. But gradually the Charter, devised to protect the feudal barons against the encroachments of the king, became the safeguard of the liberties of all subjects against the arbitrary will of the sovereign. What the Charter did was to establish the position of the king: he is subject to law, not superior to it.

The barons were pleased with Magna Charta. Pope Innocent was violently displeased. He considered himself temporal ruler of England, and King John was only his vassal. This royal vassal had no right to grant rights to *his* vassals without permission. On August 24 Innocent annulled the Great Charter, remarking that "We can no longer pass over in silence such audacious wickedness, in contempt of the Apostolic See, in infringement of the rights of the king." The whole thing was null and void. He ordered the barons to quiet down or be excommunicated, and he suspended Stephen Langton from office for two years. Stephen could not leave Rome.

Now, with the pope on his side for a change, John began to ravage his own realm, burning, killing, destroying. The Crown Prince of France, who was to become Louis VIII, landed on the coast of Kent and marched to London, where many barons swore allegiance to him. In mid-October, John led his troops across the Wash, a wide estuary on the east coast where four rivers meet the North Sea. He carried with him, packed in wagons, all his treasure, no longer trusting anything to the care of monasteries as in the past. He had gold, jewels, the royal regalia (the crown, scepter, and orb of England), jeweled gold and silver cups, a hoard of gold coins, bags of unset gems. While the treasure was being hauled across the tricky mudflats of the Wash, the wagons were engulfed by the tide. The treasure is still there.

At Swineshead the furious, raging king ate too heartily, became sick and swore that the monks there had poisoned him. In fever and pain, grinding his teeth and constantly cursing, he went in a horse litter to the palace of the bishop of Lincoln at Newark. And there, on October 18, 1216, in a howling storm that tore roofs from houses, his soul passed to wherever it was supposed to go.

John Lackland lived up to his name, for when he died no part of his realm was his at peace. He left a torn England to his son Henry, barely nine years old. Henry III reigned for fifty-six years.

John had an inherited right to the deviltry that was in him. Through his ancestor William the Conqueror he was a descendant of the Devil, and one of his female forebears, a Countess of Anjou, was peculiar to say the least. She seldom went to church and when she did, always left before mass. One day four knights grabbed her just as she was about to sweep out, but she threw off her cloak, snatched her two youngest sons up under her arm—and flew away through a high window. Richard the Lion Hearted loved this story and often remarked that he and his brothers had come from the Devil and to the Devil they were going. Presumably they did.

14
Sir James Douglas

C. 1286–1330

The Black Douglas, one of Scotland's greatest heroes, is a bloody villain to Englishmen. Much depends on one's point of view.

By the time James Douglas was born, somewhere around 1286, King Edward I of England had come within a cat's-whisker of conquering Scotland. In 1297 he proclaimed himself king of Scotland and hauled off to London the Stone of Scone, on which Scottish kings had traditionally sat for coronation. It is still used when British sovereigns are crowned and—except when Scottish Nationalists stole it for several months in 1950—has been in Westminster Abbey ever since.

Passions ran high in the Anglo-Scottish wars, and mercy to a fallen foe—on either side—was unusual. Everybody had a gripe—someone or something to avenge. Much was said of knightly virtues and courtly behavior, but these were usually drowned in a sea of blood. Murder, fighting, arson, rape, and looting were the order of the day.

It was in the Marches, the lowlands that make up the border of southern Scotland and northern England, that the fighting was the worst. The Marcher lords, of whom Douglas was one, loved war, and their incomes depended more on loot and the ransom of noble captives than on land productivity. A poor old farmer didn't stand a chance. Fighting was endemic and incessant—an active way of life. It wasn't much fun for an average man to be alive.

Occasionally, someone would do something so imaginatively horrible that he impressed himself on the consciousness of the times. It was hard, even then, but Sir James Douglas did it—

and became a devil incarnate to the English, a marvelous hero to the Scots.

James was called "the Black Douglas," either from his swarthy skin or the darkness of his deeds against the English. He was the eldest son of the fourth Lord Douglas, Sir William de Douglas, who had been one of those patriots who "hae wi' Wallace bled." King Edward captured the hapless Sir William and dragged him off to captivity in the Tower of London, where he died in 1298.

With the collapse of Scottish fortunes, his family sent young James off to Paris for safety—and incidentally for an education. James became bilingual in Gaelic and French. But he had more fun starting a career in womanizing, which he enjoyed for life. One admirer said he had the makings of a "first-rate poacher," whether of animals or women is not clear.

It is to John Barbour, the fascinating Scottish poet of the thirteenth century, that we owe our descriptions of Douglas. James was of "gray visage," presumably sallow-skinned, not handsome but with a great shock of black hair. He was the athletic type, with "well made limbs" and "great bones and broad shoulders." All his life, James preferred outdoor sports like hunting, fishing, and fighting. "He loved better to hear the lark sing than the mouse squeak." Apparently it was no drawback in his relations with the ladies that James lisped. But then, says Barbour, so did "gud Ector of Troy."

Douglas was a natural leader, and all his life men fought to serve him and under him. Says Barbour:

> All men lufyt him for his bounte [valor]: For he wes of full fayr effer [demeanor]; Wyse, curtaiss [courteous], and debonar; Larg and Luffand als [always] wes he. And our [over] all things luffyt lawte [loyalty].

He was "honest, laill [loyal], and worthy," as kind to his friends as he was terrible to his foes. Above all things, he hated disloyalty.

He was gentle and serene, unusual traits in his time. And, more than that, he had brains. Unlike the usual medieval knight whose military capacities consisted of attacking the enemy head-on, Douglas had some sense of guerrilla warfare. On one occasion he complimented one of his men on his audacity. That was fine, said Douglas, "but if you follow my advice, you will not engage unless we have the advantage. There is no dishonour in strategy seeing we are so few against so many."

Scottish historians are understandably laudatory of Sir James Douglas. "He was the greatest soldier of all, save Bruce himself." He was "the most hardy knyght, and the greattest adventurer in al the realme of Scotland." He was "the best knight of Scotland," and "no knightlier figure graced the Middle Ages." His contemporaries called him "the good Lord James."

But to the English he was something else again. He ravaged the border whenever possible, looting, burning, and killing. If an English archer fell into his hands, he was either killed outright or had his right eye blinded and the forefinger of his right hand hacked off. The black name of Douglas (from the Gaelic *dulh glas*, "dark water") became a terror on the Border, and English mothers rocked their babes to sleep with:

Hush ye, hush ye, little pet ye,
Hush ye, hush ye, do not fret ye,
The Black Douglas shall not get ye.

But all this fame was still in the future for the young lad studying in Paris. Sometime in his middle teens, James returned home to find that the usurping King Edward had given all his castles and lands to an Englishman, Robert de Clifford. Bereft of estates and power, he set out to find service under that most resplendent of Scottish heroes, Robert the Bruce, who had raised the banner of rebellion (the English version) or independence (the Scottish version).

Douglas found the Bruce and did homage to him as his true sovereign. Thus began a friendship that was to last for the Scots king's lifetime—and beyond. Years of triumphs and dismal defeats followed for both. Douglas fought in seventy battles, winning fifty-seven and losing thirteen.

On Palm Sunday, March 27, 1306, Douglas had the great joy of seeing Robert the Bruce crowned king of the Scots at Scone. It wasn't much of an affair. Only two earls, a couple of bishops, one abbot, and some odds and ends of friends and fighting men bothered to show up. The "Stone of Destiny" (the Stone of Scone) was in London, the Scottish crown was with an earl in exile, and Duncan, Earl of Fife, who traditionally crowned Scotland's kings, was too scared of Edward I to put in an appearance.

So it was a woman, Duncan's sister Lady Isobel, who crowned Robert the Bruce. It was a pretty dismal beginning for a king who was to restore Scotland's independence.

One year and two days later, the "good Lord James" pulled off a stunt that heartened the king's friends. He set out to capture his own castle.

Edward had given Castle Douglas to one of his henchmen, Robert de Clifford, who was somewhere off in the south on March 19, 1307. But he had left behind a batch of about thirty soldiers, and the castle itself was very strong—indeed, too strong for Douglas to take with the forces he then had. And since Douglas couldn't bang down the wall with his own fists, he decided on a *ruse de guerre*.

With the Bruce's consent, Douglas sneaked into Douglasdale and spied out the lay of the land and who was doing what and where and when. Deciding that he had a chance to take the castle, he revealed himself to an old servant of the family, Tom Dickson by name. Tom told him all he knew about the castle's garrison and then went out to tell everyone true to the Douglases that the young laird had come home.

Douglas stayed concealed in Tom's house, while day after day his father's old retainers rallied to his side. They loved him. As Barbour said: "Douglas in hert gret blithnes had." Douglas and his gang of cutthroats (patriots) decided to wait for Palm Sunday, when (as they assumed rightly) the English garrison would go to church. The plan was then for Sir James and his followers to set upon the English.

Although nobody mentions the weather, Palm Sunday was a nice enough day for the English garrison, carrying green boughs in their hands, to walk the mile to St. Bride's, the parish kirk. They left behind a cook preparing Sunday dinner, a few domestics, and one sentry.

Douglas meanwhile dressed himself as a simple peasant, as did his men. With concealed arms, they entered St. Bride's along with the English. The men were to have awaited a signal from Douglas, but some featherbrain called out the signal too soon. "Douglas! Douglas!" rang through the church, and a wild mêlée followed in which Tom Dickson got himself killed. But Douglas won, killing or capturing some thirty Englishmen.

Taking their captives with them, Douglas and his men had no

trouble overpowering the sentry and the cook at Castle Douglas. "The good Lord James" was home.

Not one to waste anything, Douglas first of all sat down to eat the Sunday dinner prepared for the Englishmen. Since he knew he had no chance of defending the castle, he then set about looting it of all portable valuables. He proceeded to wreck the place. He piled up all the wheat, malt, meat, and other foodstuffs in the castle. Next, he staved in the casks of wine and other liquors and added them to the pile. He then slew (some say beheaded) his English prisoners and added their bodies and blood to what was rapidly becoming a terrible mess. And at last, he set fire to the whole pile—and incidentally to the castle. As he left, he poisoned the water with salt and dead horses. The mess he left behind became known as the "Douglas larder." As Barbour wrote:

> For mele and malt and blud and wyn
> Ran all togidder in a mellyn,
> That was unseemly for to se:
> Tharfor the men of that cuntre,
> For sic thingis thar mellit wer,
> Call it the Douglas lardener.

The fame of his exploit rang throughout Scotland and England. Although Sir Walter Scott was later to call the incident "very cruel and shocking," he justified it because of Douglas' sadness over Tom's death. In any event, men flocked to King Robert's banner, and Douglas was started on a career in which he was to become the terror of the Marches.

In a short time, Clifford, the English owner of Castle Douglas, showed up with lots of men and provisions. He rebuilt the castle, purified the well, put a good soldier named Thirwall in charge (urging him to be on guard against the wiles of that black bastard, Douglas), and left for England.

Douglas soon learned of this and set out to capture his castle a second time. Again his forces were too weak to besiege it. Only another *ruse de guerre* would work. He hid some of his men in a nearby forest and sent fourteen others dressed as peasants to drive some cattle near the castle gates. Seeing only the cattle from atop the castle walls, Thirwall decided to liberate them and rushed outside with a considerable body of men. As he neared the trap, out popped the Scots. Another bloody mêlée followed, in which Thirwall and most of his men were slain. A few got back to the castle and prevented Douglas from capturing it.

Even so, Douglas had now killed two English commanders of his castle. The word got around. Soon both English and Scots called the place "the Perilous Castle of Douglas," and it was difficult to get volunteers to man the place without extra pay.

It so happened that at this time (1307) there lived in England a very rich and beautiful young lady whose head had been turned by tales of chivalry. She had lots of suitors. But she wanted not only the handsomest among them but above all the bravest. So one evening she got all her men friends together for a great dinner. After dessert she gave a little speech. She would, said the young lady, give her hand in marriage only to "ane gud beacheler" knight who could hold "the aventurous castell of Douglass, that to kep sa peralous was" for one year and one day. The silence that met this proposal was deafening, but finally one young gallant named Sir John Wilton (or Wanton) took up the dare.

So off to Castle Douglas went Sir John. He must have been very much in love or very stupid—or both. He certainly hadn't learned anything from Thirwall's fiasco. For again Douglas came home to his castle with a band of men too few to take it by siege. Again, he resorted to a *ruse de guerre*. Again he hid a number of men in a forest ambush near the castle and sent out fourteen knights dressed as peasants and leading horses laden with bags of grass. Knowing that Sir John was short on food, Douglas hoped the English would come out to liberate the sacks of "grain."

Sure enough! Out trooped Sir John with most of the garrison. As they neared the "peasants," Sir John's men were attacked from the rear by Douglas and from the front by the fourteen knights who jumped on their horses and turned on the English. Another great mêlée ensued, and poor Sir John and most of his men were killed. Douglas took the castle and burned it down. But, touched by the romantic story of Sir John and the English girl, Douglas departed from his usual custom of killing English captives and set them free.

In this year of 1307 Edward died. He was succeeded by a nincompoop, Edward II, who was determined to make a success of his father's Scottish policy. After a great deal of to and fro in the intermediate years, the Scots and English met at Bannockburn on June 23–24, 1314. With only 30,000 men, the Bruce defeated 100,000 invaders under Edward II. The victory was decisive in securing Scotland's independence, although the English were too dense to realize it. Scattered fighting in the Marches continued for a long time. But never again was Scotland in real danger. Almost 300 years later, it was a Scottish king, James VI, who inherited the English throne to become James I of England.

In 1329, Bruce fell ill and soon died—on November 7. But on his deathbed, he summoned his men and in a touching scene told them all that he had made a vow to go to the Holy Land. Now it was too late, said the king, and he asked "the Good Lord James" as a special favor to take his heart to Jerusalem. "Douglas wept bitterly as he accepted this office," says Sir Walter Scott, "the last mark of the Bruce's confidence and friendship."

King Robert's heart was cut out, embalmed, and placed in an enameled silver case, which Douglas wore around his neck on a string of gold and silk. Douglas set out from Berwick, sailed through the English (cursed name!) Channel, and eventually arrived in Seville, Spain.

It so happened at this time that Osmyn, the king of Moorish Granada, was invading the lands of King Alfonso XI of Castile and Leon. The latter asked Douglas to help him, and Douglas was never one to run away from what could be a lot of fun. He was widely applauded by Alfonso's knights, one of whom wanted to compare scars with Sir James. The man had been terribly cut up and was amazed to see a knight of Douglas' renown without a visible scar. "Praised be God!" said Douglas, "I have always had hands to protect my head."

The Christians met the Moors in battle and had little trouble defeating them. The Scottish knights, not used to the cavalry warfare of the Moors, pursued the enemy too far. The Moors turned and hit hard. Douglas, some distance away from the embattled Scots, shouted the old war cry: "Douglas! Douglas!" Taking from his neck the silver cask containing the Bruce's heart, he flung it into the battle, crying out "Onward as thou were wont, thou noble heart! Douglas will follow."

The Scots won the day, but his friends found Sir James's body lying on top of the Bruce's heart. After being disemboweled, Douglas' body was boiled until all the flesh came off the bones. These, together with King Robert's heart, were returned to Scotland, the "gud Lord James" to be buried in St. Brides, a mile from the site of the massacre of the "Douglas Larder."

15
The House of Visconti

Ca. 1200–1447

*The Viscontis were a family in which
sons excelled fathers in their capacity
for villainy. They were all mean bastards—and proud of it.*

The Viscontis were an unusual lot
even for the early Renaissance. No
historian has really put his heart into an attempt to whitewash
the family. Most other noble Italian families of the time produced
a saint or two, or at least someone—usually by comparison—
whom his contemporaries labeled "the Good," "the Well-Beloved,"
"the Magnificent."

But not the Viscontis. We search in vain through the family
archives for someone to say something really complimentary
about. They were *all* family skeletons.

The House of Visconti started in the usual way. Out of the
obscure morass of the Middle Ages, they came onto the scene
with a large birthrate, a marvelous talent for vice and improvisa-
tion, and a positive genius for betrayal and skullduggery. Most
of the Viscontis hired *condottieri* to do their fighting while they
manned a command post well to the rear of the battle. They have
often been called cruel but never stupid.

Early on, the Viscontis adopted as their badge a viper swallowing a man—probably alive—and most appropriate it was. It
became the most hated, dreaded, and menacing of the contemporary coats-of-arms. In time the Viscontis bested their rivals in
villainy, deceit, treachery, and all-round rascality and emerged
as the First Family of Milan.

Matteo, who died in 1322, was the founder of the family's
political fortune. An almost contemporary historian, Corio, mentions the sale of human flesh in Milanese butcher shops, and men

were known to have sharpened their teeth by exercising them on a dead enemy. This was extraordinary behavior in any age, but the Viscontis showed that what others could do they could improve on.

Matteo didn't do much in the villainy line, except lock up the Holy Roman Emperor Henry VII for a few days until His Majesty granted him the title of Imperial Vicar in Milan. This wasn't really out of the ordinary. Even the pope wouldn't let poor old Henry stay more than one day in Rome.

One historian admitted, in a sort of pro-Visconti way, that the crimes of Matteo's descendants made the name of Visconti "odious," but that really Matteo wasn't that bad. "He was clement, submissive to God, constant in adversity and moderate in victory." If this is true, which is doubtful, it is lamentable that Matteo's example was disregarded by those who came after him. The next three or four generations were a thoroughly bad lot.

After Matteo's death, his oldest son with his guardian ran things in Milan for a while, until his second son, Giovanni, archbishop of Milan, took over. He is best known, aside from the usual streak of family cruelty, for his great quarrel with Pope Clement VI. Archbishop Giovanni Visconti stole Bologna, one of the pope's towns, and was ordered to give it back. The pope even sent a legate to Milan to force Giovanni to do so. The archbishop met the legate in church, with a cross in one hand and a sword in the other.

"Here," he said, "are both spiritual and temporal weapons. I know how to defend the one with the other."

The pope then placed Milan under interdict (a ban restraining everyone from the sacraments) and summoned Giovanni to Avignon to answer for his crimes. The archbishop thought that was just fine and replied he would visit the pope with 1200 cavalry and 6000 infantry. At that point the pope decided to rescind the interdict and grant Bologna to the Viscontis for an annual tribute of 12,000 florins.

Archbishop Giovanni, a master of chicanery, in a most unspiritual way managed to scatter gold around the papal court, including a gift to the Countess Turenne, "the pope's director in temporal affairs," as she was called. Giovanni established bribery as a fine old family tradition.

His younger brother left three sons, Matteo II, Galeazzo II, and Bernabo—in that order of succession. Only a year after their uncle's death in 1354, Galeazzo and Bernabo got together to murder their older brother (for the good of the family, they said).

Bernabo, the more pious of the two, had thirty-two children, some of them legitimate, whereas Galeazzo's tastes ran more to literature. He founded the University of Pavia, exchanged "figs, flowers, and flattery" with the poet Petrarch, and followed the family tradition of locking up Holy Roman Emperors. When Charles IV paid him a visit, Galeazzo kept the hapless emperor under lock and key until Charles granted him the title of Imperial Vicar of Milan, in the family tradition.

Bernabo and Galeazzo are best known for their invention and perfection of the *quaresima*, a forty-day public torture of those accused of conspiring against the state. The unfortunate wretch was stripped and then placed on a scaffold in Milan's main public square. He was kept alive for forty days, which required constant attention.

One day he might lose an eye, the next a toe or an entire foot, on the third the nose, then a hand, and so on. To vary things a bit, and to keep public interest alive, the victim was made to drink noxious liquids, or was beaten almost to death, burned here and there, or had an arm or leg broken in places or pulled from its socket.

Both Galeazzo and Bernabo, out of artistry and piety, insisted the wretch's life be prolonged for forty days. When the time limit was reached, what was left of the doomed man was broken on the wheel and often disemboweled and quartered. All this was done, said the brothers, to show their concern for the safety of the state and to demonstrate that one did not lightly trifle with the Banner of the Viper.

When Galeazzo II died in 1378, his son, Gian Galeazzo, was to have succeeded him, but Uncle Bernabo thought otherwise. *He* was more competent, he said, to be Lord of Milan. And so, for the next seven years, Bernabo ruled alone, while Gian Galeazzo pursued his studies, turned to religion, and stayed out of Bernabo's clutches by living in another town. Bernabo tried from time to time to dispose of his nephew, but the lad led a charmed life.

Bernabo perfected the *quaresima*, administered justice, and indulged his taste for the chase. (Perhaps justice is the wrong word, but it was the word Bernabo liked.) Afraid of conspiracies (and he knew about such things), he enforced a curfew at sunset.

THE HOUSE OF VISCONTI

No one could say the words "Guelph" or "Ghibelline" (being pro-pope or pro-emperor) without having his tongue cut out, and Bernabo once locked up two secretaries—who had misspelled some words—with a wild boar. Their remains were buried the next day. Bernabo had other unusual ideas of justice. He burned alive a monk who had remonstrated with him for his cruelty, and a sexton who charged too high a fee for digging a grave was buried alive right next to it.

On one occasion, a young Milanese full of exuberant spirits pulled the beard of one of Bernabo's keepers of the peace. Justice demanded, Bernabo said, loss of the beard-pulling hand. A kindly judge procrastinated long enough to allow the lad's parents to appeal, whereupon Bernabo ordered the severing of the judge's right hand and, for good measure, *both* of the young man's hands. Such was justice à la Visconti, and it made quite an impression on potential wrongdoers.

Despite his great piety, Bernabo did not take any impertinence from Pope Urban V. The Holy Father sent two legates to Milan carrying a lengthy bill of excommunication against Bernabo. The latter met the papal legates on a bridge over a fast-flowing stream.

"Would you prefer to eat or drink?" Bernabo asked significantly. Surmising what they were in for should they say "drink," the two legates mumbled that they would prefer to eat. Bernabo then made them eat the papal bull, parchment, lead seals, thread and all. This was the Visconti way!

Bernabo loved the chase. He also made up his own rules. Nobody in Milan was allowed to keep a dog, but Bernabo had 5000 of them. These he quartered, as one would soldiers, in the homes of his loyal subjects, and every two weeks an inspector checked up to see how the dogs were doing. If the dog was too thin, a fine was levied, and if it was dead, Bernabo ordered confiscation of the luckless keeper's entire estate.

Bernabo so loved the hunt that he wouldn't share its pleasure with anyone. He more than once flung a hapless peasant to his dogs for having snared a rabbit. His delight at watching the peasant being torn to bits by his ferocious dogs was the talk of Milan. This became another family tradition and Giovanni Maria (his grandson and great-nephew) was to follow in Bernabo's footsteps.

Bernabo had the distinction of being denounced for his barbarity by St. Catherine of Siena, but it was his nephew Gian Galeazzo who finally gave him his come-uppance. Gian Galeazzo was only twenty-five when his father (Bernabo's older brother) died, and for seven years he led a rather retired life at Pavia. He assiduously cultivated a reputation for timidity and piety and a remarkable devotion to the Virgin. He was always telling his beads.

Uncle Bernabo thought this attitude indicated cowardice (which was true) and that Gian Galeazzo wasn't too much of a menace. Little did he guess that in Gian Galeazzo's breast beat the heart of one of the wickedest of the Viscontis.

One day in 1385, Gian Galeazzo wrote to Uncle Bernabo that he was about to make a pilgrimage to the shrine of Our Lady of Varese near Lake Maggiore, and would his beloved uncle meet him along the way? Uncle Bernabo and two of his sons met Gian Galeazzo, who affectionately embraced his uncle. While still holding Bernabo in his arms, Gian Galeazzo shouted to his German mercenaries to arrest his uncle and cousins.

This took but a moment. The old fox had been outsmarted. Bernabo and his two sons were flung into a dungeon. One attempt at poison disposed of the cousins, but it required three to eliminate Uncle Bernabo. Gian Galeazzo was now sole Lord of Milan.

Gian Galeazzo Visconti had been married while very young to Isabella of France, but after her death he married his first cousin Caterina Visconti, the daughter of Uncle Bernabo. Although he has sometimes been called the worst rascal in the family, the madness in his uncle makes his villainies seem rather pallid.

Gian Galeazzo was the type who turned white at the slamming of a door or a noise in the street below and who would shriek in terror during thunderstorms. Unusually gifted, even for a Visconti, his intellectual qualities and obvious piety seem to have obscured his natural viciousness, even to his contemporaries.

Founder of the Cathedral of Milan and patron of many artists and writers, Gian Galeazzo excelled at Machiavellianism— long before the word was invented. A great dissembler, betrayer, and deceiver, he was overweeningly ambitious, and in due course he bought the title duke of Milan from the impoverished Holy Roman Emperor Wenzel in 1395. He died of the plague at fifty-one before his enemies could get to him.

Gian Galeazzo left three legitimate children, two boys and a girl. The latter, a small girl named Valentina, was married to the duke of Orléans. Long after her death and the extinction of her house, she was responsible for great ills that befell Italy. Louis XII, king of France and Valentina's grandson, thought it only right to claim his grandmother's inheritance. Italy was invaded and devastated from head to toe, in a manner that would have appealed to long-dead Viscontis.

But back to Gian Galeazzo's two boys, both of whom were second-named because of their father's devotion to the Virgin. When Gian Galeazzo died, he left Milan and most of the duchy to his older boy, Giovanni Maria, aged thirteen, and Pavia and some other towns to the younger, Filippo Maria. At first they were too young to rule, so their mother Caterina (Bernabo's daughter) took over as regent.

Conditions were unsettled. Women were raped in the streets, towns were looted and burned, private dwellings were entered and their inhabitants put to the sword. Caterina did her best. As regent, she headed a Council of Seventeen, but all hell soon broke loose. Revolts in several outlying towns were put down with Visconti thoroughness and cruelty, while back in Milan Caterina came more and more to rely on the advice of her friend Barbavara.

People thought, quite correctly, that Caterina and Barbavara were lovers. A revolt broke out, but Caterina was not a Visconti for nothing. She kept control of Giovanni Maria, feigned submission to the rebels, tricked them into believing her a poor, helpless woman, turned the tables on them and eventually relieved them of their heads. A new council had to be formed, of course.

With this new crowd, Caterina was not quite so lucky. Another group of rebels turned up, grabbed possession of Giovanni Maria, and popped Caterina into a dungeon. She was poisoned a short time later, and a new council ruled in Giovanni Maria's name. While they governed Milan, they gave him the congenial job of handling his late mother's friends. This young juvenile delinquent immediately improved on the established methods of dealing with enemies of the state.

Even as a lad, his impatience became legendary. While his two grandfathers, Galeazzo II and Bernabo, had enjoyed the slowness of the *quaresima*, Giovanni Maria found waiting a terrible bore. Executions became hurried affairs, and the finesse of his grandfathers tended to become a lost art in the abattoir he made out of Milan.

Giovanni Maria was a latter-day Caligula. Quite mad he has been called by some, although others have been careful to note that his peculiarities could readily be accounted for because both his mother and father were Viscontis. That was a handicap for any young man, and his marriage to a Malatesta (a family hardly less villainous than the Viscontis) did not help.

After their mother's premature demise, both Giovanni Maria and Filippo Maria came under the tutelage of Facino Cane, one of the great *condottieri* of the day. As regent of Milan, he was rather indulgent toward Giovanni Maria. We might even say that Facino, like Caterina, spoiled the boy.

Giovanni Maria was allowed to establish himself as a kind of princely executioner. As long as he kept his nose out of affairs that didn't concern him (like ruling his duchy), he could do what he liked with prisoners of the state.

He loved dogs, the chase, and the Lombard breezes caressing his face as he rode down a hapless peasant. Despite charges to the contrary, his dogs were not *always* fed on human flesh, although one of Giovanni Maria's delights was to throw state criminals (man, woman, or child made no difference) to dogs especially trained to tear them into bits and gobble up the human flesh before the eyes of the fascinated duke. He kept a special kennel of dogs for this purpose.

Giovanni Maria gave the quarry a few minutes' head start and a promise of freedom should he escape. Then away they went over hill and dale. It was quite exciting for the young duke, who always saw his wolfhounds catch the "fox." The dogs had their fill of fresh meat, and Giovanni Maria returned to his palace in high good humor.

Giovanni Maria had a master of hounds named Squarcia, a man of considerable imagination. After all, killing people in the same way got on the duke's high-strung nerves. But it may be only rumor that the two of them got bored with palace parties and took out a few dogs in the dark of night to hunt down stray wanderers in the streets of Milan.

Giovanni Maria's fits of temper resulted in executions becoming more and more summary. Once, when his people were outside the palace yelling, "Peace, Peace," he sent out his mercenaries to slaughter a couple of hundred of them. He took an unreasoning dislike to the words "war" and "peace" and executed several Milanese unfortunate enough to utter them. He even changed the church service from "give us peace" to "give us tranquility."

Meanwhile, the real government of Milan was in the hands of Facino Cane, the regent. Luckily for the Viscontis, Facino had no children of his own. In 1412, he was struck with a fatal illness. For Giovanni Maria, this opened up new worlds. He faced the future with hope and great expectations. But, since his joy lay in other's agony, the prospects for his long-suffering subjects became too much to bear. Facino was bad enough, but the thought of a long reign by Giovanni Maria was impossible.

And so, on a bright spring day in 1412 (May 16), while on his way to mass (Giovanni Maria was as pious as his father and grandfather), he was stabbed to death at the door of San Gottardo.

The three conspirators were nobles who were soon captured by his brother's troops and subjected to tortures of such intricacy, barbarity, and vulgarity as to delight the shade of Giovanni Maria. The funeral was a splendid success. One of the late duke's favorite prostitutes covered the body with roses and was richly rewarded by Filippo Maria for her thoughtfulness.

With Giovanni Maria out of the way, Filippo Maria became duke of Milan. Facino, who died within hours of Giovanni Maria, had made his soldiers swear to defend the new duke and even made his wife and soon-to-be widow, Beatrice da Tenda, swear to marry him. It was hardly a marriage made in heaven. In a short time, Filippo Maria heard from one of his wife's ladies-in-waiting that a young and comely page had been seen sitting near the duchess's bed. He put everyone connected with the case to the torture, including his wife.

The page confessed, although Beatrice protested her innocence to the end. Filippo Maria found her guilty and executed wife, page, and—for good measure—all the duchess's maids. With such incidents fairly common to the time, one historian calmly remarks that "it would be unfair to judge Filippo Maria harshly." After all, he probably thought she was guilty.

Filippo Maria was notorious for his ugliness. The historian Sismondi describes him as "a strange, dingy creature, with protruding eyeballs and furtive glance." Maybe that's why he didn't like visitors. Cowardice was his outstanding trait. He, like his father, shrieked during thunderstorms, lived most of his life outside the city of Milan (he thought it safer that way), hated to see his own soldiers, and would receive no visitors. Indeed, he reversed the fine family tradition of locking up Holy Roman Emperors. When Emperor Sigismund visited Milan, Filippo Maria stayed in his room and gave out that he would have died of joy had he looked on the Emperor's countenance.

With this last of the family, the House of Visconti went to seed. Although a man of considerable gifts (he died in bed), he was more cowardly in all respects than any of his forebears. As a matter of fact, he wrung his hands at the news of his *condottieri*'s defeat (for fear they would desert him) and wrung them again at news of a victory (for fear they would take over). As a villain, he just didn't measure up. It is true, of course, that he practiced the *quaresima* and other devices of torture against his enemies, but his heart wasn't in it.

The Viscontis had fallen on evil times, and when Filippo Maria died in 1447 he left as heiress only an illegitimate daughter, Bianca. She married Francesco Sforza, and the Banner of the Viper lay in the dust.

16
Gilles de Rais

1404–1440

In need of money? There must be some
better way to get it than by bargaining
with devils.

Aaron Gilles de Rais, a marshal of
France and the friend of a saint,
was thirty-six when he was hanged and burned at Nantes in 1440.
Hanging *and* burning did not constitute overkill in his case, considering that among his crimes were the torture-murders of
something like 200 children. He doubtless had his reasons, aside
from sheer enjoyment; he was so profligate a spendthrift that he
always needed money, and in his desperation he figured the only
way to get it was through the intercession of evil spirits, who
required human sacrifices.

He started out as the heir to vast riches, broad estates, and
great power. His grandfather, an unscrupulous fellow, reared
him. For a while, when he was a young man, Gilles ran in superior company. He was the official protector of Joan of Arc, who
was to become a saint five centuries later. In those days when the
English claimed France for their infant king, Henry VI, the un-
lettered peasant girl donned armor and inspired the vacillating
dauphin to fight for his rights. Gilles de Rais, assigned to look
after her, rescued the Maid when she was wounded in battle.
When the dauphin was crowned Charles VII at Rheims Cathedral
in 1429, Gilles had the great honor of delivering the holy vessel
containing the oil of consecration. He stood at the side of the
Maid during the ceremonies. The king made him a marshal of
France and granted him the right to add to his crest the lilies
of France. His wife was rich. So it looked as though Gilles de
Rais had it made.

But no matter how much money he could lay hands on he always needed more. He loved to put on mystery plays, popular in his century; they instructed in religious or historical matters. They also entertained. So lavish were Gilles's productions that the audiences simply let their mouths hang open—because no matter how grand the spectacle, an even grander one was waiting in the wings. A stage set might have three stories out in a public street. Costumes weren't put together out of any old thing that was handy; they were of silk and satin, trimmed with gold, silver, embroidery, and precious stones. And the baron didn't permit a costume to be used twice. He had it tossed out or sold for a pittance, after paying more than it was worth in the first place.

This wasn't all. Gilles was fond of music. He established his own "college" of musicians, twenty-five or thirty men, and provided them with a portable organ for accompaniment. It took six men to carry. He traveled in style from one of his châteaux to another with comrades, servants, and his private choir, dressed in ecclesiastical splendor.

Even the king of the land couldn't afford all this, but it never occurred to Gilles to economize. He borrowed, he mortgaged some of his properties, he raised money wherever he could—and he was definitely not a good credit risk. Finally the king himself issued a Decree of Interdiction, making it unlawful for him to sell or encumber any more of his properties.

Casting around in desperation for a new source of money, Gilles hit upon an idea that looked good. Along with just about everybody else he believed the base metals could be transmuted into gold if you only knew how to go about it. What you needed was a philosopher's stone. Everybody knew this, but nobody had one. So, in the interests of science, he took up alchemy and became the prototype of the mad scientist. He didn't fool around like a well-meaning amateur. He rounded up professional alchemists, skilled in the black arts. But, for all their knowledge of necromancy, their experiments kept failing, and so he imported, to head the operation, an Italian named Francesco Prelati, age twenty-three.

Gilles moved his wife—to whom he paid scant attention anyway—to one of his remaining châteaux and installed his black magic crew in another, along with the necessary books of spells and the equipment. With appropriate lighting effects and assorted fearsome goings on they commanded the appearance of Satan, Belial, Beelzebub, and a lesser-known fiend named Barron. Apparently nobody noticed that there was something ambiguous about calling up devils in the name of the Trinity, the Virgin Mary, and all the saints. Gilles de Rais was a great one for playing both ends against the middle.

Belial was in command of 522,280 devils. Beelzebub, prince of devils, was a monster. Satan was his rival. Barron wasn't so famous, but Gilles didn't demand fame. He was a pragmatist and would settle for any power that worked. Also he considered himself a good Christian—boasted about it, in fact—so he specified to the expected evil spirits, "I will promise you everything except my soul and my life." This wasn't a very handsome offer. For hundreds of years people had pretty well agreed that devils wanted human souls and would pay well for them—Faust and Mephistopheles were after all almost historical memories. So there was a question: Just what could Gilles de Rais offer that the demons couldn't get without him?

None of them showed up, and all this black magic was ruinously expensive. He had been offering hens, turtledoves, and pigeons as sacrifices. Now Prelati made a suggestion: lay off on the poultry and offer the evil spirits something they could really enjoy, the flesh and blood of children. This was not so shocking to Gilles as you might think. For some years, ever since he was twenty-eight, children large and small had been mysteriously disappearing in the neighborhood of whatever château Gilles was inhabiting.

Puzzled peasants grieved for their little lost ones, but what could they do about it? Boys of all ages, and girls too, simply didn't come home from running errands, or a child left to look after the baby or to tend a flock of sheep wasn't there when its parents returned from working in their fields. Sometimes a boy gladly accepted an offer to become a page in the rich baron's household, or to sing in his fancy choir—but next time the baron came to that neighborhood with his entourage, the boy wasn't with him any more.

Later, when Gilles de Rais was tried for heresy and murder, the lists of missing children were long and black—at least two hundred disappeared in eight years—and there were hundreds of witnesses for the prosecution. The baron had a whole crew of kidnapers working for him. He practiced gross perversions on his little captives and thoroughly enjoyed watching a lingering death.

One of his murder methods was to have a child gagged and suspended a few feet above the floor with a cord around its neck. Choking, helpless, near to death, the child was let down—ever so grateful to the great baron, who had saved it and fondled it on his knees. When the terrified child's tears had dried, the process began all over again until it was fatal. Gilles had the child's arms and legs amputated. He sometimes lined up the severed heads of his victims, asked his accomplices to vote on which was prettiest, and then kissed that one lavishly.

For de Rais, it was an easy matter to get additional use out of the neighbors' kids by sacrificing them to the stubborn demons from the Underworld. The chanting of spells went on in the sinister hidden rooms of the baron's châteaux, the smoking incense burned, the children died—but no showers of gold rang on the stone floors, no philosopher's stone appeared. Various devils did, but never when Gilles was in the room.

The powerful evil spirits came to some of his crew of black magicians—the Devil even gave a bad beating to Prelati, the chief alchemist, who yelled in pain and a few minutes later showed Gilles his bruises. It was all very frustrating to Gilles, who never got a look at one of the dignitaries called up from hell but had to pay for all the necromancy. One problem was that the Black Baron when scared always crossed himself. His magicians kept *telling* him that that action ruined the spells and frightened off the demons he wanted to meet.

But Gilles came wonderfully close to his goal—or so he was assured by his hired sorcerers. Things kept happening when others were present, but he, alas, had just stepped out. Barron, the little-known demon, showed up as a handsome young man, but only Prelati was present. Prelati implored on behalf of his employer, and Barron pointed at a nice pile of gold ingots in a corner of the room just before he disappeared. Prelati rushed out to inform Gilles—but the gold had turned into a huge green snake. The sorcerer saw it but his master, just behind him, was cheated even of that. There was a heap of something that glittered, but it turned out to be dust.

Gilles kept trying, sometimes by himself. Two of his men walked into his bedchamber without warning one night and found him holding a cloth that contained the heart and eyes and a hand from a murdered child. The little corpse on the floor was still warm. In spite of such delicate offerings, virtually guaranteed to invoke the fiends of hell, none appeared to the Black Baron.

Now and then the baron ordered a cleanup, lest someone find the piles of stinking flesh and bloody bones in his cellars. On one occasion he set his men to gathering up skulls to be packed in boxes and sunk in a river.

Gilles was caught at last—not because the grieving voices of the peasants were answered but because he offended the duke of Brittany, to whom he owed allegiance. For various outrages— such as brutally dragging a clergyman out during high mass and desecrating the chapel—Gilles was sentenced to pay a huge fine. Of course he couldn't pay it. Now he *really* needed money, but his fate was about to catch up with him.

In the summer of 1440, the Bishop of Nantes began to look into the life and works of Baron Gilles de Rais. The bishop's officers collected a remarkable number of cases of lost children over a remarkably wide territory. In September, Gilles was ordered to appear before the bishop's tribunal. He was accused of having caused several innocent victims to perish, of committing upon them the sin of sodomy, of invoking devils, and of being guilty of heresy.

When Gilles was faced with two trials, one civil and one ecclesiastic, he made an awful discovery. He hadn't known that the practice of black magic constituted heresy. The baron had been careful, he thought, to keep in good repute with heaven at the very time he was fishing around in hell. Murder, yes, but heresy—he wouldn't have dreamed of that.

His chief alchemist, Prelati, was an important witness. Prelati admitted that he had heard of murders, but he was a clever fellow, and came through the trial smelling mighty like a rose. Prelati was sentenced to life imprisonment, but the duke of Anjou, a dedicated alchemist, rescued him and hired him. Sixteen years after the death of Gilles de Rais, Prelati was hanged for other crimes.

Witness after witness testified, each trying to save his own neck. A couple of the baron's employees admitted to packing up a bunch of skulls in one attempt at housecleaning, but neither could remember whether that lot included thirty-six or forty-six. Gilles railed and bellowed in utter fury, insulting members of the ecclesiastical court—they couldn't *do* this to him! But

there was so much testimony against him that he began to realize that the court *could* do this to him. He stopped trying to clear
himself and told all, including how he had killed children slowly
with the cord and relished every minute of it. Over and over he
confessed that he had killed for pleasure: *"pour me propre
délectation."* He named five of his accomplices. Two of them were
sentenced to be hanged and burned.

Gilles was found guilty of heretical apostasy and demonic
evocation. He was excommunicated. He wept copiously and maintained that he had never meant to be a bad boy and commit
heresy. Excommunication really scared him. The bishop absolved him and admitted him to communion. Then Gilles felt
much better.

Off they went to the civil tribunal. The courtroom was jammed.
De Rais confessed like crazy to the abominations of which he was
accused; he had already been through this and was getting the
hang of it. When the previous confession was read aloud to him,
he confirmed it. Legend says that at this point the president of
the court was so shocked that he ordered an image of Christ,
which hung on the wall, to be covered with a veil. The civil
court sentenced Gilles to pay the big fine he owed the duke of
Brittany; for his other crimes he would be hanged and burned
alive. He didn't have much time to worry about it. The execution
would take place at eleven o'clock the next morning, October 26,
1440.

There was a big audience for the execution. Gilles prayed in
public and implored everyone to pray for him, especially those
whose children he had murdered. Two of his bloody-handed employees, Henriet Griart and Étienne Corrillaut (known as
Poitou) were to die at his side. He admonished them to die like
men, following the example he was going to set for them. Then
he mounted a ladder to one of the three gibbets that awaited. A
noose was fitted around his neck. The fire below was lighted. A
stool was jerked out from under him, and he died almost instantly. He did not feel the flames that leaped up. When Joan of
Arc had died almost nine years before, that pure Maid who had
been his comrade in arms, she was granted no such mercy as
hanging. She died slowly and in agony in the flames.

Griart and Poitou were hanged and their bodies consumed by
the fire. Their ashes were scattered. But the body of Gilles de

Rais was not much burned when it was taken by several ladies of high degree for a proper funeral and burial in the Carmelite Church. Rank had its privileges.

For many years there remained in Nantes a stone Calvary, a monument to the Black Baron, built at the request of his daughter Marie. Part of it was a statue of the Virgin, which became famous as La Vièrge Cree-Lait, Our Lady the Milkmaker. It became *the* shrine for pregnant women from all over Brittany to pray for the blessing of Heaven. Nobody knows why a monument to that notorious child-killer, Gilles de Rais, should have become famous for such power. The Black Baron's tomb was destroyed when the Jacobin Terror in Nantes reached its peak in late 1793 and the church was ravaged.

As the years passed, and the names of the lost children and their grieving parents were forgotten, folk memories of the Black Baron faded, although horror did not. Dark tales clustered like bats around the crumbling châteaux where he had tried to summon up devils. The former lord had done something ghastly; that was remembered. Gradually the nature of what he had done was "remembered," too. A legend grew: he was a wicked fellow with a beard so black that it had a bluish cast, and he kept getting married and murdering his wives, except the last, the seventh one.

Baron Gilles de Laval de Rais became Bluebeard, the wicked killer of six wives, instead of the vicious murderer of some two hundred children. The real Gilles had only one wife, and she outlived him.

In 1697—two and a half centuries after the demise of Gilles de Rais—a French writer, Charles Perrault, wrote a book to amuse his children, *Contes de Mère l'Oye*, or "Stories of Mother Goose." The tale of Bluebeard was one of them. So were Little Red Riding-Hood, The Sleeping Beauty, and Cinderella. Thus the grisly tale of the demoniac mutilator of children became a bedtime story with a happy ending.

17
Tomás de Torquemada

1420–1498

There wasn't much of a choice between hell's fire and the fires of this religious fanatic!

Torquemada, that grim and pious Spaniard, did not invent the Inquisition, but he brought it to its full and frightful flowering. His victims were estimated (by another Spaniard, Juan Antonio Llorente) as 8800 burned, 6500 burned in effigy (because they had evaded him by dying or fleeing), and 90,000 penanced in various degrees. And when Torquemada put a penance on a sinner, it was considerably more than saying the rosary a few times. He didn't fool around.

A century before him, a Dominican friar named Hernando Martínez had persecuted the Jews of Spain, although both the king and the pope ordered him to desist. He defied them and went ahead. (Torquemada managed things more adroitly; he had the king, the queen, and the pope on his side.) Martínez' fiery preaching aroused a Seville mob to fury in 1390. The mob rushed into the Juderia, or ghetto, and butchered an estimated 4000 Jews just because they weren't Christians.

The Jews of Spain couldn't go back where they came from, because they had been born in Spain, like generations of their ancestors. Their only hope of safety was to become Christians. More than a million of them were baptized. They were called New Christians, except by Old Jews, who called them by a contemptuous epithet, *marranos,* meaning pigs. These converts, to the dismay of other Spaniards, achieved the same rights as Old Christians even to holding the same jobs. Several men who held high office in the court of Isabella of Castile were New Christians. Some of the Old Christians felt that things were getting out of hand, with these converts gaining equal rights and competing for advancement. The thing to do, then, was to catch them as heretics, backsliders.

The Inquisition, unlike the persecution of Martínez, was aimed only at heretics, Christians who erred. Anyone, Moor or Jew, who had never been baptized, was not questioned. But a *converso* who was suspected of being a *reverso*—that was potential fuel for the fire!

In 1478, Tomás de Torquemada came into prominence. He was tall and gaunt, slightly stooped. He wore the white habit and black cloak of the Dominican Brotherhood. He was Prior of the Convent of Holy Cross of Segovia, an austere fellow who never wore linen lest he feel comfortable, and so tough in following the rule of poverty that he wouldn't even provide his sister with a dowry so she could get married. He pinched out just enough money so she could enter a nunnery. Torquemada never ate meat. Maybe if he had loosened up enough to enjoy a good steak, he wouldn't have had to get his kicks from the odor of burning human flesh.

The Grand Inquisitor's name sounds invented; it could have been derived from the Latin *torquere* for twist (as on the rack), and the Spanish *quemada,* burned. Actually, it was simply a respectable family name derived from a Roman town, Turre Cremata, "burned tower." It just happened to fit this holy horror.

Torquemada persuaded Queen Isabella of Castile (whose husband was King Ferdinand of Aragon) that the old laws about heresy should be enforced, and he was just the man to do it. Ferdinand was more enthusiastic about the idea than his royal wife. Isabella was a gentle* sort who wouldn't even attend a bullfight unless the bull's horns were tipped with leather, but she came round to the idea that heretics ought to be cleaned out by fair means or foul. And so the Inquisition, known as the Holy Office, was launched with great fervor.

The first tribunal was set up in Seville in late 1480, and thousands of frightened New Christians fled. As the inquisitors saw

---

* An example of Isabella's tender heart is found in an anecdote about a peasant who tried to kill King Ferdinand because the Devil had told him to. The guilty man was condemned to have his fingers, toes, hands, feet, and limbs cut off at intervals. Isabella kindly ordered he be given a heavy blow on the head so that his consciousness would be dimmed while the hacking was going on.

it, this was proof that they were guilty. So orders went out that no one should give them refuge anywhere. On January 2, 1481, the inquisitors, determined to track down these heretics, commanded the nobles of Castile to take a census of everyone who had just moved into their territories and deliver them to prison for examination.

A group of wealthy, influential New Christians met in Seville at the home of one Diego de Susan to discuss defense. But Susan's beautiful daughter, in love with a Castilian, an Old Christian, betrayed her father and his friends to her lover. They were tried by the Inquisition for heresy and apostasy and—as was to happen almost always from henceforward—were found guilty.

The Inquisition didn't exactly hold trials. It simply proved, one way or another, that the accused was guilty. The Inquisition didn't shed blood. There were plenty of clever ways to torture a suspect without breaking his skin. Once he was proved guilty, the Holy Office didn't execute him; it was forbidden to take human life. The trembling sinner was handed over sadly to the secular arm, the civil authorities, and they did all that was necessary.

On February 6, Seville's first *auto da fé*—the miserably misnamed "act of faith"—took place. The accused heretics who had been betrayed by Susan's daughter were led from their prison barefoot, each wearing a yellow penitential sack called a *sanbenito* and carrying a candle. A black-robed Dominican led the procession, holding up the green cross of the Inquisition, swathed in crepe. At the cathedral, the doomed men heard mass and a fearsome sermon, full of hellfire. Then, in a meadow, they were chained to upright stakes and burned for the glory of God.

The nobles of Castile, thoroughly jarred, rounded up and delivered great numbers of accused *relapsos*. An "edict of grace" was published to encourage more to give themselves up. If *relapsos* would just confess, the edict proclaimed, and be reconciled to Mother Church, they would receive absolution and their property would not be confiscated. This had to be done within a specified time. Around 20,000 "relapsed *conversos*" flocked in, to get on the right side of the law and the Church—only to find that "grace" involved a secret proviso that hadn't been published. It wasn't enough for a suspected New Christian to confess he had erred; he had to name all his friends who might be "Judaizing," backsliding to the faith of their fathers! If he did not thus betray his own people, he would be burned in spite of his confession, and his children would be left destitute because of confiscation of property. Many of these men, tormented by fears for their children, gave in and turned traitor to their friends.

The Holy Office was really hitting its stride. Seventeen more pitiful victims were burned to death in Seville's second *auto da fé* on March 26. By November, 298 persons had been burned in Seville alone and seventy-nine others had escaped the fire by reconciliation to the Church—thus being allowed to spend the remainder of their lives in prison.

The Inquisition became big business. The Holy Office published a list of ways to prove that a *converso* was Judaizing. If a man put on a clean shirt on Saturday, the Jewish Sabbath; if a woman abstained from going to church for forty days after childbirth; if anyone held a farewell supper for a traveler leaving on a journey; if a dying person turned toward the wall or was turned by someone else; if anyone stripped the fat off meat before eating— any of these acts, which conformed with the ancient Jewish law, was proof of Judaizing, and off with him to the Inquisition.

Even the most pious and determined officials of the Holy Office couldn't look over the shoulder of every New Christian, but they certainly tried. A friar climbed to the roof of a convent every Saturday morning and carefully noted which houses had no smoke issuing from their chimneys.

Burning became such big business that a huge platform of stone, known as the *Quemadero,* or "Burning Place," was built in the fields of Tablada. It remained until Napoleon's soldiers destroyed it early in the nineteenth century.

Torquemada, appointed Grand Inquisitor by the pope, was a man who planned ahead and didn't miss any opportunities to prove a suspect's guilt. He set up four permanent tribunals and a code of rules that remained in effect for more than three hundred years after his death. A *converso* could be suspected in one of three degrees: Lightly—for this he did penance, which might be severe; vehemently—punished by imprisonment and heavy penance; violently—punished by imprisonment and the shame of having to wear the ignominious *sanbenito.* This yellow garment of scorn was decorated with a big cross front and back or with other symbols designating just how wicked the person was. Torquemada, that great administrator, was attentive to detail. The design on the *sanbenito* showed whether the person was a repented heretic, not to be burned; or a relapsed heretic who was not to die by fire although his body would be burned (the nicety here was that he would be strangled before the fire was lighted); or an unrepentant heretic, who could expect nothing but the worst of horror.

The zealous priests and laymen attached to the Holy Office were forbidden to shed blood or cause loss of life, but sometimes a suspect died under torture. That was too bad but not awfully serious for the officiating clergyman. His punishment was that he had to be absolved by another priest.

Inquisitors were not encouraged to use their imagination in the torture chamber. They didn't really need to invent anything new. Methods of inflicting excruciating pain had been developed long before and did not require improvement. Three infernal methods had been perfected: the rack, the hoist, and the water torture.

The rack pulled and twisted; it could dislocate hips and shoulders. (And while it was doing this, the inquisitors kept encouraging the suspect to tell the truth and get right with God.) The hoist was a pulley attached to the ceiling. The victim's wrists were tied *behind* him, and he was slowly pulled up with a rope. When the whole weight of his body was on his tormented, twisted arms, he was encouraged to confess his sins; dropping him a short distance could pull his shoulders apart, especially if weights were tied to his feet.

For the water torture, he was tied on a short ladder with his head lower than his feet and fastened with cords that cut when he moved. They could be twisted like tourniquets to bite into his flesh clear to the bone. His nostrils were plugged, his mouth was held open by an iron prong and linen was forced into his throat. Then water was poured in so that he almost but not quite suffocated. In a terrible effort to draw air into his lungs, he had to keep swallowing the water. The methodical tormentors kept track of the number of jars of water administered.

The devoted men of the Holy Office spent much time setting up questions according to rules perfected by Torquemada. No matter how a frightened suspect answered, he would be trapped, because under circumstances of terror he was bound to contradict himself in some detail—and that was reason enough to call him a liar and put him to torture. The Inquisitors learned to play with words so that "grace," for instance, didn't mean what the frantic suspect thought it meant when offered. It often meant that his soul would be saved if he admitted heresy, but his body would go through the fire. "Mercy" meant that he would be strangled at the stake before his body was burned.

This weasel-wording made the inquisitors feel quite calm, even benevolent, when they tortured a victim who was actually strong in the Catholic faith, the theory being that torture could not turn him against his faith. It might even strengthen him.

It was hard indeed to prove innocence. A *converso* who was actually a good Catholic might be trapped by endless, soothing questions or by a false witness frantically trying to save his own skin, but the victim was supposed to die with resignation and even rejoicing, because it was all in the cause of truth.

The confiscation of property was part of the punishment of heretics. Their children might be left impoverished, but what of that? Both the Inquisition and the government always needed money. Isabella and Ferdinand were still fighting to eject from their territories the remnants of the Moors, who had invaded and conquered Spain seven hundred years before.

A man's property could be confiscated if heresy could be "proved" against him, even after he had been dead for forty years. In this case, he would be burned in effigy, since his living body was not available. The theory in confiscating property was that this was reasonable punishment for sin. After all, Adam and Eve, the first sinners, had lost Eden.

Questioning was always secret. You might disappear and be seen no more by your friends until you tottered out of prison, wearing a *sanbenito* and carrying a candle, on your way to a lingering death at the stake. Torquemada improved upon the secrecy aspect, making "trials" even more unjust than before— if total injustice can be improved upon.

Occasionally, of course, there was attempted rebellion. Some nobles who were Old Christians had the gall to speak up. They were listed as hinderers of the Holy Office. A group of assassins tried to kill two inquisitors in Saragossa and did kill one of them, in church at midnight, in spite of the mail shirt he wore under his habit and the steel lining in his skullcap. A servant of one of the assassins was tortured and, under promise of grace, revealed the names of the others. "Grace" in this case turned out to mean that, unlike the others, he wouldn't have his hands hacked off before he was hanged, drawn, and quartered. Five men were burned. Two who escaped were burned in effigy. Another cheated by eating a broken glass lamp in prison, but the Holy Office burned his corpse. Some two hundred people were punished in one way or another for this murder. The murdered Inquisitor, Pedro Arbues de Epila, was beatified two hundred years later and canonized as a saint in the nineteenth century.

Sound executive that he was, Torquemada kept expanding business. In 1485 he established the Inquisition in Toledo. Penitents were at first invited to turn themselves in and have their souls washed. Then everyone was ordered, on pain of excommunication, to name *reversos* within a limited time. Torquemada had another trick up his sleeve: he ordered all rabbis to swear that they would denounce any New Christian who had backslid. It became a capital offense for any rabbi to protect his own people! Thus the Grand Inquisitor forced the Jews themselves to work in his secret service.

Three men and their wives fled from Toledo to Valencia, bought a yawl, and set sail to escape persecution. But an ill wind blew their boat back, and the fact that they had tried to get away was considered proof of their guilt. All six were burned.

New Christians who were willing to admit to Judaizing didn't get off easily. A really big celebration in February 1486 featured the humiliation and degradation of some 750 men and women who went through a penance known as *verguenza* or "shame." They were paraded through the streets of Toledo bareheaded, barefoot, and naked to the waist, each carrying an unlighted candle to show that the light of faith did not illumine his soul. After mass and a fearful sermon they were sentenced to fast and be whipped on six consecutive Fridays and never to hold honorable employment as long as they lived. In addition, they had to give a fifth of the value to their property to the government to help fight the holy war against the infidels of Granada, the Moors.

That was for the penitents. For the impenitent, who would not admit to hersey and say they were sorry, of course there was no such mercy. They were rounded up, paraded through the streets with great ceremony, and in Cathedral Square they were abandoned to the secular arm. In a field outside the city they were chained to stakes and burned to death by slow fires.

Because an accusation of heresy might bring horrible punishment, hundreds of New Christians turned themselves in as penitents. The best they could hope for was scourging in public and the shame of wearing the *sanbenito*, some for the rest of their lives. After the so-called edict of grace expired, it was too late to seek salvation, but it was never too late for Torquemada's industrious inquisitors to track down more *conversos* and "prove" them guilty. Burning was stepped up considerably, and the "guilty" who were not sentenced to fire spent the rest of their lives in prison.

When Pope Sixtus IV died in 1484, some eminent Spaniards suggested that Torquemada, his appointee, be deposed. But his successor, Innocent VIII, returned him to office with even more power. He had jurisdiction of all Spain, and all Catholic rulers everywhere were commanded to cooperate with him. This was Torquemada's big opportunity. Now he could clear the heretics out of Spain and pursue the survivors wherever they went.

Some Spaniards applied to the pope for secret and expensive absolution, and Innocent VIII granted some briefs of dispensation. Torquemada was furious. Rome was actually protecting these awful people! He went to see King Ferdinand about it. Ferdinand agreed; if money was changing hands, *he* wanted it. The briefs that had been granted were canceled. The New Christians who had paid heavily for safety were safe no more, and all they achieved by protesting was to make themselves known.

Torquemada was doing so great a job that Isabella urged him to accept promotion to archbishop. He was too humble for that. He would remain simply a prior—and Inquisitor General.

Torquemada's big opportunity to drive *all* Jews out of Spain, whether baptized or not, came in 1490 when the case of the Holy Child of La Guardia came to light. A four-year-old boy had been killed, and rumor had it this was a ritual murder by Jews, having to do with black sorcery.

The Inquisition's investigation went on for months in the torture chambers of the Holy Office. Suspects were given every opportunity to trap themselves and one another. And on November 16, 1491, near the church of St. Peter in Avila, eleven figures stood on a scaffold. Three of them were merely effigies of suspects who had escaped the fire by dying on the rack. All were abandoned to the secular arm and taken to the local burning place.

At the last minute some of them "accepted the spiritual comforts of the Church" and earned the mercy of being strangled before the fires were lighted. Two men remained true to the Jewish faith; their flesh was torn with red-hot pincers before the fire was lighted.

The body of the Holy Child was never found; of course it had been translated at once to heaven. This case provided the "proof" that Torquemada wanted: Jews had martyred and crucified a Christian child. Now he was ready to carry out his big plan of eliminating all the Jews. The year 1492 was not only the year Columbus sailed the ocean blue. It was also the year when the last of the Moors were driven from Granada and the year the Jews were expelled from Spain. Isabella signed the edict of expulsion on March 31.

The banished people were kindly permitted to sell their property, but there was a trick to this. They could not take any money out of Spain when they left. Some two hundred thousand men, women, and children had to leave the country where their ancestors had lived for hundreds of years. Every road to the coast was crammed with fugitives trying to carry something along to sell for support in a strange land. Nobody could help them. Everyone could abuse them. Ships' captains took most of their possessions in return for passage—and then tossed many passengers overboard. A rumor spread that some were swallowing jewels and gold pieces, so hundreds, or even thousands, were ripped open in a search for wealth.

Some went to Italy, southern France, England. Some reached the Ottoman dominions in eastern Europe and prospered. The Netherlands became an important diamond-trading center, and still is, because among the expelled artisans who found shelter there were diamond-cutters. But thousands and thousands died trying to find refuge.

Ferdinand and the gentle Isabella, prodded by Torquemada, procured from Pope Innocent VIII a bull threatening excommunication to anyone in any country who gave the refugees help. Apparently no ruler paid any attention except in Portugal, where a Spanish princess married the sovereign. Then the Jews who had found refuge there were driven out.

According to one Spanish historian, Juan Antonio Llorente, who had access to all the records, the Inquisition acquitted about one accused person in two thousand. Llorente was General Secretary to the Holy Office in Madrid from 1789 to 1792.

Tomás de Torquemada died September 16, 1498, at the age

of sixty-eight, no doubt fairly well satisfied with his success in the hideous work he had undertaken for the glory of his Maker.

Spain's last public burning was in 1781, almost 300 years after the first. In 1826 a man was hanged by the Inquisition, which wasn't officially abolished until 1834. The Edict of Expulsion against Jews lasted even longer. Francisco Franco lifted it in 1968.

18
The Borgias and Their Friends

1431–1570

Rodrigo, the Borgia pope, didn't let his bachelor status keep him from pushing his children ahead.

We tend to envision two of the Borgias as deadly dangerous: Lucrezia, the beautiful brunette, languishing toward some velvet-clad, bejeweled gallant as she drops poison from one of her finger rings into his glass; and Cesare, vulpine and insidious, urging a guest to have just a smidgen more of broiled lark while he drops poison on it from *his* trick ring.

But this image is wrong. Lucrezia was beautiful, all right; her contemporaries said so. But she was not brunette, she was a blonde with big blue eyes, and she didn't need to poison anybody. Her duty was to get married whenever her father found a new husband for her, even if she liked the one she had. Lucrezia was Daddy's girl. She did as she was told.

And her brother Cesare, although he used poison from time to time, really preferred a hired hatchet man with good strong hands. Strangling was quieter than poison, which might put the victim to yelling with pain before he could get decently home, and neater than stabbing, with all that blood to clean up. Cesare, like his sister, realized that in most cases Father knew best.

Father's name was Rodrigo Borgia. He was a Spaniard, born January 1, 1431, and adopted by his uncle, Pope Calixtus III. Rodrigo became a cardinal at age twenty-five and vice chancellor of the church the following year. Immensely wealthy from the benefices conferred on him, he was before long the second richest man in the College of Cardinals, none of whom had to pinch pennies.

Rodrigo Borgia's uncle died in 1458, and the Cardinal of Siena

became Pope Pius II. Two years later, Pius found it necessary
to write the young cardinal a stern letter, which tells us something about what kind of man young Borgia was—and he didn't
change his ways as he grew older. Here are parts of the letter:

> Beloved Son: When four days ago in the gardens of Gio-
> vanni de Bichis, were assembled several women of Siena
> addicted to worldly vanity, your worthiness, as we have
> learnt, little remembering the office which you fill, was en-
> tertained by them from the seventeenth to the twenty-fourth
> hour. For companion you had one of your colleagues, one
> whom his years if not the honor of the Holy See should
> have reminded of his duty.
> From what we have heard, dancing was unrestrainedly
> indulged, and not one of love's attractions was absent,
> whilst your behavior was no different from that which
> might have been looked for in any worldly youth. Touching
> what happened there, modesty imposes silence. Not only the
> circumstances itself, but the very name of it is unworthy
> in one of your rank. The husbands, parents, brothers, and
> relations of these young women were excluded, in order that
> your amusements should be the more unbridled. You with a
> few servants undertook to direct and lead those dances. . . .
> Our displeasure is unutterable, since all this reflects dis-
> honorably upon the sacerdotal estate and office. It will be
> said of us that we are enriched and promoted not to the
> end that we may lead blameless lives, but that we may pro-
> cure the means to indulge our pleasures. Hence the contempt
> of us entertained by temporal princes and powers and the
> daily sarcasms of the laity. . . . The very Vicar of Christ is
> involved in this contempt, since he appears to countenance
> such things.
> You, beloved son, have charge of the Bishopric of Valen-
> cia, the first in Spain; you are also Vice-Chancellor of the
> Church; and what renders your conduct still more blame-
> worthy is that you are among the cardinals, with the pope,
> one of the counsellors of the Holy See. We submit it to your
> own judgment whether it becomes your dignity to court
> young women, to send fruit and wine to her you love, and
> to have no thought for anything but pleasure. We are cen-
> sured on your account; the blessed memory of your uncle
> Calixtus is vituperated, since in the judgment of many he
> was wrong to have conferred so many honors upon you. If
> you seek excuses in your youth, you are no longer so young

that you cannot understand what duties are imposed upon
you by your dignity. A cardinal should be irreproachable, a
model of moral conduct to all. . . .

May your prudence therefore set a restraint upon these
vanities and keep you mindful of your dignity, and prevent
that you be known for a gallant among married and unmarried women. . . . Your age, which is such as still to
promise improvement, admits that we should admonish you
paternally.

Those were scandalous times. In the same year, 1460, a son
was born to Cardinal Rodrigo and an unnamed married woman.
He was named Pedro Luis and he was the first of many children
by several mistresses.

Rodrigo was, of course, a priest and a bachelor, but he was a
loving father to his many children. Just how many he had, and
by how many mistresses, is open to argument. (Clergymen were
not, in his time, expected to behave any better than laymen, and
laymen behaved very badly indeed, if they could afford it.) The
mother of most of Rodrigo's children was Vannozza de Catteneis.
She was married, although not to their father. She gave Rodrigo
at least six children, maybe seven. The most outstanding of this
brood were the notorious Cesare and the political cats-paw Lucrezia. Nobody could say that Rodrigo was a bad father; he did
more for his children than he did for the church.

He did not altogether ignore his official responsibilities, however. He should be remembered for his efforts as pope to suppress lawlessness in Italy and for his patronage of art, science,
and literature. He began the *Index Librorum Prohibitorum*, the
index of prohibited books, which continues today, after almost
five centuries. He contributed to world peace by drawing the
Line of Demarcation to keep Spain and Portugal from fighting
over the treasures of the New World, which was discovered in
the same year he advanced to the papal throne. He sent missionaries to America.

He achieved his elevation to the papal throne through simony,
being a man who believed that a thing worth having was worth
paying for. But he did not invent simony; it was an accepted
practice in his time. He failed in his first attempt at election to
the papacy in 1484, when Innocent VIII got elected. Innocent was
the first pope to admit that he had children instead of nephews,
and he loaded them with riches.

When he died after eight years in office, Rodrigo Borgia had a second chance, and some very tough competition. The king of France paid 200,000 gold ducats to insure the election of Giuleano della Rovere, and the Republic of Genoa put up another 100,000. But the College of Cardinals didn't like such interference from France, and Borgia money, although it had a Spanish accent and was therefore suspect in Italy, had a loud voice. Rodrigo had once boasted that he had enough bags of gold to fill the Sistine Chapel.

The conclave met August 8. By the tenth he had bought the votes of thirteen cardinals. Then he had a little chat with his toughest remaining competitor, Ascanio Sforza. They made a deal: in return for Sforza's vote Rodrigo would hand over a lot of cash and appoint him to the office of vice-chancellor, which paid very well to a smart man.

Now Rodrigo needed just one more vote. This he bought from the Cardinal of Venice, who was ninety-six years old and wouldn't have much longer to enjoy money but didn't mind turning a dishonest ducat. On August 11, 1492, Rodrigo Borgia of Valencia became Pope Alexander VI. Now he could *really* look after the needs of his loving family. Pedro Luis, the oldest, had already died of malaria, and two of the girls were married, but there remained several others. There is some doubt about their exact birth years, but Giovanni was probably born in 1475, Cesare in 1476; Lucrezia came along in 1480, and Giuffré a year later. In the fullness of time there were another Giovanni, born in 1498, and Rodrigo, 1503; they were sons of Giulia Farnese, who was a bride of sixteen when she became the pope's mistress. She was young enough to be his granddaughter but old enough to know just what she was doing.

Rodrigo Borgia showered wealth and honors on his children. He had persuaded Sixtus IV to bestow on Cesare, age six, the rich revenues of the Cathedral of Valencia. From there on, benefices fell thick and fast. Cesare was a canon, an archdeacon, a rector, a provost. He was treasurer of the church of Carthagena at age nine. This job, like the others, didn't require any effort on his part; but the appointments brought in a nice fat income. At fifteen Cesare was bishop of Pamplona and was said by his father to be "distinguished for his virtues and his learning." On the day Rodrigo became pope, he appointed Cesare bishop of Valencia. Not bad for a sixteen-year-old kid who had not the slightest interest in the religious life! And there was more to come.

Rodrigo had big things in mind for little Lucrezia. When she was eleven, and her father was still a cardinal, he arranged her betrothal to a Spaniard with a promising future. Then a better opportunity came along, so Rodrigo broke that contract—although betrothal was much more binding than a present-day engagement—and the dutiful little girl was promised to another Spaniard. But the following year, when her father became pope, her value in political horse-trading was sharply increased, so her second betrothal was canceled and she was promised to Giovanni Sforza. They were married June 12, 1493, when the bride was thirteen.

In September of that year, the pope appointed Cesare a cardinal. Cesare at seventeen was described as lively and merry, and "he bore himself like a great prince," not necessarily a prince of the church.

In spite of the shopping around that their father had done, before and after he became pope, he kept on looking for more golden bargains for Lucrezia. He found one in the Duke of Bisceglie, son of the king of Naples. Alexander VI had in mind that with Lucrezia married to the king's son and a hoped-for marriage between Cesare and the king's daughter, Cesare might very well, in the fullness of time, mount the throne of Naples himself some day.

There were a couple of stumbling blocks in the way. Cesare was a cardinal and couldn't marry. Lucrezia was already married. She was willing to do whatever Daddy said, even if it involved annulling her marriage to Giovanni Sforza, but Giovanni dug in his heels. This left Lucrezia in an unenviable situation. Because of her stubborn husband, it was difficult to obey paternal orders.

Lucrezia was able to warn her husband in a roundabout way that he was in a dangerous spot. In a normal family, a wife would simply *tell* her husband something like that, but the Borgias preferred subtlety. One day when her husband's chamberlain was in her apartment, the imminent arrival of Cesare was announced. "Pssst," she hissed to the chamberlain, "my brother's coming. Get in that cupboard and maybe you'll hear something interesting."

He did. Cesare strode in, with his sword clanking, and raved and ranted that if that blank-blank Giovanni Sforza knew what was good for him he would quit arguing about wanting to stay married. "If he doesn't get out of your life," roared Cesare, "I'll kill him myself!"

Exit Cesare, raging. Exit the chamberlain, gasping. The threatened husband left town in a hurry. Lucrezia's clever father found a way for her to get out of the marriage, but the scandal was terrific.

A few days after Lucrezia got the message to her husband, a murder shook not only the Borgia family but all of Rome. Vanozza, mother of the brood, had a party for Cesare and his brother Giovanni, duke of Gandia, at her home on June 14. Afterward the brothers, with some friends and servants, took horse and started back to the papal palace. Before they got there, Giovanni said good-night and, with a groom and a masked man who was never identified, separated from the others. Nobody thought anything of that. Any young blade might be planning a night on the tiles. He wasn't home by morning, but the pope didn't worry much, assuming that Giovanni had stayed with some girl, overslept and didn't want to be seen leaving by daylight.

That night Giovanni's groom was found, badly wounded and unable to tell what had happened. The pope sent out a big search party. They found a wood dealer on the bank of the Tiber who had seen something interesting. About midnight, two men had appeared and cautiously looked around. Then they left. Next came a rider on a white horse with a dead body on it and two men, one on each side, to keep it from falling off. They backed the horse into the river and the two men threw the body as far as they could. The cloak floated, and they threw stones until it sank. Then they left. The wood dealer didn't think much about the incident. He had seen at least a hundred bodies consigned to the Tiber in his time.

The pope had the river dragged, and the duke of Gandia's body was pulled up out of the sewage that passed for water. He hadn't been robbed; but his throat had been cut and he had nine other big wounds. Anybody who had reason not to like him was suspected, but the murderer was never found. After a while whispers began to circulate: *That Cesare, he's the one who killed his brother. Why? Because he was jealous. Their little sister, Lucrezia, you know. . . .*

Cesare did have something to gain by his brother's death. He was still a cardinal and didn't want to be. He was rich, but the benefices his father had given him could be taken away by some later pope. As a layman, Cesare could hope for more permanent sources of wealth (by marrying money, for instance), but, as long as Giovanni lived, Giovanni would be their father's pet.

When the furor, and the pope's honest grief, died down, there still remained the problem of getting rid of Lucrezia's stubborn husband. It was arranged. An official commission of cardinals met, consulted, and announced that Lucrezia, wed these four years, was still a virgin. How could that be? Because, the commission solemnly explained, the marriage had never been consummated, the reason being that her husband was "impotent and cold by nature."

All Rome howled with laughter at this shameful accusation. *Poor Giovanni! Impotent, can you imagine?* Giovanni was furious. His first wife had died in childbirth (and his third one— Lucrezia's successor—presented him with an heir), but it suited the convenience of the Borgias to claim that he lacked virility. Nobody important went to argue for him, and it was dangerous to argue with Borgias, so he finally signed a statement admitting that he had been Lucrezia's husband in name only. He hinted around among the right people that the reason the pope got rid of him was that the father wanted the daughter himself. The Romans adored nasty gossip. Giovanni's accusation grew to a belief that both the pope and Cesare had committed incest with Lucrezia.

Anyway, the marriage was annulled December 20, 1497, and Lucrezia, now seventeen, was free to marry again. But a strange event occurred. In March 1498 Lucrezia, so recently declared a virgin, became a mother. Two ambassadors stationed in Rome wrote home to their governments that her child was illegitimate. About this time a couple of bodies were reclaimed from the Tiber, those of a man known as Perotto, a member of the pope's household, and one of Lucrezia's maids. There were those who said that Perotto was father to Lucrezia's child and that the maid knew too much, so Cesare had got rid of them both.

The record of this child is clouded, because the Borgias were very good at covering their tracks. A mysterious boy called the *infans Romanus* was born about the same time—or was it the same child? He was known as Giovanni di Borgia, and he became part of the swarming Borgia family and eventually duke of Nepi. Alexander VI confused history by issuing two bulls about the *infans Romanus*. One, which was published, said the child was the son of Cesare and an unmarried woman. The other, filed away in secret, said he was Alexander's own child. But gossip said that little Giovanni was the son of Alexander *and* his daughter Lucrezia. The child became part of Lucrezia's household after her second marriage and was treated as her little brother.

The July after the annulment of her first marriage, Lucrezia quietly married the duke of Bisceglie, son of the king of Naples.

A few weeks after Lucrezia's second wedding, Cesare was permitted to relinquish his cardinalate. Thanks to the king of France, he became duke of Valentinois in another of the high-level horse trades so beloved to noble Italian families. Cesare would now marry the daughter of the king of Naples, Carlotta, who was being brought up at the French court. He would also hand over the pope's dispensation for King Louis XII to get rid of his unwanted wife so he could marry another girl.

But there was a hitch. Carlotta wouldn't have Cesare. She put down her little foot and said no, no, and no. There were other fish in the sea. Cesare married Princess Charlotte d'Albret, age seventeen. He stayed four months—just long enough to make sure she was pregnant—and then rode off with King Louis to invade Italy on the pope's orders. Charlotte never saw him again.

Cesare attacked Milan; no problem there. The people welcomed Louis of France as their duke. Then Louis helped Cesare attack some of the cities of Romagna, the excuse being that the pope said their lords hadn't paid their feudal dues. Cesare won a hard-fought battle and conquered Imola and Forli, although Caterina Sforza, who ruled those cities, kept fighting even after most of her people deserted her. She was brought into Rome in golden chains when Cesare made his grand, triumphal entry.

The Borgias were riding high. Cesare, furious at a drunken man who mocked him, had the man deprived of his tongue and one hand. Another man, who circulated a pamphlet criticizing Cesare, was drowned in the Tiber.

As time passed, it became apparent that Lucrezia's marriage to her second husband, the Neapolitan heir Alfonso, was no longer useful to the Borgias. His family had been toppled off the throne of Naples by the combined efforts of the French and the Spanish. Suspecting that he would be safer out of the hands of the Borgias,

Alfonso, now nineteen, left Rome but unwisely returned at his father-in-law's bidding. On the night of July 15, 1500, while walking down some steps from the Vatican to the Piazza of St. Peter's with two companions, he was attacked by several men armed with swords. Alfonso and his escort fought gallantly, but he was desperately wounded in the head, right arm, shoulder, and hip. Covered with blood he tried to escape—but every street was blocked by men determined to kill him. With the help of one of his companions, he staggered back into the Vatican and collapsed.

The pope, who had been sick in bed with a fever, rushed to him. Lucrezia fainted when she heard the news. The Ambassador from Venice reported to his government, "It is rumored that he who wounded the duke was the same who killed Gandia and threw him into the Tiber." The duke of Gandia, it will be remembered, was Cesare's brother. This same ambassador reported that Cesare said after the attack on Lucrezia's second husband, "I did not wound the duke, but if I had, it would have been no more than he deserved."

Alfonso didn't quite die that time. He began to mend. Cesare busily ordered that nobody without proper authority was to carry arms in the area of the Vatican. The pope set up a guard. Lucrezia and Alfonso's sister Sancia nursed the wounded man with loving care and even supervised the cooking of his food for fear someone might take a notion to poison him. But Alfonso, duke of Bisceglia, had to die, so of course he did.

Much of the low-down on the Borgias comes to us from a private journal kept by John Burchard, a Swiss who served for many years as Master of Ceremonies in the Vatican. Burchard held office under five popes, two before Alexander VI and two after him. In dead-pan style he wrote down events that he considered interesting, such as the death of Lucrezia's unlucky second husband:

"On Tuesday, 18th August, 1500, Alfonso of Aragon, who had been brought after his recent injuries to the tower above the chapel cellar in the main garden of the Vatican, and had been carefully guarded, was strangled in his bed at four o'clock in the afternoon, as he did not die of his wounds."

When the fracas began in the sickroom, Lucrezia and Sancia ran to the pope for protection. When they came back, Lucrezia was a widow. Alfonso's doctors and a hunchback who had nursed him were questioned but released as innocent—"A fact," remarked Burchard, "that was very well known to those who had made out the warrants."

Another account said that Cesare came to call on his ailing brother-in-law but Lucrezia and Sancia drove him out. Whereupon he called his guard captain, Michelotto, who quietly strangled the duke. Later this Michelotto was officially charged with killing Alfonso, the duke of Gandia, and half a dozen other men. On the rack he claimed that the pope himself had given the order for Alfonso's death.

With Alfonso dead, Lucrezia was free to be married off again. This time her father chose another Alfonso, of the d'Este family, heir to the dukedom of Ferrara. He wasn't at all enthusiastic, and neither was his family, but they sniffed the good, rich smell of money, for with Lucrezia went a very large dowry.

Lucrezia's brother saw to it that her time of waiting wasn't too dull. One of Burchard's journal entries goes this way:

> On the evening of the last day of October, 1501, Cesare Borgia arranged a banquet in his chambers in the Vatican with fifty honest prostitutes, called courtesans, who danced after the dinner with the attendants and the others who were present, at first in their garments, then naked. After the dinner the candelabra with the burning candles were taken from the tables and placed on the floor and chestnuts were strewn around, which the naked courtesans picked up, creeping on hands and knees between the chandeliers, while the Pope, Cesare and his sister Lucrezia looked on.

There was more, and you would blush to read it. There is no record that the fair Lucrezia blushed. She married her third husband, the second Alfonso, on December 30, 1501.

Hanging around with the Borgias was a dangerous occupation. One of Lucrezia's ladies was a relative, beautiful Angela Borgia, who caught the admiring eyes of two of Lucrezia's new brothers-in-law, Giulio d'Este and Cardinal Ippolito d'Este. One day Angela teasingly remarked to Ippolito that Giulio had beautiful eyes. Ippolito seethed with jealousy. He did more than seethe. He hired assassins to grab his brother and tear out those beautiful eyes. A doctor succeeded in saving the sight of one eye.

The d'Estes were a nest of snakes. Giulio demanded that one

of Ippolito's eyes be torn out in retaliation, but Alfonso only banished him. Ippolito's friends thought this punishment was much too severe. So Giulio set up a plot to depose Alfonso from the dukedom; Ippolito the cardinal would be poisoned and Alfonso would be killed at a masked ball. Alfonso's brother, Ferrante, would become duke. This didn't work out. The cardinal got wind of the plot and told Alfonso. Some of the plotters escaped, some had their heads cut off, and Ferrante and Giulio were imprisoned for life. They outlived Alfonso himself. Ferrante died at sixty-two, and Giulio was released when he was eighty-three.

It was getting unsafe to write poetry in praise of ladies, although that's what poets were supposed to do. Ercole Strozzi admired Lucrezia and praised her in something he wrote. Soon after he was married in May 1508, his body was found, wrapped in a mantle that concealed twenty-two wounds. Lucrezia's husband, Alfonso d'Este, was credited with that murder.

One fine summer evening in 1503, Cardinal Adrian Corneto gave a dinner party to celebrate his appointment as cardinal. The pope and several other prelates were there, and so was Cesare Borgia. It was a good party—but afterward several of the guests became very sick. The cardinal himself broke out all over and suffered so much from that and from "sudden heat of the viscera" that he was put into a big tub of cold water. All his skin peeled off.

Cesare Borgia, robust and in his prime, almost died. His skin peeled off, too. The pope was stricken, as well. He lingered for days, horribly sick. The symptoms indicated poisoning. But the new cardinal hadn't poisoned himself, so the Borgias got the blame. Not that they had suicidal inclinations, but it seemed perfectly clear that they had meant to poison Corneto and the lethal draft went into the wrong cups. There was talk that Cesare had sent over some poisoned wine by a servant who got confused about what he was supposed to do.

Poison was so often used that any death in the higher circles of society that wasn't obviously due to violence or the plague was usually attributed to it. The popular poison was a white powder, a crude preparation of arsenic. How soon acute arsenic poisoning takes effect depends on what's in the stomach at the time it is taken. If the stomach is empty, the symptoms (difficulty in swallowing, burning throat, nausea, cramps) may begin within ten minutes. If the stomach is full, symptoms won't occur until ten or twelve hours later.

Whether poisoned or not, and he probably was, Pope Alexander VI became horribly ill after the Corneto banquet. Several bleedings didn't help at all. Vatican servants reported that they heard the pope on his deathbed pleading with the Devil for more time. A story spread that the Devil had promised him a reign of eleven years and one week in return for his soul, and that was just what he had had. Another story said that, as he died, the Devil in the form of an ape leaped out a window. After his death, water boiled in his mouth and his body steamed. Seven devils were seen in his chamber, another horrified tale-teller related.

Alexander breathed his last August 18, 1503. While he was dying, Cesare was himself close to death's door, but he had strength enough to send some men over to plunder the pope's apartments of all its movable treasure. Included were two chests each containing 100,000 ducats.

John Burchard has described the events following Alexander's death in some detail. As the body lay near the main altar in St. Peter's with four torches beside it, said Burchard, "The decomposition and blackness of his face increased constantly so that he looked at eight o'clock, when I saw him, like the blackest cloth or the darkest negro, completely spotted, with nose swollen, the mouth quite large, the tongue swollen up, doubled so that it started out of his lips, the mouth open, in short so horrible that no one ever saw anything similar or declared to know of it."

Burchard simply could not get the late pontiff's funeral arranged in seemly fashion. Six porters carried the body, laughing and joking, to put it in the coffin, which turned out to be too small. They laid Alexander's miter beside him, covered him with an old carpet, and pounded with their fists to make the body fit the box. *Sic transit gloria.*

Cesare recovered, but he did not live to a ripe old age like his father. Everything he had fought for was lost with his father's death. For Cesare had not succeeded in finding himself a kingdom while he had the powerful backing of Alexander VI. The next pope was Pius III, who died after twenty-six days in office. His successor was Cardinal Giuliano della Rovere, who was elected November 2, 1503, and took the name Julius II. This was the man Rodrigo had defeated when both were candidates for the office twelve years before. Julius II had no use for Borgias.

He not only didn't coddle Cesare, he imprisoned him briefly in the same room where, three years before, Cesare's hatchet man Michelotto had strangled Lucrezia's second husband.

Released, Cesare fled to Naples. He was arrested there in the name of Ferdinand, king of Aragon and Castile, and hustled off to Spain, where he was imprisoned in the very top of a high tower. More than two years passed before he escaped October 25, 1506. The arrangements were made by a Spanish count, not because he loved Cesare but because he didn't like King Ferdinand. A servant of the jail keeper smuggled in ropes—which turned out to be not quite long enough. Three men waited down in the moat to rescue Cesare.

A servant slid down first but had to drop from the rope's end. He was severely injured by the fall. By this time the alarm had been raised. Just as Cesare was ready to drop, someone cut the rope from above and he fell, badly injured. The unlucky servant who had gone down ahead of him was executed on the spot, but Cesare, held on a horse by his rescuers, reached safety. After a month he was able to travel, but who wanted him? Certainly not the king of France, to whom he applied. He found a job as captain-general of the forces of a brother-in-law, King John of Navarre. During a seige of the Castle of Viana, in Navarre, Cesare was ambushed and hacked down by twenty swordsmen. He died March 12, 1507, still in his early thirties.

The inscription on his tomb read: "Here in a little earth lies one whom all did fear, one whose hands dispensed both peace and war. O you who go in search of things deserving praise, if you would praise the worthiest, then let your journey end here nor trouble to go further."

Nearly two hundred years later a bishop who didn't agree that Cesare Borgia had been the worthiest ordered the tomb destroyed. Nobody knows of what little earth his dust is now a part.

Lucrezia, the dutiful daughter, didn't do anything spectacular after she married her third husband. Her real career was maternity. By her second husband she had one son and a miscarriage. By her third she had four sons, two daughters (one stillborn), and four miscarriages. Some researchers attribute the miscarriages to what the French called the Italian disease, the Italians called the French disease, and we call syphilis. It was common, and many cardinals as well as lesser persons suffered from it. Probably Alexander VI and Cesare Borgia did; anyway,

Alexander had a chronic ailment that fitted the symptoms and Cesare had telltale sores on his face, which he sometimes covered with a mask.

Lucrezia died in childbirth at thirty-nine.

But the Borgias weren't all bad. One great-grandson of Alexander VI was about as different from his papal forebear as you can imagine. His name was Francesco Borgia. He was born October 28, 1510, a grandson of the duke of Gandia, who had been unloaded into the Tiber. Francesco was duke of Gandia, too. He fathered a large family, but unlike his grasping great-grandfather he was respectably married.

He held high appointments at the Court of Charles I of Spain, but after his wife died he renounced the world, entered the Society of Jesus, and was ordained a priest. He rejected honors, refusing the red hat of a cardinal. When he died in 1572 he was general of the Jesuits. In 1670 he was canonized as St. Francis. Two of his descendants in the eighteenth century became cardinals.

In spite of these good apples on the family tree, the name Borgia has come to stand for murder and treachery. Of course the Borgias had a good start in making some kind of mark on history. They were rich and noble to begin with. But the name Machiavelli has gone further; it has become part of the English language in its adjectival form. An underhanded, tricky person is Machiavellian, but you don't call anybody Borgian, do you?

Whereas more than one high-ranking plotter contributed to the infamy of the Borgias, it took only one Machiavelli to make his family name immortal—and he wasn't underhanded or tricky. He was just a realist. The Machiavellis were nobody until Niccolò came along. In addition to his famous work *The Prince,* he wrote several others including plays and poetry, but nobody reads them any more.

The names of Cesare Borgia and Niccolò Machiavelli are intertwined in the vague recollections of people who suppose that Machiavelli wrote his *magnum opus* as a kind of textbook for Cesare to follow in attaining political power. Not so. It was written several years after Cesare's hacked body was enclosed in its little earth.

Niccolò Machiavelli, born in 1469, was a few years older than Cesare. For some thirteen years he held an important post in the government of the Republic of Florence in a department that had charge of foreign and military affairs. In 1512 the Medici family returned to power and Niccolò, age forty-three, was out of a job. He was arrested, officially tortured, and released. The following year, living quietly in the country, he wrote *The Prince,* a handbook for men who hunger for political power. Cesare Borgia was his hero but was only one of several leaders whose success and failure he mentioned and explained.

Cesare's strong suit was his great cunning. He had changed allies and plans when change suited his purpose. He had played one government against another. He had been vigorous in attack. He had killed most of the lords whose possessions he conquered, had won most of the nobles of Rome over to his side, and controlled a majority of the College of Cardinals. Everything was moving along nicely toward a union of many small states, but when his father died Cesare had only Romagna firmly in hand. His other schemes were incomplete, so everything fell apart. Cesare was too sick to take appropriate action. Machiavelli wrote:

> Since he was able if not to make whom he would Pope, at least to prevent the election of any whom he disliked, had he been in health at the time when Alexander died, all would have been easy for him. But he told me himself . . . that he had foreseen and provided for all else that could happen on his father's death, but he had never anticipated that when his father died he too should be at death's door.

The Prince sets forth the science of politics, sixteenth-century style. Its theme is how to win and hold power. Right and wrong have no place in it. All that counts is *Will it work?*

Machiavelli related with approval an anecdote about the way Cesare changed policy when it looked like a good idea. Romagna, when he conquered it, was lawless because it had been ruled by weak lords, so he assigned stern, decisive Remiro d'Orco to restore order. When d'Orco's brutal methods had done their work, Cesare undertook to gain the good will of his subjects by showing that his administrator's severity wasn't *his* fault. So one morning he "caused Remiro to be beheaded and exposed in the market place of Cesena with a block and bloody ax by his side—a savage spectacle," purred Machiavelli, "which at once astounded and satisfied the populace." It must have astounded Remiro d'Orco, too. He had only been following the boss's instructions.

The Prince, still read in various translations and editions, will shock modern readers because of the author's placid acceptance of villainy. Political morality simply didn't matter. What counted was success. Machiavelli knew what goodness was, but he didn't think princes should be stubbornly addicted to it:

> The manner in which we live, and that in which we ought to live, are things so wide asunder, that he who quits the one to betake himself to the other is more likely to destroy than to save himself; since any one who would act up to a perfect standard of goodness in everything, must be ruined among so many who are not good. It is essential, therefore, for a Prince who would maintain his position, to have learned how to be other than good, and to use or not to use his goodness as necessity requires.

The Prince is one of a handful of books that have profoundly influenced Western thought and—heaven help us—may continue to do so. About thirty years after Machiavelli's death in 1527, it was added to the Church's Index of forbidden books, although both religious and secular princes went right on following the recommendations cogently set forth in it. The Inquisition ordered the destruction of *all* Machiavelli's works. But in 1869, the 400th anniversary of his birth, Italy honored his memory with a national celebration.

19
Selim I, the Grim

1467–1520

No matter how hard your lot in the corporate rat race, your boss isn't likely to send you a curt note to commit suicide, as Sultan Selim did to seven of his prime ministers.

His grandfather was the great Turkish sultan, Mohammed II, who captured Constantinople in 1453 and made it the capital of the Ottoman Empire. His father was the amiable and cultured Sultan Bajazet II, who reigned from 1481 to 1512 and whose most significant contribution to Turkish history was the rebuilding of Constantinople after the disastrous earthquake of 1509. Selim was the third of Bajazet's surviving sons.

In his fight for the throne, Selim had nothing to fear from his sisters. Women didn't exactly count in the Islamic world, and no woman has ever been sovereign of a Moslem state. Nor did any law of primogeniture (whereby the sovereign's eldest son automatically ascends the throne) exclude Selim. It was the custom for a reigning sultan to choose among his sons, one boy getting the whole works.

Sultans used to dole out provincial governorships to various sons, and sultan-watchers with lots of political savvy picked the heir as the one who got the province nearest to Constantinople. When a sultan died, he who got to the capital first had the best chance to be the next ruler. Sons customarily maintained first-class spy systems in Constantinople to keep track of Papa's health. They also bred fast horses. To get power became a race with time.

Selim's grandfather (Sultan Mohammed II) had decreed the ghastly *kanun*, which required each new sultan to kill all his brothers. The intent was to remove all danger of a civil war. But it also engendered a certain restiveness among younger sons as they grew to manhood. Prospects of their dying in bed of old age were bleak indeed.

By 1510 or thereabouts, Selim's father (Sultan Bajazet) was an old man, feeble and in uncertain health. He had already named as his favorite and successor, his second son—Ahmed. Selim's future didn't look so rosy, so he decided to take things into his own hands. He visited his father with a retinue large enough to be a regiment but failed in the bluff. Much of the army remained loyal to Bajazet, and Selim fled to the Crimea to think things over.

In 1512, he gave it another try. He showed up in Constantinople, this time with the full support of the army, especially of the Janissaries, who were the sultan's own special troops—Turkey's Praetorian Guard or *corps d'élite*.

At Selim's insistence, the Janissaries demanded audience of Sultan Bajazet. He received them seated on the throne. What did they want, he asked? "Our Padishah is old and sickly," they said. "We will that Selim be sultan." Without hope of support from any part of the army, Bajazet surrendered: "I abdicate," he said, "in favor of my son, Selim. May Allah grant him a prosperous reign."

But Bajazet asked one favor. He wanted to retire to the small town of his birth and there live out his years. Selim was graciousness itself, accompanying his father with great deference to the outskirts of Constantinople. But three days later, ex-sultan Bajazet died. Some said it was of a broken heart. Everybody else knew that Selim had had him killed.

Selim's two older brothers, Khorkand and Ahmed, rose in revolt against the upstart. With lightning speed, Selim turned on Khorkand and took him prisoner. He graciously allowed his brother an hour before having him bow-strung (strangled by the string of a bow). In his last hour on this earth, Khorkand wrote a poem denouncing his brother's cruelty. Selim read the poem, wept, had Khorkand killed, wept some more and ordered a state funeral. He proclaimed three days of mourning and killed fifteen of Khorkand's soldiers who had helped betray their master into Selim's hands.

At Brusa, Selim really hit the jackpot. Five nephews, ranging in age from five to twenty, fell into his hands and he ordered them all strangled. The twenty-year-old put up a hell of a fight, while the youngest wept. Selim couldn't have cared less.

He still had one brother, Ahmed, to dispose of—Ahmed, who had been his father's favorite and heir to the throne. After some fighting, Selim won. Ahmed, too, was strangled, and Selim wept. By this time, Selim had killed off most possible rivals for the throne. And he began to be called Selim Yavouz—the Ferocious.

Now forty-seven, Selim was undisputed lord of the Turkish world. Unlike most members of the Osman family, he cared little for sensual pleasures. He visited the seraglio (harem) infrequently, preferring to spend his nights in literary and theological studies. A poet himself, Selim wrote in Turkish, Persian, and Arabic. As one critic said, some of his odes "were exquisitely beautiful."

The sultan enjoyed reading about the lives of Alexander and Caesar, and he preferred the company of scholars to soldiers, appointing many to high positions in the government. He particularly liked to discuss fine points of Moslem theology with his scholars and holy men.

But discussing religion with Selim could be dangerous. Not only did he have a short fuse on his temper, but he was also a bigot. The Mohammedan world was riven into two major sects, the Sunnites, who believed in the words of the Prophet Mohammed alone, and the Shiites, who in addition to the Prophet's words accepted those of his four immediate successors. Selim was a Sunnite (as were most Turks), and anyone who strayed from the orthodox in discussing religion with the sultan was killed on the spot—often by Selim himself.

The more he thought about it, the more concerned he became about those of his subjects who were heretical Shiites. He set up an army of spies and then ordered the capture of 70,000 of them. He wanted to kill them all, but he settled for the slaughter of 40,000 and imprisonment for the rest. For this, he became known as Selim the Just.

Selim disliked his Christian subjects almost as much as he hated the Shiites. He pondered the problem and finally decided the best thing was to kill them all—at least those who would not embrace the true faith. He was diverted from this aim by complicated arguments that his grandfather, Mohammed the Conqueror, had granted special rights to those Greek Orthodox Christians who accepted him as master. Selim was outraged.

But he spared the Christians, although he desecrated most of their churches and turned them into mosques.

His approach to governmental and political affairs was equally straightforward. His first act on becoming sultan was to kill with his own sword a Janissary who asked for a pay hike for the corps. Selim had firm ideas on how to control inflation. He was equally firm with corrupt judges, making them pass sentence on themselves before handing them over to the executioners. Selim was known to laugh a lot.

The sultan was not one to drag out an issue. He kept a gaggle of executioners, called mutes because they had no tongues, around him for purposes of swift justice. Trials often took just long enough for Selim to say two words: "Kill him." He didn't like long-drawn-out arguments, and those protesters who took too long in talking were often decapitated, stabbed to death, or strangled on the spot. It is no wonder that what passed for cabinet meetings at Selim's court were marvels of brevity.

So short became the tenure of office that his ministers took to carrying their wills with them. To be called to Selim's court unexpectedly might mean anything from instant death to being appointed grand vizier (prime minister). In any event, it was customary to take a formal, tender, and sometimes permanent farewell from one's loved ones each time Selim summoned anyone to the palace.

No other ruler in history was so hard on his prime ministers. Selim went through seven of them in eight years. One after another, seven were decapitated, until Turks took to cursing their enemies: "May you be vizier to Sultan Selim."

Around the court, it became a jesting matter. To be Selim's prime minister was to be appointed for life—but life might not last more than a few months. One grand vizier even joked about it. As he said to Selim: "My Padishah, sooner or later you will put your faithful slave to death. Give me a short interval to arrange my affairs and prepare for the next world."

Selim almost split his side laughing. Soon he choked out: "I have long been thinking of killing you, but no one at present is fit to take your place, so I cannot now oblige you." He did later.

It was on the battlefield, however, that Selim earned historical fame. In a reign of less than eight years, he almost doubled the size of the Ottoman empire. He started with a war against Persia. Not only was Persia governed by a bunch of scruffy

Shiites, but it had helped out brother Ahmed. In 1514, Selim massed 140,000 men, 300 guns, and 60,000 camels near Constantinople and began a march of well over 1000 miles to Tabriz, then Persia's capital. He took Tabriz, but his soldiers started grumbling about spending the winter there, so Selim returned home. He annexed Turkestan and Diyarbekir.

Egypt, Syria, Arabia, and northern Mesopotamia were next, They were run by the Mamelukes, soldiers recruited from slaves, who elected their sultan for life. In 1516, when Selim entered Syria, he was opposed by eighty-year-old Sultan Ghowri, a man of almost nonexistent military talents. Selim lost no time in demanding from Ghowri the cession of Islam's two holiest cities, Mecca and Medina.

Ghowri sent a magnificent embassy of one envoy and ten Mamelukes with a negative response. Selim was furious. Since his regard for the rules of diplomatic intercourse was never very high, he ordered the immediate execution of the ambassador's entourage. Only with difficulty was he talked out of killing the ambassador. But he ordered that unfortunate's face and head shaved, his head covered with a nightcap, and had him mounted on a moth-eaten donkey to return to his master.

It was near Aleppo that the two armies collided. In an hour it was all over. The Mamelukes broke and fled, trampling Sultan Ghowri to death in the process. The whole of northern Mesopotamia and Syria (including modern Syria, Lebanon, and Israel) fell to Selim.

By now it was December, a good time to cross the desert into Egypt. On the way, Selim paused long enough in Gaza to commit one major and one minor atrocity. First, he ordered all the inhabitants of Gaza to be slaughtered. Then he killed one of his generals who was indiscreet enough to mention to Selim that conquering Egypt might not be a picnic.

It took Selim's forces ten days to cross the Sinai desert. No Egyptians were around, but there were plenty of Arabs who would attack in clouds of dust and then disappear. They were beneath Selim's contempt so he paid them little attention. This led to a sad episode. The current grand vizier, seeing a lot of activity on the horizon, warned Selim the Egyptians were coming. After mounting his war horse, Selim discovered that all the fuss was over some Arabs. That ended that grand vizier's term of office—and his life.

The Egyptians of those days apparently weren't any better at fighting than they are today. Near Ridania, Selim destroyed the Egyptian army, killing 25,000. He then advanced on Cairo. For a while, there was great confusion. Selim took the city at first without opposition, then the Mamelukes reoccupied it. They barricaded the streets and turned each house into a mini-fortress. It took Selim all of three days to capture Cairo.

Even so, three days were two days and twenty-three hours too long by Selim's reckoning. He ordered an indiscriminate massacre of 50,000 Cairoenes. He executed one of his generals who had secured the surrender of 800 Mamelukes by promising them their lives. And he did the same to the 800 Mamelukes. Egypt and all her lands were added to Selim's dominions.

After setting up an administration in Egypt (partly consisting of Mamelukes who had betrayed their own sultan), Selim headed for home. He crossed the Sinai once more and at the head of the army, and Selim pleasantly observed to his new grand vizier, Younis Pasha, who was riding beside him: "Well, our backs are now turned on Egypt, and we shall soon be at Gaza." Not as smart as he should have been, Younis—who had opposed the whole expedition in the first place—couldn't resist replying:

> And what has been the result of all our trouble and fatigue, if it is not that half our army has perished in battle, or in the sands of the desert, and that Egypt is now governed by a gang of traitors?

Selim's retort was to whack off the grand vizier's head.

Now undisputed master of Mecca, Medina, and Jerusalem—the three most sacred cities in the Moslem world—Selim took the title of caliph. He thus became the Law Giver of Islam and took over the Standard, Mantle, and Sword of the Prophet.

Returning to Constantinople in 1518, Selim spent the last two years of his life preparing for an attack on Rhodes—which was still in Christian hands. But in 1520 he fell seriously ill and died in great pain. His son and successor, Suleiman the Magnificent, built a great tomb for his father's body, which bore—so people said—seven bloody marks as a sign of blood guilt for the murder of his brothers and nephews.

Selim had once said: "Nothing is sweeter than to reign without fear or suspicion of one's kinsmen." He knew what he was talking about.

20
Sawney Beane

Dates (and Facts) Uncertain

Troubled about the high cost of living?
The Beane family got around it by
living off other people.

The story of Sawney Beane is a neat chronicle of togetherness. He and his wife (girl friend, really) and their descendants lived together (in a great big cave), ate together (human flesh), slept together (the Beane children had children although they never met any boys or girls except their own brothers and sisters), and died together in a mass execution.

That's *how* they lived—if they really did live outside the world of penny-dreadful pamphlets that chilled readers in the late eighteenth century. There is considerable doubt about when they lived or where. One account, published in 1810, says the Beanes flourished during the reign of James I of Scotland and Elizabeth of England—hardly likely since Scotland's James I lived two centuries earlier than the Virgin Queen. He was crowned in 1424. But Scotland's James VI, son of Mary Queen of Scots, became England's James I in 1603, succeeding Elizabeth.

One hazy record says the incredible Sawney Beane was born in East Lothian, a few miles from Edinburgh, and raised his criminal family in a seaside cave in Galloway. But William Roughead says the cave traditionally associated with this interesting predecessor of Murder, Inc., is at Bennane Head, three miles north of a fishing village in southern Ayrshire.

Anyway, Sawney (short for Alexander) was born in some century or other, somewhere in Scotland. He was a lazy lout, disinclined to work at hedging and ditching as his parents did, so he teamed up with a girl, whose name has long been forgotten, and ran away. They moved into a big cave by the sea and, casting around for a source of sustenance, hit on a career of highway robbery and murder. For some twenty-five years none of their hold-up victims lived to tell the tale. The Beanes took their money (even cannibals need a little cash for special treats), wore their clothing, and ate their flesh.

In the 1810 account, the old "long s" is used; it looks like *f*, so we have thif ftatement: "As foon as they had robbed anyone, they ufed to carry off their carcafes to their den, where cutting them in quarters they would pickle the mangled limbs, and afterwards eat them, thefe being their only fubfiftance."

Naturally, the neighbors began to notice when people they knew were missing. Some of those who went searching for their friends never came back. Several honest travelers were arrested on suspicion and hanged. The same melancholy end came to some innocent innkeepers, suspected of having done away with travelers lodging with them overnight. A few innkeepers along the ocean road closed up and went into safer occupations, causing no end of inconvenience for travelers who were already thoroughly scared and now found no place to stay overnight.

As Sawney's family increased and his kids got big enough to help, they attacked groups of five or six persons who were traveling on foot, but they prudently avoided horseback parties of more than two. It was important, Daddy no doubt warned the children, never to take a chance on letting a victim get away to spill the beans.

Their cave was on the seashore and the tide washed far into it. Search parties passed right by the entrance, convinced that nobody could be hiding in that wet place. But the cave extended far under a cliff—200 miles, says one enthusiastic chronicler; one mile, according to a more conservative estimate—so there was plenty of room for housekeeping and for storing provisions, the remains of unlucky travelers. In twenty-five years, it is said, at least a thousand men, women, and children mysteriously disappeared.

The industrious Beanes finally made a fatal error. One potential victim got away. This was a man who, with his wife behind him on the same horse, was returning from a fair. He fought his attackers furiously, but his wife fell off the horse. The Beane girls cut her throat and butchered her, "which difmal fight caufed the man to make the more refiftance."

A party of twenty or thirty travelers galloped up, attracted by the noise of battle, and rescued the bereaved widower. The Beane party hastily retreated through the woods, leaving the late wife's mangled body. Obviously, it wasn't ghoulies or ghaisties that had been causing all those missing people to disappear. Somebody rode hard to Glasgow to report to the provost, who immediately sent word to the king

His Majesty came in person with a posse of four hundred men and a bunch of bloodhounds. The man who had escaped was their guide. They searched and searched but couldn't find a thing. When they came to the mouth of the Beanes' cave, they were going to ride right by, because obviously nobody could be in that wet hole, but the hounds, sharp noses alert, set up a great yelping. Carrying lighted torches, the posse splashed through the entrance and followed the winding passages of the cave.

And, lo, they "faw the difmal fight, and were ready to fink into the earth to fee fuch a number of arms, legs, thighs, hands and feet of men, women, and children, hung up in rows like dry'd beef, and a great many lying in pickle." They also found money, watches, rings, swords, pistols, and clothing—a treasure trove.

Naturally they arrested the whole Beane crew—"eight fons, fix daughters, eighteen grand-fons, and fourteen grand-daughters begotten in inceft." They must have been a pallid, unhealthy-looking lot after all those years of keeping house in a deep, dark cave.

After decently burying the anonymous human remains, the king's triumphant party set off for Edinburgh with Mr. and Mrs. Beane, their eight fons, fix daughters, and all. At Leith this unwholesome crew was executed without any trial. The men's hands and legs were cut off, so they bled to death. The women and children, after being forced to watch this edifying spectacle, were burned in three big fires. "They all died without the leaft fign of repentance," says the gory chronicle, "and continued venting the moft horrid imprecations to the laft gafp of life." It seems unlikely that the onlookers expected cheers, but no doubt the enthusiastic audience did it for them.

Many a villain has had his later defender in print; Cesare Borgia, Gilles de Rais, the Marquis de Sade, and others have been painted as not bad, really. Nobody has leaped to the defense of Sawney Beane and his helpmeet, who grew up in civilization and knew that murder is not nice and cannibalism is downright nasty. But it has been pointed out that their children and grandchildren didn't know any better. (Give little Willie a finger to gnaw on; that'll keep him quiet.)

And in 1907 a letter from an angry Scot residing in Melbourne, Australia, who signed himself "Alba," was published in *Scottish Notes and Queries* arguing that the story of Sawney Beane was "a clumsy Cockney invention, without any foundation whatever in fact." Alba raged that English writers were always downgrading Scots "with a desire to pull us down below the English level—and that is low enough. . . . Let any English wastrel circulate a trashy falsehood to the detriment of an entire nation, the vagabond will receive credence."

He was answered temperately by "W.S." in the magazine's next issue with a reminder that the English and Scots now formed one people under the same king and the same laws. "What though there be some stupid Englishmen who, disliking the Scots, pretend to believe them cannibals or the descendants of cannibals!" commented this writer. "Leave them to stew in the juice of their own childish imaginings."

What provoked Alba's outburst was the publication of a novel, *The Grey Man,* by S. R. Crockett—a tedious book by our standards, but it purported to explain the legend of Sawney Beane. "W.S." pointed out that Crockett's story was placed in the wrong century, during the reign of Scotland's James VI and England's James I, rather than in the earlier, more savage era of Scotland's James I. William Roughead, however, thinks the later period of Scotland's James VI was right for Sawney Beane. It was savage enough, although this is the King James for whom a still-popular translation of the Bible was named. Although the King didn't do the translating himself, he was a very literary man, author of sonnets and other works including the famous *Counterblaste to Tobacco,* as well as a man of action who (perhaps) presided at the harvest of the Beanes.

21
The Duke of Alba

1508–1582

The next time a general runs for president, think before you vote. Someday we may run into a duke of Alba type, so watch out!

One of the most infamous men of the sixteenth century was Fernando Álvarez de Toledo, duke of Alba (or Alva). Old Blood and Guts Alba was a respectable general, perhaps the greatest of his day, but he had all the political savvy and understanding as Pithecanthropus Erectus. As governor of the Netherlands, he made many other tyrants in history look like models of propriety. In a way, he out-Neroed Nero.

The duke lived in troubled times. The Protestant Reformation began while he was still a boy—he was born in 1508—when Luther tacked up his ninety-five Theses on the church door in Wittenberg in 1517. Luther's hammer-blows shook Europe to its foundations, and during his entire life Alba was involved in fighting—as he saw it—heresy, subversion, and treason. Alba was a "good'" sixteenth-century Roman Catholic, which meant in those days that anyone who departed from the "true faith" should be killed. And in the most painful way possible. Suffering improved the soul.

In the duke's early days, Carlos I, king of Spain, ruled the Holy Roman Empire (mostly present-day Germany) as the Emperor Charles V. His Spanish mother Juana la Loca (Crazy Jane) bequeathed him Spain, the Indies, and various Italian states. His father, Philip the Handsome, left Charles his German estates and the seventeen provinces known as the Low Countries or the nether-lands.

Of these seventeen, the northern seven now comprise the Kingdom of the Netherlands—or Holland, as we usually call it. One, Luxembourg, is today an independent Grand Duchy, and the other nine make up the Kingdom of Belgium. In Alba's day, the king of Spain ruled all these provinces, and what he said was the law. Or so Alba argued.

It wasn't that simple. Although Charles ruled in Germany as Charles V and in Spain as Carlos I, he ruled in the Low Countries as lord paramount of each of the seventeen provinces—and as nobody else. In other words, he ruled in Holland as count of Holland but not as either Carlos I or Charles V. The same for Brabant, where he was duke of Brabant, and so on. It was terribly confusing to everybody, not least of all to narrow-minded Spaniards like the duke of Alba.

Two events in the Low Countries were above all to influence the duke. In the first place, Protestant reformers, especially Calvinists, made great headway in all seventeen provinces. They did all sorts of dreadful things to Catholic churches and citizens: burning, murder, and looting were the order of the day. When told of these events, Alba was adamant: the heretics must be squashed—and at once.

The duke took this attitude not only because he hated religious dissenters, but also because of the second important development in the Low Countries affecting his career. In 1556, Carlos I (Charles V) abdicated. He left Spain, the Indies, various Italian provinces, and the Low Countries to his son, Philip II.

As a grandee of Spain, one of the greatest nobles of the realm, the duke of Alba proffered allegiance to Philip. The new king is now best known for sending the Spanish Armada against England. And losing his shirt doing so. As a matter of fact, Philip wasn't very bright—about mediocre—and he was a religious bigot. He took any difference of opinion in religious matters as a personal affront. No, by God, it was heresy and treason. He was the perfect master for a simplistic man like the duke.

On the one hand, many people in the Low Countries were heretics—and thus enemies of God. On the other, because of their disagreements about religion with Philip II, they were subversives at best, traitors at worst. And what do you do with heresy and treason? The problem is as old as history itself. Philip and

Alba didn't invent it, but they knew just how to handle it. Their answer was to kill all the heretics and traitors they could get their paws on.

Alba, this defender of the faith, was a strange man. He loved to have his picture painted. He left over 100 portraits for posterity to admire. In them, he appears thin-faced and tall, his skin somewhat sallow, his head rather small. His eyes dominate each picture; they are dark but alive and agleam with intelligence. His mouth is good but partly obscured by a black moustache that joins a bristling black beard. If you looked at any of the paintings without knowing they were of the duke, the impression would be of a man of power and dignity. But most people think of Alba first and then read into the paintings all kinds of dreadful things: his lips are cruel, his eyes menacing, his wrinkles fearful. One such historian summed up an Alba portrait: "It is the face of a strong, evil man who thinks the world is not good enough for him."

Alba was almost sixty when, in 1567, he began his career as one of history's monsters. From the age of sixteen, he had fought for God and King all over Europe. He had proved a pretty good general, and he seemed just the man to do Philip II's dirty work in the Low Countries. Prudent on the battlefield, he saw no virtue in slaughter for slaughter's sake—only if the result justified it.

This is not to say that he was tender-hearted. A disciplinarian of the old school, an off-with-their-heads type, Alba didn't believe in fooling around. When Philip chose him to crush the revolt in the Low Countries, the duke remarked that he had spent his life subduing "men of iron." He wouldn't have any trouble taming "men of butter" in Brussels and Amsterdam.

As a man of war, Alba was a simpleton when it came to government. As he said, it all boiled down to this: "Kings are born to give orders, subjects to obey them." This accounts for Carlos I's advice to his son Philip II at the time he abdicated the Spanish throne:

> Alba is ambitious, sanctimonious, and hypocritical; and perhaps may even try to tempt you by means of women. But he is a grandee and must not be allowed to have any share in the internal government of the kingdom. In foreign

affairs and war make use of him and respect him, as he is the best man we now have.

Some people said Alba lacked imagination. This wasn't entirely true. In the Low Countries, he showed considerable inventiveness in putting the rebels to death. And then there was that time when he pulled off a caper that captured the heart of every love-sick maiden in Europe. He married at twenty-two and was immediately posted for military duty in Hungary. The more he thought about it, the more he thought it was a helluva way to spend a honeymoon. In seventeen days—on horseback yet—he rode from Hungary to Spain and back again just to spend a few hours with his bride.

Of all his vices, pride was Alba's worst. He never tired of reminding people that he was a duke, a grandee of Spain, and a descendant of an imperial Byzantine family. He was a real bore. In Spain, he had the right to keep his hat on in the king's presence, and when he was in Germany court functionaries kept telling him to remove his hat in the presence of the Holy Roman Emperor, whom Alba thought of only as king of Spain. And, as governor of the Low Countries, he disdainfully addressed everyone with the familiar "thou."

After his first victories over the Protestant rebels, Alba got the idea of having a huge statue of himself made out of the guns he had captured. It was set up in Antwerp. In his left hand, he held a marshal's baton, while his right hand stretched out over the town in a gesture of "protection." At his feet lay a two-headed body representing the aristocracy and common people of the land. The inscription modestly reminded all and sundry that here stood the duke of Alba, the man who had restored peace and justice, exterminated rebellion and heresy, and was the best servant of the best of kings.

It was in April 1567 that Alba left Spain for Italy with Philip's commission to raise an army. With his accustomed efficiency, the duke raised a force of over 10,000 battle-trained veterans. It was the custom in those days for ladies of dubious virtue—otherwise known as camp followers—to march with the troops. Alba rounded up 2000 of these girls, organized them into troupes and companies, and assigned them to the men. And so troops, guns, and whores all headed for Brussels to do God's work.

Alba reached Brussels on August 22, 1567, and was itching to go. His first problem was the king's bastard sister, Margaret, duchess of Parma, who was a favorite-aunt type. Margaret was governor-general of the Low Countries and Alba's boss. Since her policy was to treat the Protestant rebels with reasonable kindness, Philip fired her and gave the job to Alba. Philip told him to be firm, something the duke knew how to be. As he said to Margaret, "I am prepared to take all the odium upon myself."

While still in Spain, Alba had developed a long-distance hatred for three of the greatest men in the Low Countries. Most prominent was the prince of Orange, William the Silent (soon to be father of his country). Count Egmont and Count Hoorn, two knights of the Golden Fleece and nominal Catholics, were also on Alba's hate list. He wanted Philip to kill all three:

> Every time that I see the missives of these three Señores, they fill me with rage, so that, unless I exerted the utmost control over myself, my opinions would appear to Your Majesty those of one frenzied.

Who should ride out to greet Alba on his arrival in the Low Countries but Egmont and Hoorn. (William had more sense.) "Ah," said the duke on seeing Egmont, "here comes the great heretic." With a warm smile he threw an arm around Egmont's neck and spoke pleasantly to him.

Alba settled in in Brussels and then threw a dinner party for Egmont and Hoorn on September 9, 1567. Everybody had a good time, although somebody warned Egmont during the dinner to make his getaway. Egmont wavered for a little, hopped up and ran out, and then decided to return. Soon after the brandy, the duke's soldiers arrested both Egmont and Hoorn. Alba wrote to Philip, apologizing for the delay. He had "wasted" seventeen days.

While the two counts languished in jail for the next nine months, Alba took the field in person. He captured all sorts of noble Protestants and executed them, at the same time banishing William of Orange, and confiscated all their property. Then, on June 5, 1568, he stunned all seventeen provinces by decapitating both Egmont and Hoorn in public. It was a spectacular production, and Alba showed talents that in later years would have brought him fame in Hollywood. He placed the scaffold, suitably draped in black, in the middle of the great square in Brussels and surrounded it with troops. Two velvet cushions were at hand for the victims to kneel on. A grimmer note was two pikes on which the heads of Egmont and Hoorn were soon to be displayed. There was also a table with a crucifix. Both traitors died well, "very Catholically and modestly," as Alba wrote to Philip.

The executions shook the whole of Europe. If two such noble lords could be killed, then nobody was safe. That was the impression Alba wanted; he hoped the example would be "fruitful."

While this was going on, Alba set up one of the most infamous kangaroo courts in history. He created out of thin air the Council of Troubles, or, as everybody else called it (more accurately), the Council of Blood. It was in fact extra-legal, Alba's own invention, although Philip knew all about it and approved of its work. Alba appointed himself to be its head. There were twelve other members, ten of them residents of the Low Countries who couldn't vote and performed solely a window-dressing function, and two Spaniards who alone could vote. One of the locals, a sleepy old fool named Hessels, resembled nothing more than the dormouse at Alice's tea party. Every now and then, he woke up to mutter: "To the gibbet, to the gibbet." But, just in case the Council got any ideas of its own, Alba reserved the right to approve its every decision.

Soon after he set up his Council, Alba happily learned that the papal Inquisition had sentenced to death the three million people of the Low Countries—with some minor exceptions. This was great. Now the Council didn't have to fool around trying to convict its victims of heresy. Almost everybody was guilty before they were even arrested. Alba thought the permanent atmosphere of terror was all to the good; he wrote to Philip: "Everyone must be made to live in constant fear of the roof breaking down over his head."

The two Spaniards on the Council, Del Rio who didn't matter very much, and Juan de Vargas who did, were Alba's own stooges. Del Rio did as he was told. So did Vargas, but he loved the job. He hardly had the background to be a judge. As a young man, he had raped an orphan girl who had been placed in his care and had fled to the Low Countries. He became Alba's alter ego. An execution really sent him. It was grand sport, and every now and then Vargas had to admonish the prosecutors for sending him a favorable report on an accused. Such dossiers were returned for "correction."

Vargas didn't know French or Flemish, and he used to harangue his colleagues in bad Latin. But whatever the language he got across the idea that he had no truck with mercy. He thoroughly enjoyed doing the duke's dirty work. On the one hand was the dignified, serious, and haughty Alba. On the other was the joking, vicious, and dreadful Vargas. They were brothers in blood.

Vargas and the Council of Blood didn't waste time getting down to business. There were three million people to try. And the richer they were the better, because Philip's projects cost lots of money and he was always broke. It was good to kill poor heretics, of course, but since rich ones couldn't enter the Kingdom of Heaven anyway it was more fun and a hell of a lot more profitable to try them.

Alba ordered the Council to try all those accused of heresy to the "True Faith" and opposition to Spain. He banned all emigration and ordered ship captains to be hanged if caught aiding escapees. He sent into every town in the Low Countries investigators who paid informers to squeal on their relatives. And he commanded every town government to suppress heresy and rebellion on pain of the most dreadful retribution.

The Council proceeded to arrest thousands of people; on one day alone it jailed 1500. It soon found that trying each person was a waste of time. The land teemed with heretics and traitors. There was so much to be done and so little time to do God's work. The obvious solution was to try and execute (often the same thing) in batches of ten, fifty, eighty, or a hundred souls.

In the Council's first three months, it executed 1800 persons. At Shrovetide in 1568, Alba killed another 1500, and after Easter another 800. When he went home to Spain in 1572, Alba boasted that he had executed—not counting those killed in battle and murdered later as POWs—over 18,000.

The Council ran into one snag early on. As the condemned were dragged to the scaffold through the streets—sometimes tied to a horse's tail—they often convinced bystanders of their innocence. This would never do, and a new gag had to be invented. Each prisoner's tongue was fitted into an iron ring and then burned with a white-hot iron. The poor tongue swelled and rendered speech impossible. The good duke was delighted. This was just the way to frustrate the wiles of heretics and traitors.

The Council, and its agencies all over the Low Countries, heard some pretty peculiar cases—and handed down even odder decisions. A Frau Juriaen, in the presence of her maid, had slapped (with a slipper) a wooden image of the Virgin Mary. Her maid didn't report her, but the story got out. The executioner drowned both women by sticking their heads into a hogshead full of water.

In Amsterdam, a Peter de Witt talked a rioter out of killing a judge. Alba had him beheaded because he obviously had influence with traitors. In another case, the Council "examined" four noble heretics so strictly that each had to be tied to a chair and hauled off to the scaffold to be decapitated.

An Anabaptist escaped from prison, and like little Eva and Simon Legree he fled across the ice pursued by his jailer. He got off scot free, but the ex-jailer fell through the ice. The poor escapee rescued his pursuer, only to be caught, of course, and for his kindness burned at the stake.

In its haste to mete out justice, the Council often drew up its decisions before trial. Occasionally a complete innocent would go to his death. "No matter for that," joked Vargas, "if he has died innocent, it will be all the better for him when he takes his trial in the other world."

The Council hanged Blaise Bouzet, a cobbler, for having eaten meat on Friday. It convicted a sixty-two-year-old man for not stopping his son from serving with the rebels. And more and more its evil hands touched the rich. Frau van Dieman's son, without her knowledge, had lodged a heretic preacher in her house for the night. She was a devout Catholic—but she was also rich. At age eighty-four, she went to the scaffold, muttering: "I understand very well why my death is considered necessary. The calf is fat and must be killed." She was an original. As she bent her neck to the headsman, she asked him about the sharpness of his ax. He was apt "to find her old neck very tough."

As time went on, Alba and Vargas seemed to think more of confiscating property than rooting out heresy and treason. As one agent, Noircarmes, wrote to the Council:

> You can do me no greater pleasure than to make quick work with all these rebels, and to proceed with the confisca-

tion of their estates, real and personal. Don't fail to put all those to the torture out of whom anything can be got.

Alba was not averse to feathering his nest in a good cause.

As the bloodshed and horror increased, the temper of the people altered. Despair changed to anger, anger to hatred, and hatred to hope. If Alba was to carry out the Inquisition's murderous edict, it was better to die fighting than to be burned at the stake. Rebellion in all the provinces spread like a giant flame.

It wasn't long before the duke realized that he was onto a sticky wicket. The more people he killed, the more resistance he met. William of Orange was always to be found lurking on the frontiers—and occasionally dashing inside with armed men—and more and more towns rose in rebellion. Bands of rebels inside the Low Countries, the Beggars, and, outside, the Sea Beggars, posed a real military problem.

As usual, Alba's only solution was to meet force with great force—and terror. Sometimes he had recourse to the Council, but more often it was now military justice: rape, looting, the shooting of prisoners, and the slaughter of civilians. In town after town, Spanish soldiers committed—usually on Alba's orders—incredible crimes.

Alba burned Naarden to the ground and killed all its citizens. The same in Mechlin and many other towns. At Zutphen, Alba's troops burned most of the houses and tied hundreds of its inhabitants in twos and threw them into the canals. Others were chopped down in the streets, lots were hanged naked from the city's trees, and others were stripped and forced out into the fields in winter weather. Terror begat terror. Especially in the Dutch provinces, where the horrors were greatest, Dutch cities besieged by the Spaniards began to retaliate in kind. Spanish prisoners were often hanged and mutilated in sight of their brethren—and their heads flung into the enemy's camp.

Alba continued to ask Philip for more money and troops. He got royal permission to impose some taxes—including what amounted to a ten percent sales tax. All hell broke loose. It was one thing to go around killing people for religion and treason, but to attack the Dutch in their pocketbooks was something else. Some historians have even been so unkind as to suggest that it was taxation, not religion, that led to the independence of Holland.

In 1570, Alba—on orders from Philip—announced an amnesty. Complete repentance and full acceptance of the Roman Catholic faith were the terms. Not many people took advantage of the amnesty. It came too late.

Seven years of fighting for God and King had failed. Alba was getting old and ravaged by gout. He finally called it quits and asked Philip to recall him. He wanted to go home.

In 1573, Philip replaced the old warrior, the "decrepit old bird" as he called himself. Don Luis de Requesens was Alba's successor in the Low Countries. He too failed to squelch the Dutch, and in 1648 they were to gain their independence. Requesens also failed to protect Alba's giant statue. The rebels broke it to bits.

As for Alba, Philip received him with honor and favor. A few years later, he asked the duke to conquer Portugal, a task which Alba ended with a massacre of the people of Lisbon. At the last, the old boy died secure in his faith in God and loyalty to his king.

22
Ivan IV, the Terrible

1530–1584

The worst of us are perfect angels in comparison with Tsar Ivan, called the Terrible.

L ots of historical characters have special titles attached to their names. Alexander the Great, Charles the Bald, Ethelred the Unready, Louis the Fat, Basil the Squint-Eyed, and William the Silent are but a few. Ivan IV of Russia is the only one to be called "the Terrible." And don't think he didn't earn it.

Nowadays, almost any murderer is excused for his fall from grace if he had an unhappy childhood, especially if he can prove just a whisper of insanity. Were these criteria applied to Ivan, he would qualify on each count. His childhood left much to be desired—he was scared witless much of the time—and after his first wife's death he was clearly touched with madness.

In Russian, Ivan's nickname was actually "Grozny," a man "to be feared" or "the Dreaded." His stern and able grandfather, Ivan III, was sometimes called "Grozny," but he is now known as Ivan the Great. When Ivan IV was first called "the Dreaded," it seems he was to be loved and feared in the Christian sense.

Some historians have gone so far as to suggest that the sobriquet "the Terrible" is an error in translation for "Grozny." But during his own lifetime Ivan's reputation both inside and outside Russia was not pretty. No doubt his numerous enemies painted him in the darkest hues, but the truth is bad enough. He was a terrible man who did terrible things.

Unlike many of history's stinkers in whom the qualities of great ancestors are watered down to mediocrity or worse, Ivan was lucky. Both his grandfather, Ivan III, one of Russia's best rulers, and his grandmother, Sofia Palaeologa, a daughter of the last great Byzantine imperial family, were strong and intelligent. So were his father, Vasily III, and his mother, Elena Glinskaya. Ivan was fortunate to have inherited many strong qualities.

Ivan was nobody's fool. He had intelligence, strength, and ability in abundance. That he often misused these great qualities is incontestable, but even to the Soviet Russians of today he is something of a national hero. The distinguished Russian film director, Sergei Eisenstein, made a superb movie about Ivan.

When Ivan was born in Moscow in the Kremlin on August 25, 1530, the first son of Vasily III, his father was known as the Grand Prince of Moscow, or Muscovy. The night of Ivan's birth was one that Muscovites were long to remember. His yowls of entry to this world were accompanied by terrific thunderclaps and hideous lightning bolts. A year later, his brother Yuri was born.

His first three years were Ivan's happiest. Then his father died, and Ivan became Grand Prince Ivan IV. The next five years, during his mother's regency, were pretty good. But suddenly on April 3, 1538, his mother complained of cramps and died. She was probably poisoned, for her funeral was a most hasty affair. She was sick, dead, and buried in a matter of hours.

Ivan, now eight years old, obviously needed a guardian, a strong man who could rule Russia during his minority. This materialized in the person of Prince Ivan Shuisky, an able enough boyar (noble), but a coarse, rough man who probably influenced Ivan more than anyone else. He did this by alternately treating Ivan with contempt and then ignoring him. Both hurt the boy. Ivan never forgot. The two brothers were singularly neglected. Shuisky showed them all the tender, loving care of a wolf for the lamb. They often went hungry and thread-bare. A quarter of a century later, Ivan still remembered. "What sufferings did I not endure," he wrote, "through lack of clothing and through hunger."

Even as a boy, Ivan loved the hunt. In this he took after his father. Shuisky encouraged the boy's fondness for killing animals and apparently brought out a sadistic streak in Ivan. So the grand prince and his young playmates often hauled cats, bears, and dogs to the tops of the Kremlin towers and flung them to the ground. Ivan loved it. He also liked to gallop through Moscow's streets, knocking down old men and women. We don't know when Ivan lost his virginity, but with Shuisky as a tutor it must have been very early indeed. And by the age of twelve Ivan had become an accomplished drinker.

But the most mind-shaping feature of Shuisky's regency was fear. From Ivan's account, the boy never knew a moment of repose. At any time, as he later recalled, he thought he might be thrown into a dungeon or killed. In this sense, one incident affecting the boy lived on in the man's mind. It concerned Shuisky's attempt one night to kill some of his enemies. In search of one of them who had fled into Ivan's part of the palace, Shuisky's assassins invaded the grand prince's room and scared him half to death. He thought they had come to kill *him*.

In 1543, Ivan was twelve years old and a precocious lad, to say the least. On December 29, after insuring that the soldiers around him were loyal, he asked to see Shuisky. Pointing a finger at the prince, he ordered his arrest and immediate execution. To everybody's surprise—not the least Shuisky's—the guards carried out the command. They seized Shuisky, killed him, and then, on Ivan's orders, threw the body to the dogs. The dogs ate Shuisky, and Ivan became master in his own house. It wasn't a bad beginning for a twelve-year-old.

Having rid himself of Shuisky, Ivan never again turned over control of affairs to a minister of state. For the next few years while he grew into a man, he had advisers who ran things while Ivan was busy having fun and raising teenage hell.

Although for long periods Ivan conscientiously addressed himself to governmental affairs, every now and then he really cut loose. He would join a bunch of drunken friends and spend a night on the town. Staggering from tavern to tavern, Ivan and his pals drank and raped their way across Moscow. Ivan became a real juvenile delinquent as thoroughly as, later in life, he was to be an extremist. He never knew the meaning of moderation, and when he played he really lived it up. He drank too much. He laughed too loudly, and he hated and loved too fiercely. As his cruelties turned to sadism, so his sexual exercises became parodies of the normal.

The sex life of kings has been as interesting throughout history to their subjects as are the progressive polygamy and sexual escapades of movie stars today. All Europe waited breathlessly for the latest news of Ivan's peccadillos. He reportedly kept a stable of fifty whores whom he badly misused in a mixture of lust and sadism. He often disposed of rape victims by having them hanged (in the presence of the husband), stabbed, stran-gled, exposed naked to the Russian cold, buried alive, or thrown to the bears. Variety was the spice of Ivan's life.

Everybody tut-tutted when England's Henry VIII took a total of six wives. But Ivan went Henry one better—to a total of seven.

Ivan was seventeen when he first announced he ought to get married. As was the custom in Russia in those days, orders went out to all fathers with socially acceptable virgin daughters. Thus began a kind of Miss Russia contest—with the winner getting Ivan. The girls were first brought to regional towns where Ivan's agents could look them over. The lucky girls passing this first test went to Moscow. There experts chosen by Ivan examined the young ladies for chastity, beauty, health, and so on.

For his first marriage, the choice was Anastasia Zakharyin, a boyar's daughter. On this occasion at least, God smiled on Ivan. She was very beautiful, and Ivan fell head over heels in love with her. They were to have thirteen years of wedded bliss, dur-ing which Ivan was a changed man. He gave up his coarse ways, lewd conduct, and sadistic habits and became gentle, loving, tender, and—it's hard to believe—endearing.

Some of Ivan's biographers divide his life into a "mild" and a "harsh" period. His "mild" period coincided with marriage to Anastasia, during which she bore him six children, two of whom lived. When she died in 1560 (Ivan was thirty years old), his "harsh" period began. He never loved again as he had Anastasia.

Ivan's second wife, Maria, was a real beauty too. She died suddenly (it wasn't Ivan's fault) in 1569, and eighteen months later he tried again. After the usual regional heats, 2000 virgin winners gathered for Ivan's inspection. He picked twelve of them. He assigned his doctor and some old hags at court to ex-amine them intimately. Among other qualities—such as beauty and intellect—Ivan stipulated that he didn't want anybody who snored in bed. He finally chose Marfa, a daughter of a Novgorod merchant.

Marfa's reign as third wife was short but not sweet. She got the fashionable "vapors" almost at once and went into a decline and died. Some historians speculate that the thought of marrying Ivan literally scared the poor girl to death. Ivan was sure she had been poisoned—or killed by witchcraft—by the relatives of his first two wives. Now well into his "harsh" period, Ivan had Maria's brother, Prince Mikhailo Temgrukovich, impaled.

This was a form of torture and execution that Ivan relished.
A sharp greased stake (sometimes a spear with a heavy shaft)
was rammed up Mikhailo's rectum and then placed upright in a
hole in the ground—with the Prince's weight slowly driving the
stake closer and closer to his heart. It took Mikhailo some time
to die.

Canon law in Russia forbade a fourth wife, but Ivan, ignoring
that, married the beautiful Anna Koltovskaya, and regretted his
"sin" almost at once. Anna didn't last long. She bored Ivan, and
he dumped her in a nunnery. Ivan didn't marry wife Number 5,
another Anna, in a church ceremony, and thus she may be regarded as just another mistress. The same was true of Number
6, a widow named Vassilissa Melentievna, who was usually called
at court just "the woman." Number 7 was a girl called Maria,
whom he married in 1582, two years before his death.

In this same year, while marrying Number 7, Ivan got the
idea of trying an Englishwoman, Lady Mary Hastings. She was
Queen Elizabeth's cousin. He had never met her, but he nevertheless proposed. Neither Lady Mary nor Elizabeth was amused.

Although Ivan's marriage to Anastasia had been happy, the
main lines of his character had been set earlier. He was never
to outgrow his boyhood experiences of terror and mistreatment.
Anastasia only lessened his fears; she didn't get rid of them.

Basically Ivan was a paranoid who saw treason and treachery
everywhere. The personal friendships he formed from time to
time were of short duration. The friend usually ended up getting impaled, stabbed, hanged, or poisoned. Ivan was no Damon
to anybody's Pythias.

Even at his worst, when spells of madness and ferocity overcame his judgment, Ivan never forgot who he was and what had
been done to him. He never forgot anything. This was pretty
awful for people who had slighted him when he was young,
argued with him in his teens, or given him the wrong advice in
later life. They ended up dead. But Ivan was no illiterate barbarian who killed only for pleasure. He enjoyed watching people
die, but it was only because he was sure they *deserved* to die.
He could always find some political, religious, or intellectual
reason to justify his blood-letting.

Somewhere along the line, he had been well grounded in Russian grammar and religion. He memorized long pages from the
Bible and religious works and developed quite an interest in his-

tory and theology. He liked Greek and Roman writers and *The Book of Kings*. Ivan loved to identify himself with earlier greats: David and Solomon, Augustus and Constantine, and so on. He adopted them as his own spiritual ancestors.

From his rather haphazard and undisciplined education, Ivan based his rule on three main tenets. The first was that he had been chosen by God to rule Russia, and anybody who opposed him was guilty of apostasy, of trying to frustrate God's will. Secondly he laid claim to be the direct heir of the Byzantine empire, now ruled by the Turks. Moscow was the "Third Rome." Ivan and Russia were the only legitimate defenders of the true faith; the rest of Europe was heretical and schismatic. And, third, he was the rightful ruler of all Russia, even those parts ruled by somebody else like the Turks and Poles.

For these reasons, Ivan decided to change his title. Grand Duke of Moscow wasn't enough. So he had himself crowned Tsar (Emperor) of All the Russias, the first Russian ruler to be so crowned. This was in 1547 when he was seventeen. The new tsar had fierce gray eyes that always looked at friend and foe with suspicion. Ivan was tall and well-built, quite handsome, with lots of hair on head and face. His good looks didn't last long. By the time he was thirty-five, he was an old man, almost bald and with a scraggly beard. But people grew up fast in his time. After all, he had become a man with his first killing at age twelve.

Despite its cruelty, Ivan's reign is a great one in Russian annals. Ivan was smart, no question. On the foreign front, he fought the Poles and Swedes in a great effort to push Russia's boundaries to the Baltic, although he failed in this. By his conquest of Khazan, he won control of the entire length of the Volga River from Moscow to the Caspian Sea. His agents established posts east of the Urals, while in other arrangements he welcomed contact with the English in the White Sea and Archangel.

It wasn't all pleasant sailing. Ivan was no general and had to rely on his boyars to run the army. They didn't do very well. In 1571 Tartars from the Crimea conquered and sacked Moscow, while in 1582—two years before the tsar's death—he had to accept the reality of Polish and Swedish control of the Baltic coast. But what Ivan started, Peter the Great was to finish more than a century later.

Although Ivan was involved with foreign problems during his entire reign, he had time to carry on a ferocious vendetta with his nobles and other rebels. He had started his personal reign by killing Prince Shuisky. He was twenty-three when he caught a bad cold—with a very high fever—and thought he was going to die. He asked his boyars to swear allegiance to his son Ivan. Most refused, including his chief minister, Adashev, and the metropolitan (bishop), Sylvester.

Unfortunately for these gentlemen, Ivan recovered. He exiled poor old Sylvester to an island in the White Sea, where he soon died. Adashev went into hiding and died. Ivan was furious. He wanted to kill him himself. Left were the widow and five sons. Ivan had them all killed, including a brother and his family, a father-in-law and his three brothers, and various assorted relatives.

Much earlier Ivan had formed his *corps d'élite*, a band of thugs called the Oprichniki. He thought a thousand might be enough, but he finally settled on six thousand. These lads were a singularly evil lot. They dressed in black and all rode black horses. On their saddles were a dog's head and a broom, which meant that they hounded traitors and swept them out of Russia. One summer night in 1658, several of these temporary favorites organized a night on the town to which Ivan was invited. They assured him they knew whose wives were beautiful. There was nothing to it but to round up the girls. The tsar was a little late for the ceremonies, but he arrived in time to take the pick of the lot. The raped beauties were later returned to their homes, an unexampled act of clemency on Ivan's part.

Ivan's madness—or was it just cruelty?—grew apace. Once, in 1565, he abdicated. That shook everybody, and all Moscow begged him to return. He was the king-pin of Russian society, and Russia would be lost without him. People counted his personal cruelties as nothing against what might happen without him.

Ivan's sadism was pretty rough on his victims. He impaled all sorts of people, since this was his favorite sport. He had one boyar set on a keg of gunpowder and blown to bits. As the tsar remarked: "Thus he will get nearer to heaven and the angels." One of his best officers, Prince Michael Vorotynsky, fell from grace, and Ivan had him lashed to a stake between two roaring fires. Ivan stoked them himself, for he thought it great fun. It took Vorotynsky long to die.

As time went on, the tsar more personally involved himself in the tortures and executions. He liked to see men's tongues cut out. Or how about old princes stabbed before the altar during services on Sunday? He liked to use hot needles on criminals, as well as hot tongs to tear them apart.

The tsar once got mad as hell at the people of Pskov who presumed to argue with him about their rights. Seventy of them came to see him. Ivan was outraged. After yelling at them and accusing them of treason, he had boiling red wine poured over their heads. He had a few beards singed by fiery torches and finally ordered them all to strip and lie naked in the snow. A miracle saved them. As they lay expecting execution, a messenger rode into camp with the news that Moscow was on fire. Ivan rode off into the night, and the considerably tamed protestors of Pskov rode home. They never again questioned the tsar's justice.

Of all of Ivan's atrocities, his treatment of the rebellious citizens of Novgorod most horrified Russia and the civilized world. The year was 1570. Ivan and his troops moved north out of Moscow and finally overcame Novgorod. For 175 miles outside the doomed city, the tsar burned and destroyed every village in his way.

Once in Novogorod, Ivan began the massacres. To begin with, all abbots and monks accused of treason were beaten to death with their pastoral staffs. The tsar personally tortured many a victim. Some had red-hot tongs pull ribs out of living bodies. In a ghastly parody of Chinese acupuncture, Ivan used nails and spikes to rip off finger- and toenails. Many were flogged until the whips laid bare the bones beneath the flesh. Ivan then had the wounds scorched with heated pans and other devilish implements. As usual, he had a lot of people impaled.

Novgorod's river proved useful. It was a relatively sanitary way of disposing of corpses. The massacre lasted for five weeks, and blood and bodies almost gagged the executioners. Lots of people, after being tortured, often by the tsar himself, had their legs and arms all folded up and tied to their necks. They were then dumped in the river. Ivan often had babies tied to their mothers' backs and thrown into the water. With great forethought he posted rowboats full of soldiers on the river to kill any victim who showed signs of life.

We don't know how many people the tsar killed in Novgorod. Contemporaries said 60,000, although some modern historians say only 2000. Whatever the figure, it took sanitation squads some six months to remove bodies, heads, arms, and legs downstream of the city.

Soon after his taming of Novgorod, Ivan returned to Moscow with blood in his eyes. The Muscovites, so he said, hadn't been exactly loyal. So in what is now Red Square he ordered eighteen gallows to be set up, plus a great cauldron of boiling water. It was clear the tsar had something on his mind.

Everybody disappeared. They went home and locked every door and window. This sort of unsportsmanlike behavior enraged Ivan. Always the ham actor, he wanted an audience. Soldiers went up and down each street ordering people to witness Ivan's punishment of traitors.

Quite a crowd turned out in these circumstances. Ivan started off by pardoning 180 prisoners. In the tsar's eyes they weren't very guilty. Dramatically, it was a good beginning; there's nothing like hope to generate interest. But Ivan soon showed he meant business. He had one of his ex-treasurers stripped and dipped first into a vat of boiling water and then into one of ice water. He also had an ex-favorite stripped, strung up by his feet, and slowly cut into fondue-sized pieces. Others were more simply butchered, so it only took Ivan four hours to dispose of 400 victims.

The tsar was always a man of uncertain temper, and that quite unpredictable. Prince Kurbsky, one of Ivan's cronies, decided to take off before he, too, became a victim. He wrote a four-page letter to the tsar telling him what he thought of him. When Kurbsky's servant brought the letter to the tsar, Ivan was so mad that he took his favorite spear and pinned the messenger's foot to the floor. It took Ivan eighty-six pages to tell Kurbsky what *he* thought of *him*.

With this same staff the tsar was to kill his favorite son— the heir to Russia's throne. Young Ivan (the tsarevitch or crown prince) was a chip off the old block. He inherited Ivan's intelligence and forcefulness, and he never showed much distress, if any, at his old man's method of disposing of enemies. Father and son had a good relationship, and even liked each other. Young Ivan had proved himself at Novgorod. He approved of Papa's ferocious ways of getting rid of traitors.

The famous murder happened in November 1581. We aren't sure why. Some contemporaries suggested that the tsar had struck young Ivan's wife. Others said that the tsarevitch had inadvertently criticized his father on some matter or other. The tsar flew into a rage and struck his son in the head with his spear.

To give the devil his due, Ivan was shaken. He wept and wailed loudly. As the blood oozed from his son's head, the tsar prayed to all for forgiveness. The boy, oddly enough, kissed his father's hand and asked for his blessing. Then he gave up and died. Ivan was disconsolate. The prince was twenty-seven and Ivan had three more years of life.

But Ivan was a dying man. He showed some evidence of internal disease—we don't know what—and died in great pain in 1584. In 1963, the Soviets exhumed his remains. A somewhat belated autopsy on Ivan showed an above-normal amount of mercury. He could have been poisoned but probably wasn't; doctors in those days used all kinds of mercury compounds as medicines.

The corpse, after almost 400 years, showed Ivan to have been a man about six feet tall. He was muscular. He had a sharp nose, heavily lidded eyes, and a small mouth. The position of his right arm was odd. Instead of being folded on his chest, it was raised as though in a gesture of defense.

23
Lord Chief Justice
George Jeffreys

1648–April 8, 1689

*If you think the courts coddle criminals,
stop worrying. Everybody is better off
than they were under the harsh jurisdiction of George Jeffreys, the Hanging
Judge.*

This is a story of treason and plots,
of hatred for religion's sake, of
rascality, rank injustice, rebellion, and sadism. Lord Chief Justice George Jeffreys made his bloody mark on history's pages in
1685, but we must begin the tale a few years earlier.

Let us go back to 1649. On January 30, Charles I, king of Great
Britain and Ireland, was beheaded by Oliver Cromwell. Someone
broke the news to his older son Charles, then a refugee in the
Netherlands, by addressing him as "Your Majesty." The prince,
uncrowned and unwanted by a great many angry people in his
own country, burst into tears. He was only eighteen.

In April of the same year he became the father of a boy who
was named James for his fifteen-year-old uncle, he who later
ruled as James II and heartily hated the younger James by that
time. The mother of the baby was an ambitious girl from home
named Lucy Walter. The child grew up to be made duke of Monmouth and to become the author of Monmouth's Rebellion, the
cause of the Bloody Assize, a memorable term of court that followed his defeat and death.

Young as Prince Charles was, the infant James may not have
been his first child. When Charles was only sixteen, he was
credited with fathering a boy by Marguerite de Carteret during
a few weeks he spent on the Isle of Jersey. Little James, Mon-
mouth-to-be, was by no means the last, either. Not even counting

Marguerite's baby, Charles II had eight sons and five daughters, all illegitimate, by eight mistresses, and so many problems with their demanding mothers that it's a wonder he had time to rule his realm; but he was a pretty good king. His best-remembered girlfriend—best, remembered by history, anyway—was a saucy actress named Nell Gwyn.*

In the same year the bastard James was born in Rotterdam, a boy was born to the Oates family in Oakham, England, and was named Titus. He developed great talent for ferreting out plots, whether they existed or not. He was a failure at everything he undertook until, later in life, he conceived the idea of spying, lying, and tattling to gain public attention. Titus Oates was a rascal. He suffered for it, but he was responsible for the deaths of several men more worthy than himself.

George Jeffreys was a year older than Titus Oates and James, the future duke of Monmouth. He studied law and was called to the bar at twenty. He moved right along in his chosen profession, became solicitor general to the duke of York (Charles II's brother James) in 1677, and was knighted. He bought a fine house and even entertained King Charles and one of the king's mistresses at dinner. He became a judge. The laws were barbaric, and Judge Jeffreys took full advantage of their harshness. He was still under thirty when he showed his enjoyment of other people's torments in winding up a sentence against some women accused of thievery:

> And I do charge him that puts the sentence into execution to do it effectually, and particularly to take care of Mrs. Hipkins, scourge her roundly; and the other woman that used to steal gold rings in a country dress; and since they have a mind to it in this cold weather let them be well heated. [This was his idea of a good joke.] Your sen-

---

* Charles never tried to hide his indiscretions. He admitted that his children were his, and after he became king took care of his brood by making the boys dukes. Nell Gwyn got a dukedom for her elder son by saying, in the royal presence, "Come here, you little bastard." When the child's father reproached her, she replied, "What else can I call him when he has no name?" So Charles created the duke of St. Albans.

James, grim brother of good-natured Charles, was not so notorious for his extramartial affairs, but he had a lot of them. His mistresses were notably unattractive. Charles once remarked, "I think his confessor chooses them for him as a kind of penance."

tence is that you be taken to the place from whence you came and from thence be dragged, tied to a cart's tail, through the streets, your bodies being stripped from the girdle upwards, and be whipt till your bodies bleed.

As time passed and the convictions were for greater crimes than stealing gold rings, Jeffreys delighted in showing what he could *really* do.

His big opportunity grew out of the religious and political strife dividing the British Isles. These divisions had already been responsible for the Civil War, the execution of Charles I, and the Protectorate of the Puritan Cromwell from 1649 to 1660, when Prince Charles was restored to the throne as Charles II. The Catholics thought the Protestants (the established Church of England) should be burned, the Protestants thought the same about the Catholics, and both groups detested the Dissenters— the Protestants who had broken away from the established church. Almost nobody adhered to the startling idea that freedom of religious belief might be beneficial to all concerned. Mine is the true faith, and if you're too bull-headed to accept it, I'll make you just as miserable as I possibly can. It's all for your own good, even if it kills you.

Even the royal family wasn't all in the same pew. King Charles was naturally Church of England because he was nominally head of it, but he had old-style Catholic leanings. His queen, Catherine of Braganza, was Portuguese, hence Catholic. His brother, James, duke of York, became Catholic in 1669. And Charles's favorite bastard son James, duke of Monmouth, was Protestant.

Titus Oates was a born liar. He was also a homosexual, a bad-mannered oaf, and an odd-looking fellow. A contemporary described him as a "low man"—that is, short—with a very short neck and his mouth right in the middle of his face. He was a failure in life until he seized on the idea of making a name for himself in this turmoil of religious beliefs. By the time he was twenty, he had been thrown out of two schools, including Cambridge, and was in debt. He became his father's curate (his father was an Anabaptist preacher, one of the radical sects of the time), then joined the navy and was expelled from that.

Oates got into the service of the duke of Norfolk as a Protestant chaplain—and then joined the Roman Catholic church with the intention of finding out what plots were being talked about to restore that faith as the official religion of England. He was sent to an English Jesuit seminary in Spain but after a few months was expelled. Then he was tossed out of another seminary in France. But in both these places he listened carefully to talk about plans for promoting Catholicism in England, and Titus Oates was a man who could add two and two and get seven.

After all his failures, it was time he achieved some success and fame, no matter how much he perjured himself to get it. In 1678 he was back in England, talking behind his hand to one of the few men who would bother with him, the Reverend Israel Tonge, a fanatical hater of Catholicism. Oates claimed that he had uncovered, during his spying among the Jesuits, a terrible plot to make all England Catholic. He wrote a *True Narrative of the Horrid Plot,* and he and Tonge laid his discoveries before a magistrate, Sir Edmund Godfrey. They swore that the king was to be killed, his brother the duke of York was to be placed on the throne, the entire ministry of government was to be replaced with Catholics, and Protestantism was to be forcibly rooted out.

Oates and Tonge visited Godfrey September 6. Chief among the men they accused was Edward Coleman, an earnest convert to Catholicism who was a friend of Godfrey. He had been secretary to the duke of York, the king's brother, and was by this time secretary to the duchess. Coleman was arrested on a charge of high treason September 30, and about two weeks later Godfrey's body was found in a ditch; he had been strangled and his neck was broken. A sword had been thrust through the body after death. (At the murder trial of three suspects the following February it appeared that Godfrey had indeed been killed by Papists.)

Godfrey had been a good man, much admired, and his unnecessary murder inflamed the furious Protestant mob. Coleman's own papers betrayed his guilt in a plot to restore the Catholic faith. He was tried at Westminster in November 1678. Titus Oates testified under oath that during his spy days he had been present at a treasonous meeting, with Coleman present, at which the assassination of the king was discussed.

The Lord Chief Justice, Sir William Scroggs, pronounced sentence, and, horrible as it was, it was not out of line for high treason. Coleman was condemned to be hanged, drawn, and quartered. That is, he was hanged by the neck but cut down while still alive. Then his bowels were burned before his face and his quarters were severed.

Titus Oates, spy, informer, and sometime perjurer, leapt to fame for exposing the "Popish Plot." Recognition was something he had always longed for and had been denied. Now he was a public figure. Statutes against Catholic priests were vicious. It was high treason, punishable by death, to celebrate mass in England, but courageous priests continued to do it secretly. An underground priest named David Lewis was reported by Oates and convicted of high treason in March 1679. Oates found himself the hero of the panic-stricken non-Catholics. At dinner in London, men drank his health immediately after the king's. Now he was one of the great, with hosts of admirers and a fat pension from the king's privy purse.

Then a case went against him. A man accused of intent to poison the king was found innocent by a jury. Oates began to slide down the ladder of public esteem. He lost his pension and his retinue of servants. But he continued to proclaim, as he had done before, that the duke of York was a traitor. York was a Catholic, but he was the king's brother, and there was a law to take care of anyone who made such an accusation. The law of *scandalum magnatum* made any words spoken of high personages actionable because the king himself was concerned.

George Jeffreys, now Lord Chief Justice, heard the case in June 1684. Jeffreys was the duke of York's man, although their religious beliefs differed. Titus Oates didn't even try to defend himself—under the ancient law of *scandalum magnatum*, the defendant was not allowed to justify his statements, although he might try to explain them away. The jury in his case, directed by Jeffreys, found him guilty, and set the damages at £100,000, the normal amount in such cases.

Oates could not pay, of course, so on June 18, loaded down with shackles, he was thrown into prison, to the great satisfaction of the duke of York.

King Charles had done some plain and fancy plotting himself, for the peace of his country and his own advantage. In 1670 he and Louis XIV of France had signed the very secret Treaty of Dover, in which Louis promised Charles men if he needed them and a fine fat sum of money in return for Charles's promise to declare himself Catholic and restore the true religion to England.

Louis agreed, however, that the time was not ripe for Charles to disturb his unruly subjects by doing this right away, so Charles postponed his declaration indefinitely while continuing to collect payments from Louis. (He needed the money because Parliament was stingy about voting taxes.) On his deathbed—he died February 6, 1685—Charles was received into the Catholic Church.

Furious disagreements further tore the kingdom apart after his death. Who should succeed him? For all his illegitimate progeny, he had no lawful issue. Poor Queen Catherine had miscarriages but had borne no living child. The late king's Catholic brother James, duke of York, was therefore pretty obviously next in line for the throne. But Charles II's Protestant son James, duke of Monmouth, maintained that *he* was the legitimate heir, not a bastard, because of a secret marriage that he claimed had taken place between Charles and Lucy Walter. There was much talk about a black box in which the record of the marriage was hidden, but it never came to light.

So the duke of York became King James II. He dusted off his hands and prepared to persecute the enemies of his church. One of these was Titus Oates, still in prison. He was indicted for perjury, found guilty, then tried on another perjury charge. Now the grim Lord Chief Justice came into his own.

Jeffreys did everything according to law, but if he had a choice of penalties he chose the harshest, and if a jury showed tendencies toward mercy he roared execrations. His sentence of Titus Oates for perjury was utterly barbaric, a scheme of repeated torture that would naturally result in death. It began in a relatively easy way, with Oates locked in a pillory for an hour Monday morning and an hour in the afternoon. This was uncomfortable and humiliating, even dangerous because passersby threw rocks and filth at the helpless man.

On Wednesday, Oates was to be whipped from Aldgate to Newdigate, and on Friday from Newdigate to Tyburn. If he lived through that horror, he was to be imprisoned for life, but— just in case he got the idea that the court was finished with him— he was to come out on several other occasions to be pilloried.

The far-famed Jack Ketch, official executioner, was in charge of the show. Mobs—most of them supporters of Oates—surged yelling through the streets. The prisoner collapsed after the Wednesday whipping, and the king was petitioned to cancel the

Friday whipping. King James refused, saying, "He shall go through with it if he has breath in his body." The king and Judge Jeffreys had one strong trait in common: they took pleasure in the torture of others. Bloody-minded James, when he was still duke of York, had gone to some trouble in order to watch prisoners being put to the torture of the boot.

A man who saw Oates brought out for the second whipping said his back looked as if it had been flayed. This time he could not stand up to be dragged at the tail of a cart, so Ketch loaded him on a sledge and lashed his mangled body all the way to Tyburn, past throngs of groaning spectators. Someone calculated that he received 1700 blows of the six-thonged whip. It is hard to believe, but the suffering wretch lived through all this.

This ghastly affair of Jeffrey's punishment of the perjurer Titus Oates preceded the horror known as the Bloody Assize. Jeffreys was just warming up to his big moment.

Back to the duke of Monmouth, Lucy Walter's son. Monmouth had strong Protestant backing in his endeavors to succeed to his father's throne. He plotted and drummed up considerable support. He invaded England after James became king, but he was defeated at the Battle of Sedgmoor in Somerset and taken captive.

Monmouth went to his death with dignity on July 25, 1685, at age thirty-six. He tipped Jack Ketch, the headsman, six guineas and handed his servant several more, saying, "Give him these if he does his work well." Strange as it seems to tip one's executioner, a man who went to the block naturally wanted the quickest death possible, so the headsman's good will was desirable. Ketch promised to do his best, but he took five strokes, lost his temper and threw down the ax after the second one, and ended by cutting off Monmouth's head with a knife. The furious crowd tried to lynch the executioner for botching the job, but his armed guards saved him. Whether he received the additional tip is not on record.

With Monmouth's Rebellion put down, Jeffreys had a chance to show what he could really do under the guise of punishing the new king's enemies. He was a man full of hatred and spite, empty of mercy. His goal was not justice but agony for the helpless. He was appointed head of a special commission to try Monmouth's supporters. The commission carried on a campaign of retaliation and revenge, Jeffreys enjoying every minute. Jack Ketch, that willing but clumsy executioner, and his assistants traveled in Jeffreys' retinue during the term of court that became known as the Bloody Assize.

The commission's first case was heard at Winchester, where a widow over seventy, Alice Lisle, was tried for sheltering two rebels. Jeffreys' purpose was to terrorize the other accused persons awaiting trial. Alice Lisle was known as a good woman and a kind neighbor; her son had served in the king's army against Monmouth, but that didn't save her. The only wrong she had done was to give shelter for a night to two fleeing refugees after Monmouth's defeat at Sedgmoor. Lord Chief Justice Jeffreys' speeches to witnesses were full of abuse, invective, and blasphemy. At the end, the jury was doubtful, but Jeffreys insisted that the old lady—who was too deaf to understand what was being said to and about her—was guilty of high treason.

Jeffreys admonished the jury; he couldn't see why they hesitated. Accordingly, the jurors found old Mrs. Lisle guilty. "If I had been among you," he told them, "and she had been my own mother, I should have found her guilty."

He jubilantly sentenced her to be drawn on a hurdle (a sledge) to the place of execution and there burned alive. Other prisoners in the lot hauled up before the court were rogues and vagabonds whom the Lord Chief Justice was satisfied to condemn to plain hanging.

The most important reason for executing poor old Alice Lisle was that she owned some valuable property that King James had his eyes on. He had to make some big payoffs to the men who had supported him against Monmouth. But the reason for condemning her to so ghastly a death was hidden in the black heart of the madman judge.

Mrs. Lisle did not appeal to the king for mercy, but she did petition to be beheaded instead of burned. This grace was granted, and she met her bloody death courageously on September 2, 1685.

The special commission went on to Salisbury, where there were no accused traitors waiting, and then to the greener fields of Dorchester, where more than three hundred prisoners had been rounded up. Thirty of them were accused of high treason, and the triumphant Jeffreys—who acted like a prosecuting attorney rather than a judge—got twenty-nine convictions in a hurry. Sometimes he played a scene for laughs. When one poor fellow was said by witnesses to be on welfare, alms from the parish, Jeffreys said, "Do not trouble yourselves; I will ease the parish of that burden." And he did.

Jeffreys was inspired to work harder by news that King James was going to appoint him Lord High Chancellor as a reward for his efforts thus far.

Before he was through in Dorset, Jeffreys had the nasty satisfaction of sending dozens of victims to the executioner. To terrorize the people around Lyme Regis into loyalty to the king, he had twelve prominent men hanged on the very spot on the sands where Monmouth had landed for his ill-fated invasion. This multiple execution was more than just hanging, of course. The tormented, disemboweled bodies were also quartered by Jack Ketch and his merry men, the quarters seared in a cauldron of pitch to preserve them, and hung up in public places as a grisly reminder of royal justice.

It was sometimes possible for relatives of the victim to avoid this nastiness and get a body buried in the family plot by crossing the right palms with enough silver. The sister of one of Dorset's victims paid a thousand pounds not to have her brother's body cut up.

One prisoner whose sentence from Jeffreys was a near-fatal whipping was a boy of fourteen who, unfortunately, had learned to read. His only crime was that he had read aloud a proclamation by the duke of Monmouth at the request of a group of people who were not so literate as he. So much for education!

Another, a man named Tutchin, infuriated Jeffreys because there was really no evidence that he had committed treason. The judge sentenced him anyway to imprisonment for seven years and to be whipped once a year through all the Dorset market towns. There were many such towns, and this sentence meant that he would be whipped about every two weeks. Tutchin petitioned the king to be hanged instead but was told to wait with patience. He beat the rap by coming down with smallpox and later his sentence was reversed.

The special commission moved on from town to town in the southwest with pomp and ferocious intent. If suspects couldn't be proved guilty enough to execute, Jeffreys and his four fellow magistrates had another string to their bow: transportation. There was a brisk market for white slave labor in the West Indies.

Some little girls at Taunton, who had made a banner to welcome the duke of Monmouth, were haled into court along with their schoolmistresses. One teacher died of smallpox in jail. One child died of pure fright a few hours after the raving Jeffreys had her thrown into prison. The others were given, like so much merchandise, to the queen and her ladies, to be ransomed if their parents could raise money enough or, if not, to be sold as slaves and transported to the West Indies. William Penn, the Dissenter who later founded Pennsylvania, was (strange to say) on good terms with James II; he had something to do with getting the ransoms reduced. James's queen made some nice pin money by selling to their families the human merchandise that he bestowed on her as a gift.

The Bloody Assize lasted just about four weeks. Nobody could accuse Jeffreys of loafing on the job. It has been estimated that 331 persons were executed, 849 transported to slavery, and thirty-three fined or whipped.

King James was now triumphant over some, at least, of his enemies, but his power was ending. Some of his frantic Protestant subjects invited William, Prince of Orange—husband of James's elder daughter, Mary—to invade England. He was glad to oblige. The king, afraid for his life, escaped by night and abdicated by tossing the Great Seal into the Thames. That was the Glorious Revolution of December 1688. James died in France on September 6, 1701.

George Jeffreys was the last rat to leave the ship. Anyway, he *tried* to get out of England. But before he could escape he was captured, in disguise and filthy. He was actually relieved to be locked up in the Tower where the enraged populace couldn't get at him. There he died in April 1689.

Titus Oates, the self-appointed spy whose testimony had brought fatal disaster to some three dozen persons, who had himself suffered punishment that should have killed him, outlived the other major actors in this grim drama. The government of William and Mary released him from prison and gave him a pension. He even outlived those two sovereigns: Mary II died of smallpox December 28, 1694, and William III died March 8, 1702.

By the time Titus Oates died, July 12, 1705, Mary's sister Anne was queen. The only one of her seventeen children to survive infancy died when he was ten, so the throne of Protestant England passed to a Hanoverian.

24
Blackbeard the Pirate

?–1718

*So you bought a used car from Honest
Bob and he turned out to be a pirate?
Be comforted by what happened to
Captain Teach.*

Early in the eighteenth century, at
the close of a colonial fracas
known as Queen Anne's War (in Europe it was the War of the
Spanish Succession), a great many privateers turned pirate.
There wasn't really a great deal of difference. A privateer was
more or less respectable; he sailed the ocean blue in his own
ship, making war on ships of a hostile power. He had a letter
of marque—a license—from his own government entitling him
to do this. A lot of British privateers had a good thing going;
they captured and plundered French and Spanish ships along
the Atlantic Coast of North America and among the islands. But
the war ended in 1713, and what were the unemployed privateers
to do then?

George I, who succeeded Queen Anne in 1714, offered his
subjects in the American colonies clemency if they would now
stop capturing and robbing and sinking their erstwhile enemies'
ships. Many of them, rather than face unemployment or the
tedium of life as merchant seamen, went right on doing what
they had been doing. The only difference was that without the
royal license they were now pirates instead of privateers.

One of the bold fellows who had no use for dull peacetime
pursuits was named Teach or Thatch or Tash, or possibly Hyde
or Drummond. By the time he became notorious, everybody was
too scared of him to care about his real name. He was known as
Blackbeard, and honest sailors had a hard time deciding whether
they'd rather meet him or the Devil.

His habits were as fearsome as his beard, which grew even under his eyes and was very long. He spent time prettying it up, braiding it into a lot of small plaits that he tied with bright ribbons. He tucked these beribboned strands behind his ears. In preparing for battle, he sometimes lighted a couple of slow matches, loosely twisted cord dipped in saltpeter and lime water so that it burned about twelve inches an hour, and stuck the ends under his hat. Smoke curled around his frightening face, and the slow matches were right at hand for touching off cannon. In action he wore a bandolier over his shoulder to support three pairs of loaded, primed, cocked pistols, and in a belt around his waist he thrust daggers, a cutlass, and more pistols. His fire-power was considerable, and he was a sight to behold.

Edward Teach, as he called himself, may have come from Bristol, in England; pirates were Bristol's principal product for export. Maybe he came from Virginia or Jamaica. He served in the crew of a privateer during Queen Anne's War, and early in 1717, when he began to attract horrified public attention, was with Captain Benjamin Hornigold (or Thornigold), sailing from New Providence Island in the Bahamas to the continent of North America. They captured a vessel laden with 120 barrels of flour. This bit of piracy sounds no more romantic than hijacking a wholesale-grocery truck, but they usually did better, with plunder including gold, plate, silks, and jewels. Teach showed such talent that Hornigold gave him a ship of his own. This was no great sacrifice on Hornigold's part; he had captured the ship from the French. Hornigold then sailed off for New Providence to take advantage of the king's clemency and promise not to be a pirate any more.

Woodes Rogers, Governor of the Bahamas, landed with considerable pomp in July to arrange for the rehabilitation of the repentant pirates. Hornigold and the other captains lined up their brutal rogues in two long columns, and Governor Rogers and his entourage marched between them. The pirates kept firing guns over their heads—just venting boyish high spirits, of course, but this greeting must have made the governor a little nervous.

The governor set about repairing the fort and building accommodations to lodge the reformed pirates, but they found honest labor dismally dull and in a few months most of them had left. A new war came along quite soon, and the governor granted commissions for privateering, so the unemployed pirates went back to work at their chosen profession.

Captain Teach had no truck with the idea of reforming. While other pirates were shooting over the governor's head and being officially forgiven for past sins, Teach was building his reputation. He had, as his stake, the ship Hornigold had given him. He attacked, defeated, and captured more vessels and moved their guns to his own until it was well armed with forty of them. He captured a fine ship named the Great Allan, removed its cargo, put the crew ashore (instead of killing them), and burned the ship. Then he really made a name for himself by defeating an English man-o'-war in a bloody battle lasting several hours.

Soon after this he captured a sloop of ten guns commanded by a most peculiar pirate, Major Stede Bonnet, a well-heeled gentleman who had a fine estate on the island of Barbados but found life there rather dull. Bonnet had the inclination of a pirate captain but lacked proper training. For one thing, he didn't know the first thing about operating an ocean-going vessel. He did all sorts of queer things, like paying his crew wages out of his own pocket instead of dividing up the loot he collected.

Edward Teach made him a deal: Bonnet should turn over his ten-gun sloop to one of Teach's men, named Richards, and move onto Teach's ship, where he wouldn't have all the worries of being captain.

It was fashionable for privateers-turned-pirates to surrender to the king's mercy. It could be profitable, too, as Captain Teach proved. He sailed to Bath, North Carolina, and made a very satisfactory arrangement with Governor Charles Eden and the governor's secretary, Tobias Knight. They would protect him, as an officially retired pirate, and he would divvy up the plunder with them. Bath had plenty of merchants willing to buy stolen goods at bargain prices and ask no leading questions.

Before long, Teach had a nice fleet and plenty of men for his crews. Sometimes he sold his plunder in Havana, but North Carolina seemed like home because the people he dealt with at Bath were so nice about everything.

Blackbeard was an ingenious fellow, always thinking up some interesting sport to relieve the monotony of shipboard life when there were no throats to cut. One day a bunch of the boys were whooping it up on stolen rum and getting quarrelsome. "Let's find out what hell is like," cried Blackbeard, "and see who can stay in it longest!" He took several of them down into the hold, closed the hatches and set fire to some pots filled with brimstone. Before long his coughing, strangling men begged to come out. Blackbeard went out last. He had won that game, and proved his toughness—a good idea for a pirate captain, because his men thought *they* were tough. One of his men remarked, "Captain, you look as if you had come straight from the gallows." Instead of tossing him overboard for *lèse majesté*, Teach replied, "That's a capital idea. Next time we'll play at gallows and see who can hang the longest without being throttled."

On another occasion Blackbeard sat at a table in his cabin drinking with two of his cronies from among the crew. He suddenly drew two of his pistols and cocked them under the table. One of the men moved in a hurry. The other didn't—and Captain Teach fired under the table. The man he shot in the knee was lame for the rest of his life. Later, when Teach was in a more benevolent mood, someone asked him why he shot his good friend. "Because if I don't kill one of you now and then," he replied, "you'll forget who I am."

Charleston Harbor was a dandy place for Teach's activities. In May 1718 he took three fine ships with rich cargoes— fourteen slaves in good condition, fifteen hundred pounds in gold, and so on—plus five or six smaller vessels that sailed out innocently and fell into the pirates' hands. Eight or nine more ships ready for sea did not dare to venture out.

Either because of a sudden epidemic or because some of his crew members were wounded, Blackbeard sent one of his commanders, Richards, into town with a few other pirates to demand medical and surgical supplies. Keeping two important passengers as hostages, he sent word that their heads would be delivered to Charleston if his request was ignored; furthermore, he would burn the town. He got his chest of medicine, worth £300–400, and let his prisoners go after stripping them half naked and robbing one of them of £6000.

Teach was so successful at piracy that his eager followers became too numerous. The more men he had, the smaller the shares of the loot all around. Resolving to rid himself of some of these men, he talked Stede Bonnet into going overland to Bath to surrender to Governor Eden under the royal Act of Grace. Bonnet did, only to be hanged. With Bonnet out of the way, Teach loaded all the supplies and plunder from Bonnet's ship onto his own and fired a bunch of the men. Some, who didn't want to be fired, he marooned on a lonely beach.

So he sailed on and on, attacking any likely-looking ship, and never mind whether it was English or from one of England's former enemies. Also, he got married—to his fourteenth wife, one contemporary said, a girl of fifteen or sixteen—and bought himself a fine home to live in when he wasn't out on the bounding main. He sometimes invited his crew members to take turns with his bride while he looked on. Also, he pursued the wives and daughters of his neighbors with evil intent.

Law-abiding colonists got pretty tired of having to worry about their womenfolk. They held a meeting, agreed that it was no use complaining to their own governor, who was in cahoots with Blackbeard, and decided to take their problem to the governor of Virginia, Alexander Spotswood. He arranged for two small sloops—shallow enough to run over the shoals where Teach had his ship—and crews from man-o'-war vessels with a pirate-hater, Lieutenant Robert Maynard, to command them. A proclamation was issued on November 24, 1718, offering suitable rewards for Teach and other pirates and their ships. When Tobias Knight got wind of this, he sent a warning to Teach, who laughed in his beard and stripped his vessel for action. After all, he had cannon, Maynard had none.

The night before the battle, Teach drank steadily until morning. One of his men asked whether his wife knew where his money was, in case he got killed. He replied that only he and the Devil knew, and the one who lasted longest would have it all. There were some mutterings among the crew that one more person was on board than was actually numbered in the ship's company. Nobody recognized the fellow, but none of them had ever seen the Devil before.

When Maynard encountered Blackbeard, a brisk exchange of threats ensued. The pirate captain greeted his Nemesis in uncordial terms: "Damn you for villains, who are you and from whence?"

"You can see by our colors we are no pirates," jeered Maynard. Blackbeard ordered him to send over his boat, but Maynard maintained he would come aboard soon enough. Teach swallowed a slug of liquor and roared, "Damnation seize my soul if I give you any quarter or take any from you!" Maynard told him he needn't worry about giving or getting quarter.

Then Maynard ordered his crew to man the sweeps and row toward the pirate vessel. Teach let loose with a broadside that killed or injured twenty-nine of Maynard's crew and damaged one of his two sloops. The wind freshened, so the remaining sloop could approach Teach's ship. Maynard was smart. He ordered all his men below; only the helmsman and himself were in sight on deck. His sloop looked pretty helpless. The pirates were waiting. When the sloop was near enough, they heaved hand grenades onto the deck. Very little damage resulted, but when the smoke cleared Teach assumed just what he was supposed to assume: that, because he couldn't see a bunch of men on board, the crew must have been just about wiped out.

"Let's go aboard and cut 'em to pieces!" Blackbeard howled. As the two vessels got close together, he and fourteen of his merry men jumped across—while Maynard's men, who had been hiding below decks, came pouring up the hatchways to meet them.

The battle was brief but bloody. Maynard and Blackbeard fired at each other. Blackbeard missed. Maynard didn't. Blackbeard, with a tremendous sweep of his cutlass, broke Maynard's weapon at the hilt. As he heaved back for another cutlass stroke, a British marine dealt him a hard blow on the throat. Blackbeard had five pistol wounds and twenty saber cuts when he began to falter. He fell dead at Maynard's feet on the bloody deck, and his men started to yell piteously, "Quarter! Quarter!"

Blackbeard had arranged for his own ship to be blown up if worst came to worst, but the man he left ready to touch off the stored gunpowder was prevented by a prisoner who had been captured the night before. So Maynard captured the ship with everything on it, including friendly letters from various leading citizens along the Atlantic Coast and documents that showed up Knight and Governor Eden as rascals.

Maynard had Blackbeard's head cut off and hung from the bowsprit of his sloop, and thus he sailed triumphantly into Bath.

There was much yammering between the two colonial governors. Eden indignantly insisted that Spotswood of Virginia had exceeded his authority. Tobias Knight was tried on a charge of conspiring with pirates and went scot free. But a man who had tried to get evidence against Governor Eden was fined £100! There were complaints and counter-complaints, accusations and law suits. And the nine pirates who had survived Blackbeard were hanged.

Legends naturally cluster around men who strike fear into human hearts. One legend about Blackbeard is that he did some pirate business way up north at the Isles of Shoals off the coast of New Hampshire. There he put a woman ashore to guard a treasure of buried silver until he came back. He never did, but she faithfully stayed and finally died there, and her ghost haunted the place for a hundred years.

25
Anne Bonny and Mary Read

Early Eighteenth Century

Does the Women's Lib movement jar you? Shouldn't its adherents demand the right to be hanged with their friends?

Equal rights for women hadn't been heard of when two girls made their mark as pirates. That profession was normally restricted to men—and rough, tough, nasty men, at that. Both Anne Bonny and Mary Read had been reared as boys, so they either didn't recognize, or manfully overcame, both natural prejudice and most of the handicaps of being female.

Anne Bonny was born in Cork, the by-blow of an attorney and a servant girl. Mr. Bonny was in the habit of sneaking along to the servant girl's bedroom in the middle of the night, and he had been ignoring his wife for a long, long time. Consequently, when his wife had twins shortly after baby Anne's arrival, he was furious. He accused Mrs. Bonny of carrying on with someone else. What he didn't know was one night *she* had been in the maid's bed when he went tiptoeing down the hall. His mother, who had the money in the family, died leaving it to his legal wife and the legitimate twins, but the wife kindly made him an allowance, although they lived separately.

After some five years of this financial dependence, the attorney decided to take little Anne into his home and bring her up. He was very fond of the child. But all the neighbors knew of the scandal, and that he had a daughter by the former maid servant, so he dressed Anne like a boy and let on that he was rearing the child to be a clerk in his office.

The wife found out that her husband's foster son was none other than his bastard daughter, and naturally she raised the roof. She cut him off at the pockets by stopping his allowance.

This made him mad, so he moved little Anne's mother into his home, causing a great scandal. Naturally his law business fell off, so he resolved to move to greener pastures. He chose the Carolinas and took mother and child off to the Colonies with him. Anne kept house for him after her mother died, by now dressing more like a girl. Anne was a muscular maiden with a quick temper. When a young man approached her with rape in mind, she beat him so badly that he was a long time recovering.

Like any other girl, Anne had romantic dreams. She married a young sailor who didn't have a shilling, and her angry father told her never to darken his door again. Anne and her husband sailed for New Providence Island, that nest of piracy in the Bahamas. There, tiring of her penniless sailor, Anne ran off with a privateer captain, John Rackam. By this time she was dressing like a man again. Rackam, too, had a peculiarity of dress: he was known as Calico Jack because he always wore calico jackets and drawers. (He must have made a habit of appearing in his underwear; otherwise, who would have known or cared what his drawers were made of?)

Calico Jack had already reformed and claimed the king's pardon when he met Anne, but she was an expensive toy, so he had to go back to piracy to keep her supplied with luxuries. Without much trouble he rounded up some other retired pirates to help him steal a fast sloop that was in the harbor. Anne went on board several times, seemingly just to be sociable but actually to count the number of hands who slept aboard and check on how close a watch they kept. One dark night the captain and his Anne, with eight associates, rowed out to the sloop when only two seamen were aboard. Both were asleep in a cabin. Anne, with a sword in one hand and a pistol in the other, awakened them and announced that if they resisted she would blow their brains out. They didn't resist, so after the sloop was safely out to sea Rackam let the two captives go in a small boat.

Calico Jack and Anne Bonny, along with their pirate crew and the ship they were on, were captured about the beginning of November 1720. Rackam was permitted to visit her in prison the day before he was hanged, but she didn't give him much consolation. She remarked that she was sorry to see him in such straits, but if he had fought like a man he wouldn't have to hang like a dog.

Captured along with Anne Bonny and Calico Jack and the

crew was another female pirate, Mary Read. She had been
brought up as a boy to conceal her mother's misstep, as Anne
had been to hide her father's peccadillo.

Mary's mother was married to a sailor named Read. She was
pregnant when he went to sea, and he never came back. The
widow lived with her in-laws and in due time was delivered of
an infant son. But, as time passed, the unfortunate Mrs. Read
found herself pregnant *again*. What to do? She bade her husband's parents farewell with the excuse that she was going to
live with a friend in the country. Her baby boy died. The new
baby was Mary.

When Mary was three or four years old, her mother ran out
of eating money, of which the in-laws had plenty. She could go
back to her mother-in-law, but how was she going to explain
that her little boy had become a girl? She dressed little Mary as
a boy and took her off for London. Grandma was quite willing
to bring up the child, but that wouldn't do at all; young Mrs.
Read talked her into allowing a crown a week for maintenance
and moved back to the country, where she reared Mary as a boy.

Little Mary grew up, went to Flanders and enlisted in an
infantry regiment. She acquitted herself bravely as a soldier.
Then she joined a cavalry regiment and did very well again.
But alas, she fell in love with a tent-mate. The two troopers
caused quite a lot of talk by getting married, with the bride
dressed like a girl for a change. The newlyweds resigned from
the service and settled down to run a pub. But Mary's husband
died, business at the pub fell off, and back she went into the
army.

Then peace broke out and a lot of soldiers were discharged,
our Mary among them. So she set sail for the West Indies, looking for new adventures. Her ship was captured by English
pirates, and Mary realized that this was really the life she was
cut out for.

The story goes that she kept her sex secret while pirating
until Anne Bonny, in the same crew, fell in love with her. Mary
said, "Er, I have news for you," to keep Anne from wasting
her time and affection. But Anne's protector, Captain Rackam,
turned green with jealously, so the secret had to be confided to
him to keep him from killing the handsome young pirate who
was Mary Read.

The pirate crew captured a great many ships in the West

Indies, recruiting from among their captives. One of these recruits, Mary realized with a sigh, was a young fellow she simply couldn't live without. He liked her, too—as another fellow. She managed to disarrange her shirt one day when nobody else was around, and when he saw that she was a girl he liked her better than ever.

Her lover quarreled with another member of the crew and, according to the pirates' code, agreed to go ashore with him to fight a duel. Mary, a managing type, picked a quarrel with the same pirate and arranged to fight him two hours before the time set for her admirer's confrontation. She fought with sword and pistol and laid the nasty pirate dead at her feet.

Once, before Captain Rackam found out that she wasn't a man, he asked her why she followed a pirate's life when it was so notoriously dangerous, and, if caught, she would certainly be hanged. She answered stoutly, "Hanging's no great hardship, and if it wasn't for that every cowardly fellow would turn pirate. Then us men of courage would starve." Mary obviously favored capital punishment—but when it came to the crunch she weaseled out of it.

When Rackam's ship was captured, the last three persons to be taken were Anne Bonny, Mary Read, and a seaman. Along with Rackam and other captured crew members, Anne and Mary were sentenced to hang. Then they realized that being female was an advantage, not a handicap. Both girls were pregnant, and in those days a pregnant woman condemned to death could at least delay the fatal day by a legal gimmick known as pleading her belly. Anne and Mary told the judge, "Your Lordship, we plead our bellies," and were reprieved.

26
Henry Bouquet

1719–1765

You're angry when people don't go by the same rules you do? Some British officers in the American colonies got mad enough to fight Indians with germ warfare.

Warfare between the whites and the Indians in North America before the American Revolution—as later—wasn't very nice. It's fashionable nowadays to talk about the "poor Indian," but lots of them were pretty bad. The whites weren't much better. Whites usually treated whites better than they did Indians. The Indians were at least consistent. They killed other Indians as readily as they killed whites.

Who first did what to whom is a problem historians will long discuss, but by the time Colonel Henry Bouquet appeared on the scene both Indians and whites had perfected their m.o.'s. Atrocity and counter-atrocity became the name of the game in this period right after the end of the Seven Year War (1756–1763)— Americans call it the French and Indian War.

The British won the war and kicked the French out of most of North America, taking over their colonies in Canada and elsewhere. (To keep what we call the Louisiana Purchase out of British hands, the French gave it to Spain. Napoleon later got it back and sold it to us.) Although most Indians fought on the French side, many supported the British. But, by the time the war ended, there were lots of British officers who took a dim view of Indian "rights."

One was General Lord Jeffrey Amherst, commander-in-chief of British forces in North America. A forceful, stern, and energetic general, Lord Amherst didn't like Indians. He thought they were "insatiable animals" and "disgusting creatures." Amherst once wrote, "When men of what race soever behave ill, they must be punished but not bribed." He didn't pussyfoot around. "I am determined to take every measure in my power," he wrote, "not only for securing and keeping entire possession of the country, but for punishing those barbarians who have thus perfidiously massacred his Majesty's subjects."

One of Amherst's ablest officers (some thought he ought to be commander-in-chief) was a soldier of fortune who had been born in Rolle, Switzerland, in 1719. He was Henry Bouquet. As a youngster, Henry entered the Swiss army and saw action in Holland and Sardinia. In 1754, he enlisted in the Royal American Regiment (a British unit) and by the time he arrived in North America in 1756, was a lieutenant colonel. He fought all over the colonies, from Georgia to Michigan, and in the process didn't acquire a high regard for either the Indians or the Colonials— all of whom he thought were a shiftless lot.

As soon as he arrived in America, everybody filled him in, of course, with the usual tales of Indian barbarity. It didn't take Bouquet long to learn the rules of fighting Indians, and he got a lot of experience fighting France's Indian allies. At the end of the French and Indian War, he was pretty much an expert on Indian atrocities.

He had seen first-hand the results of Indian raids on outlying settlements—with their grisly scenes of horribly mutilated bodies. And he had seen the scalped remains of women and children and been told by former Indian captives of what they had been through—like having been stripped and forced to run between two lines of Indians armed with knives and clubs.

And now in 1763, with the French and Indian War at an end, the famous Indian chieftain, Pontiac, organized as many of the tribes as he could (Indian individuality made them hard to discipline) in what has been called "Pontiac's Rebellion" or "Pontiac's Conspiracy." He himself attacked Detroit (and failed) and other Indians attacked Fort Pitt, which Bouquet had commanded for three years in the late war.

As soon as the news of Pontiac's uprising reached Lord Amherst, he ordered Bouquet back to Fort Pitt. On the way, he and his men ran into an Indian ambush at Bushy Run. His 460 troopers fought off the ninety-five attacking redskins with the loss of only sixty men! This was hailed as a great victory, and Bouquet got through to Fort Pitt with his remaining 400.

And now we get to the complicated part of the story. Did Colonel Bouquet actually exchange germs for bullets and try to infect the Indians with smallpox?

On his way to Fort Pitt, Bouquet received plenty of advice on how to treat the Indians. Some of it came from Lord Amherst. On June 23, 1763, the general wrote to Bouquet that should any "Savage" fall into his hands "a Quick Retaliation" must be made for their "Barbarities." Two days later, he was even more specific, noting that Bouquet should "extirpate that Vermine from a Country they have forfeited, and with it all Claim to the Rights of Humanity." On June 29, he wrote: "I wish to Hear of no Prisoners, should any of the Villains be met with in Arms...."

While getting Lord Amherst's advice, Bouquet also heard from a farmer named John Hughes who recommended the use of dogs to hunt down the Indians. He elaborated an eight-point program of how the dogs were to be used, ending with the suggestion that if Bouquet managed to kill two or three Indians on a raid he should let the dogs "tear them to pieces." He argued heatedly that 500 men with 500 dogs would be "more dreadful" to 2000 Indians than 1000 soldiers. Bouquet toyed with the suggestion, then told Amherst about it. The general liked the idea but said there weren't enough dogs around, and England was too far away to get any.

Earlier, Lord Amherst had written to Bouquet: "Could it not be contrived to send the small pox among the disaffected tribes of Indians? We must on this occasion use every stratagem in our power to reduce them." He later suggested, "You will do well to try to inoculate the Indians by means of blankets."

The general would never have proposed the use of such extraordinary wartime measures in Europe, where "gentlemen" (officers) led "the scum of the earth." But fighting in Europe was stylized and formal and everybody followed the rules. America was something different. The Indians had never heard of the rules and fought as they pleased. This enraged Lord Amherst more than anything else.

In any event, Bouquet wrote to the general: "I will try to inoculate the Bastards with Some Blankets that may fall in their

Hands, and take care not to get the disease myself." After all, one had to be careful about such things, since a smallpox germ might not know the difference between a red skin and white skin.

The argument among historians does not involve the *intent* on the part of Lord Amherst and Colonel Bouquet to introduce biological warfare in fighting the Indians. That seems pretty clear. The real question is: did Bouquet actually *try* to infect the Indians?

Among Bouquet's papers, one historian found an interesting bit of evidence. It's a bill that Bouquet sent to headquarters for reimbursement for two blankets, one silk handkerchief, and a piece of linen which he had used "to Convey the Small-pox to the Indians." The fact that smallpox did break out among the Indians around Fort Pitt—and raged for about a year, seriously hampering their military activities—is not conclusive evidence that Bouquet's scheme was successful. Smallpox was everywhere in those days.

Bouquet himself didn't catch the disease. After a year or two, he journeyed to Pensacola, Florida (then in British hands), where he became a general and died in 1765.

27
Jean Baptiste Carrier

1756–1794

If you are irritated with the slowness of clogged courts, remember that Carrier speeded them up so efficiently that "justice" became a grand-scale disaster.

By 1789, most Frenchmen were fed up with the inequalities and misgovernment of the Old Regime—the equivalent of what is known today as the Establishment. In those days, it was hard for a poor boy to get anywhere. Everybody in France belonged to one of three estates, or classes. The clergy, making up the first estate, had all kinds of privileges, including no taxes. The nobles made up the second estate, and they weren't taxed either. Everybody else—banker and farmer, merchant and serf, lawyer and fisherman—made up the third estate. They paid through the nose.

At the top of the heap was King Louis XVI, an amiable guy with a stupid wife, Marie Antoinette. Louis wasn't a bad king. He was just dumb. His grandfather, Louis XV, had said: "After me, the deluge." And poor Louis XVI didn't know enough to stick his finger in the dike. He didn't know a dike when he saw one.

But Louis was a good-hearted man and realized that a lot of people were unhappy. He would have liked to be called "Louis the Good." In 1789, he called the Estates General into session. It wasn't much of a legislature, for it could only advise the king, and it hadn't met for 175 years.

Everybody got excited. Reform and change were the order of the day. The only trouble was—this seems to be true of all revolutions—that there was no agreement on what the changes and reforms should be. In all the confusion, the hot-headed extremists came more and more to the fore, until finally they threw out Louis XVI, established a republic, and cut off the heads of their political opponents, including Louis and Marie Antoinette.

One of the radicals was Jean Baptiste Carrier, a Jacobin (as his party was called) who went around demanding that heads should roll. He was hardly discriminating. His advice in every speech was: "Kill, kill, kill!"

He wasn't much to look at. As a member of the National Convention (the legislature of the new republic), he was described as being all arms and legs, with stooped shoulders, deep-set yellow eyes, and thick lips. Also he fidgeted. He hadn't very much chin but his ears were big, unshapely. His voice was normally shrill, but when he was in a temper his words "seemed to come from his bowels."

The future "Great Exterminator," as Carrier has been called, was born in Yolet, a small village in the Upper Auvergne, in March, 1756. He was the third of five children. His father was of the lower middle class but had enough money to educate his children—with a little help. The help came from the local gentry, the Marquis de Miramont, and his gentle wife.

The marquis's chaplain was a Carrier relative, and young Jean Baptiste was often a guest in the chateau. The marquis and marquise treated him kindly. And it paid off. In the dark days ahead, when all aristocrats were suspects, Carrier apparently went out of his way to save the marquise's life. Such an act of clemency and gratitude was totally out of keeping with what we know about Carrier. It was an aberrant act of mercy in a career soaked in innocent blood.

Jean Baptiste's father, the marquis, and the chaplain decided that the boy would make a good priest. He was intelligent and quiet, sometimes even sullen. His table manners were atrocious—he ate like a pig—but this could be corrected. So they sent Jean Baptiste to a Jesuit college in Aurillac where he did well enough.

But the boy had a mind of his own. After a couple of years, he announced that he wanted to be a lawyer. And so Papa, the marquis, and the chaplain sent him to the University of Paris. He returned to Aurillac, married a merchant's daughter—she was to have no importance in his life—and signed on as a clerk in a prominent lawyer's office. He had already begun to drink heavily, and from time to time he got a little violent in his cups.

He didn't last long on this job. His boss soon fired him. Nobody knows why for sure. Later, after he had become notorious, people said that he had forged some documents. Maybe so, but the evidence points to his boss's poor income. Jean Baptiste was an unnecessary expense.

At about the same time, the chaplain died, and Jean Baptiste produced a will in which the departed cleric left him lots of money. Again he was accused of forgery, but handwriting experts supported his argument, and he was never tried.

At the outbreak of the Revolution in 1789, Carrier was thirty-three years old. He was often drunk, and his legal practice suffered. He was a man of mediocre intelligence and no great will-power. Although he showed some tendency toward extremism as a solution to life's problems, nobody who knew him in 1789 guessed what a monster he was to become in four years.

The calling of the Estates General and the fall of the Bastille —a mob took this royal prison on July 14, 1789, and the French still dance in the streets on every July 14—excited all France. In his little provincial town of Aurillac, Carrier was caught up in the national hysteria. At first he liked "Good King Louis." But it wasn't long before he demanded the king's overthrow and the wholesale liquidation of traitors.

On August 10, 1792, the Paris mobs overthrew Louis and destroyed the monarchy. Carrier was elected to the new republican legislature, the National Convention. He never became much of an orator, but his extremism was genuine enough. He always went the other fellows one better. He proposed the creation of a Revolutionary Tribunal to try suspects. Although the Convention adopted his idea, it did so in a much more moderate form than Carrier liked.

In any event, Carrier became a national figure. In January 1793, he voted for Louis' death and demanded the adoption of the extreme measures against the Republic's foreign and domestic enemies. It wasn't long before more than half of France was in the hands of other countries (France was now at war with most of Europe) or counterrevolutionaries horrified at the king's death.

For France, for the Revolution, it was a time of extreme danger. But the National Convention, led by Robespierre, Danton, and other revolutionary heroes, was up to the challenge, and they mobilized the country. The *levée en masse* (mass military conscription) made every French man, woman, and child a soldier. And the foreign invaders were flung out of the Republic.

Among many measures taken to suppress the counterrevolutionaries, the National Convention adopted the system of deputies-on-mission. The Convention sent various of its members, armed with full powers of life and death, to troubled provinces and questionable generals. Each Deputy-on-Mission could set up a revolutionary tribunal and the guillotine (a humanitarian device concocted some years before by a Dr. Guillotin to cut off heads swiftly and painlessly), and adopt the necessary measures to stamp out treason.

During all of the years the Revolution flourished, the worst area for counterrevolution was in the Vendée, a region to the west of Paris and on the border of Brittany. Thousands of people and whole armies were engaged on both sides. Atrocity was the name of the game, and it is impossible to indict Royalists over Republicans or vice versa.

As part of its program to destroy the traitors in the Vendée, the National Convention sent out several deputies-on-mission. One of them was Jean Baptiste Carrier, soon to be known as "the Tiger of the West."

Carrier first arrived in Nantes in the fall of 1793. He toured Brittany and even entered the Vendée. Later he boasted of having a horse shot from under him at the "battle" of Cholet while "stemming the flight of cowardly Frenchmen." It was nearer the truth to say that he fled in panic and hid out in a farmhouse until it was safe to come out and concoct his "victorious" story.

He soon returned to Nantes where he set up a revolutionary tribunal and the guillotine. For the moment, things went well for the Republicans in the Vendée, and thousands of Vendéans (estimated at 80,000) fled into Brittany, where it was Carrier's job to round them up.

He also collected a bunch of town toughs and formed them into a Compagnie Marat, his own version of vigilantes. They sneered at Carrier behind his back, flattered him to his face, and carried out his orders. They were boon drinking pals, and as the terror in Nantes grew worse Carrier was drunk most of the time.

Not only did Carrier suspect the locals in Nantes—indeed in all Brittany—of treason, but now his bailiwick was deluged by the Vendéan refugees. Thousands were arrested, the regular jails overflowed with suspects, and all kinds of extraordinary measures had to be taken, like locking up prisoners in other public buildings.

Carrier was worried. He wrote that "on all sides a counter-revolutionary commotion threatens to burst forth." As he informed the government in Paris: "My revolutionary operations are in full swing; there are arrests every day; the guillotine is permanent; miscreants suffer capital punishment; monopolists are discovered. . . ."

Poor Jean Baptiste! *So* many suspects in jail. And the court and guillotine were *so* slow. He had never had to face such a problem before. He did his best to speed up justice and empty the jails. When some of the thugs around him demurred against guillotining of children, Carrier steeled his heart. They were traitors, he said; they must die like the others. But killing the kids took more time than ever. One child's head was too small to fit "the national razor," as Carrier called the guillotine. The blade split his skull instead of cutting his neck, and the result was an awful mess and more delay.

Food shortages in Nantes and danger of cholera and typhus outbreaks forced Carrier to extreme measures. It never occurred to him to empty the prisons by freeing the victims. He said that they were all guilty, anyway, and trials took too long. As he wrote to a friend: "Prisoners are being led to Nantes in hundreds; the guillotine cannot suffice. They are being shot. Long, long life to the Republic!"

Prisoners were tried in batches and sent to the quarries by the hundreds to be shot. Carrier was becoming more and more unhappy with the slowness of his revolutionary tribunal. He got so mad finally that he wrote to Paris that "instead of amusing myself by bringing them to trial, I shall send them to their own homes to be shot." This, he thought, would be a good example to others. Meanwhile, he continued to rail at the judges. To one, he shouted, "You, you old rascal, you old bastard, you want verdicts, do you! Go ahead! If the whole pen is not emptied in a couple of hours I will have you and your colleagues shot!"

After some experimenting, Carrier decided that the fusillades, while helpful, were not the whole answer. It took a lot of time and more help than he had at hand to dispose of the bodies. Somewhere he got the idea—maybe it was the fruit of his own increasing madness—of drowning his prisoners in the Loire River. Thus began the infamous *noyades,* or judicial drownings. He had the scuttle-holes in a lot of old barges pierced and temporarily stopped up. Carrier's men then loaded a boat with prisoners (ninety priests on the first round) who were tied in pairs. The barge was taken to the middle of the river and sunk, with what Carrier called its "cargo."

These victims were sentenced by Carrier himself. No use having them tried. In one batch, he sentenced twenty-four "brigands," one of whom was thirteen and two who were just fourteen. Carrier praised the "Miracle of the Loire," and decided it was a practical method. Some witnesses (and there were few of these because the atrocity was always done at night) said there were more than twenty such mass drownings. Some historians have said that only four are verifiable, others that there were only seven, and that the number of victims ran from about 2000 to 4860, of whom 148 were priests.

Meanwhile, the executioners were having some fun. Some victims floated in the water and yelled for help. The answer was a good bash on the head with an oar. Some managed to free themselves of the ropes and swim to the boats filled with executioners. They lost a lot of arms from hanging on to the rowboats. Every now and then, the murderers amused themselves by stripping their victims naked, choosing the best-looking man and loveliest girl and tying them face to face before flinging them into the Loire. They called this grim jest "a Republican marriage."

An English poet, Algernon Charles Swinburne, who thought the Revolution was grand—it was safely over before he was born—wrote a long poem, *Les Noyades*, about these "marriages." It includes these verses:

> In the wild fifth year of the change of things,
>   When France was glorious and blood-red, fair
> With dust of battles and deaths of kings,
>   A queen of men with helmeted hair;
> Carrier came down to the Loire and slew,
>   Till all the ways and the waves waxed red:
> Bound and drowned, slaying two by two,
>   Maidens and young men, naked and wed.

People downstream from Nantes complained that the river banks were littered with corpses. Carrier was furious. He told them he was too busy defending the Republic to worry about minor matters. As the butchery went on, Carrier began acting a little strangely. In and out of court, he raved and ranted more than ever. "You judges must have verdicts," he once yelled; "pitch them into the water, which is much more simple." At various meetings, he would get carried away and start screaming, "Kill, kill, kill!" Once he got so excited that he took out his sword and began waving it around. His only victims were the candles nearby.

He took to locking himself in his rooms and issuing wild orders by proxy: "Burn all the houses of traitors with the victims inside," read one such command. He turned more and more to brandy and sluts.

It was no way to administer a great province, and complaints against his atrocities and misrule began to reach Paris. By this time, the little lawyer from Arras, Maximilian Robespierre, was almost a dictator. He sent a young friend, Jullien, to Nantes to check up on Carrier. Carrier arrested him, and there were some frightful scenes of bluff and outrage. He freed Jullien, who returned speedily to Paris. Robespierre demanded Carrier's recall.

And so ended the great atrocities in Brittany. Carrier returned to Paris just in time to witness Robespierre's fall and get caught in its backlash. Many old-line terrorists were brought to trial, Carrier among them. He put on a pretty good show but was condemned anyway. The "National Razor" cut off his head too as the crowds shouted "Death to assassins!"

28
The Marquis de Sade

June 2, 1740–December 2, 1814

What's in a name? This man will always be remembered for dedicating his life to the pursuit of vice.

Donatien Alphonse François, Marquis de Sade, was born in a palace in Paris. His father was a count, his mother related to the royal Bourbons. One of his distant ancestors was Madonna Laura, the lady beloved of the poet Petrarch in the fourteenth century. At age four, the boy was packed off to live with an uncle, the Abbé de Sade, a rounder who didn't let religious duties cramp his style. Women guests were always scurrying up the back stairs of the abbé's big, gloomy château.

The boy went to school in Paris, then trained for the cavalry. Before he was sixteen he was a sub-lieutenant. He fought in Germany during the Seven-Year War and was a captain when discharged. He was then twenty-two, rather fat, about five feet one or two inches in height. The French army was an excellent school for depravity, but what he learned there was elementary compared with the self-guided post-graduate study to which he devoted his life.

He married at twenty-three, unwillingly; his father needed money and the Montreuil family had it but yearned for a titled son-in-law. The Comte de Sade made a deal with them: "My son will marry your daughter, and never mind that she is plain and skinny and he doesn't like her." The young marquis, madly in love with his current mistress, growled but married Renée Montreuil on May 17, 1763.

Poor Renée was hardly used to being the Marquise de Sade when her new husband went to jail. Paris was full of *petites maisons*, "little houses," where all sorts of shocking things went on. Sade was arrested for going beyond the bounds of propriety in one of them, indicating an early genius for refinements of vice. He was released after two weeks in the pokey, not one whit reformed.

Even if he had known that he would spend twenty-seven years in various prisons and an insane asylum, he would probably not have changed his ways.

The Marquis de Sade was by no means the only vice expert in France. Louis XV (who died in 1774) has been called France's most corrupt monarch. He had a private bordello known as the Deer Park, which cost the nation a fortune in tax money. The Deer Park was set up for him by his mistress, Madame Pompadour. This king also had his *Intendant de Menus-Plaisirs,* or Minister of Dainty Pleasures, a cabinet post that his grandson and successor, Louis XVI, abolished. Ordinary poor people, with the examples of royalty and the nobility before them, did the best they could in the way of sin.

Sade fell in love at the drop of an eyelid, to the growing annoyance of his mother-in-law. There was, for instance, the actress Colet, who was already being kept by a marquis and a comte. She took on de Sade too, but continued to live with one of her other loves, who kindly hid whenever de Sade called.

Then the marquis took up with a girl named Beauvoisin. This time he really made his mother-in-law furious, for he took Mademoiselle Beauvoisin to his château at La Coste in Provence where he introduced her as his legal wife. That put-upon lady and her mother were far away in Normandy.

Renée and her mother moved to Paris, where Renée bore a son. De Sade paid no particular attention. He had rented a furnished house, a *petite maison,* in Arcueil, just outside Paris, and was raising such hell that the police warned keepers of bordellos not to send him any more girls. He had viciously whipped at least four of them. His father was dead by this time, and the marquis was now the Comte de Sade, but he had established himself in the public eye with his original title and is still known by it.

He had almost reached the ripe old age of twenty-eight when he made himself notorious. There are several versions of the Keller case, all deserving the term sadism, which derives from the marquis's own family name. De Sade, all dressed up, went for a stroll on Easter morning in 1768. Times were hard, and thousands of poor people were out begging while the rich went to church in splendor. Rosa Keller, a widow, an unemployed seamstress, asked de Sade for money.

"Come along with me," said he. She testified later that he offered her housecleaning work. He testified that, on the contrary, she knew very well what he wanted, and it wasn't housecleaning. The marquis took the dressmaker in a carriage to his *petite maison* in Arcueil, and there he ordered her to strip. She protested, but he threatened to kill her if she refused. Terrified, she obeyed, but kept her shift on. Sade tore it off, made her lie face down on a sofa, tied her up, and then lashed her with a whip of knotted cords while she scremed. De Sade anointed her cuts with some salve that he said would cure them right away, and then whipped her some more.

While he was out of the room, she snatched up the bed coverings, made a makeshift rope, forced open the window shutters, and let herself down to the garden. When she reached the street, she was cut from the whip and scraped and skinned from climbing over the garden wall. De Sade's valet—no-good servant of a no-good master—offered her money to return to the house, but she refused. Terrified but free, she took refuge with some sympathetic women of the village and as soon as possible filed charges against the marquis.

His wife, Renée, anxious to hush up the scandal, saw to it that Madame Keller received a substantial sum of money to drop the charges. But the affair had gone too far. By order of the king, Louis XV, de Sade was imprisoned in solitary confinement. The confinement wasn't totally solitary, however. His valet was allowed to tend him, and his wife visited him and became pregnant again. The marquis's imprisonment was gradually relaxed. He went deeper into debt by producing various entertainments for which he wrote the scripts.

Renée, already mother of two boys, gave birth to a girl in 1771. For a while the marquis behaved pretty well, for him, but behaving like other people was simply not his line. When the baby was a few months old, he moved his family from Paris to his own château at La Coste—and took his wife's young, pretty sister along. Julie was a born flirt, and before long their affair became scandalous. Poor Renée would put up with almost any bad treatment, but her mother wouldn't.

While this affair was building up steam, the marquis took himself off to Marseilles, in June 1772, for a few days of his special kind of fun and games, accompanied by his valet, Latour. Little did he suspect that he was going to get into a mess that would land him in prison for years with a death sentence hanging over him.

Latour set off to make arrangements for de Sade's latest idea of entertainment. He lined up four young prostitutes—Mariette, Marianne, Marionette, and Rose—and rented a small house. Some of the demands de Sade made were too much even for professionals. Three of the girls refused indignantly, no doubt inquiring loudly just what kind of girls he thought they were. Marianne, however, took part in an act of sodomy, which was legally punishable by death at the stake.

Among other activities, de Sade had the girls whip him with a blood-stained device studded with nails. During time out for a rest he dealt out some bonbons. Either the candy (which may have contained an aphrodisiac) or the horrors of the day made two of the girls sick. He invited them all back for later that evening, but they had had enough. Latour the valet hastily lined up a girl named Marguerite. She too ate some candy and became horribly sick.

De Sade and his valet went merrily back to La Coste and the charming Julie. De Sade was astonished to learn that two of the girls had filed charges against him, claiming that he had tried to poison them and had committed sodomy. The loyal marquise, Renée, rushed off to Marseilles to try to get the proceedings called off, but she failed. De Sade and Latour were tried *in absentia*, found guilty, and sentenced to death. De Sade was supposed to confess his sins publicly and then be beheaded. Latour was to be hanged. Both bodies were to be burned. But in their absence stuffed effigies were solemnly executed at Aix.

De Sade didn't care. He was safe in Italy with his adoring sister-in-law, and that was where he made his big mistake. Julie's mother, his mother-in-law, had influence and could probably have helped clear him of the criminal charges, but when he ran off with her younger daughter he had gone too far. Madame de Montreuil might have forgiven adultery (there was a lot of it going around), but custom designated it, in this case, as incest as well. She undertook the complete ruin of her erring son-in-law. All she needed was a *lettre de cachet* signed by the king. This was a handy device for getting people put away, a kind of private warrant for imprisonment without trial. The king signed it willingly, and Madame de Montreuil used it with vicious consistency until such warrants were abolished eighteen years later, after the fall of the Bastille.

Julie flitted away from the marquis after a few months, but her mother never got her married off. She spent some time in a convent and died of smallpox at about thirty-six.

De Sade thought he was safe in Savoy, out of France, under an assumed name, but he underestimated his mother-in-law's fury and ingenuity. She appealed to the king of Sardinia, who was duke of Savoy, and had him extradited. Bad as he was, perhaps he deserves a little sympathy for being saddled with such a spiteful mother-in-law.

He was locked up again, with his faithful valet as cell mate, and was by no means a model prisoner. He complained and protested constantly, pointing out that a man of his social standing shouldn't have to put up with close confinement. He drove the commander of the prison half crazy. The commander would have given almost anything to have him moved.

De Sade did move—to the commander's great embarrassment. With Latour and an imprisoned baron, he escaped through a built-in privy, which had an unbarred window. De Sade made his way to his home at La Coste, where his faithful wife protected him. The château was so big that he could always find a cranny to hide in when police approached. After some legal shenanigans, Renée learned that the *lettre de cachet* might be annulled if de Sade would officially deny the charge of sodomy, the poisoning charge being no longer valid.

The de Sades lived quietly, even secretly, at La Coste. The marquis didn't dare go out looking for excitement, so his enterprising wife shopped around and brought in half a dozen young girls and a young male "secretary." De Sade bought some human skeletons to decorate one of his orgy chambers. That was quite a winter at the old château, interrupted at last when some of the girls' parents found out what was going on. De Sade quietly left for Italy to do some post-graduate reading on the erotic customs of the ancient Romans.

Back home once more, life was a series of girls (and occasional boys) brought into the château. In January 1777, new servants moved in, two boys and two girls. Three of them moved out the next day, having fought off de Sade's indecent suggestions, but one girl stayed on. De Sade called her Justine, and the heroine of his first and most famous novel, written later—in prison— bore that name. The girl's father made a fuss when he got wind of what was going on at the château; he even fired a shot at the marquis. But Justine stayed on voluntarily for quite a while.

The de Sades took a chance on freedom and went to Paris. Madame de Montreuil found out and brandished her *lettre de cachet*. De Sade was arrested and imprisoned at Vincennes. He was thirty-seven years old, with half his life still ahead of him. He spent most of it in prison.

The verdict that resulted from the Marseilles scandal looked bad on the family record, so de Sade's mother-in-law, much as she hated him, pulled strings to have it annulled. She succeeded. De Sade no longer had a death sentence hanging over him. But Madame de Montreuil never forgave him for running off with her younger daughter. She was determined to keep him locked up until he rotted.

He escaped but was recaptured and, solely by power of the *lettre de cachet*, was tossed into prison again at Vincennes. There he was lodged in a dungeon with no heating system but plenty of mice and rats. When he asked for a cat, the prison authorities informed him pompously that animals were forbidden. He yelled, "You stupid fools, if animals are forbidden, how do I have mice and rats?"

Renée wrote him loving letters. He wrote her cruel ones, accusing her of carrying on with a lover. He raged at the prison authorities; he wrote: "You imagine you have done wonders, I wager, in reducing me to a terrible abstinence as to the sins of the flesh. Well, you are mistaken. You have heated my mind, you have made me form phantoms that I have to bring forth."

Soon he was to bring them forth on paper. At the end of February 1784, Vincennes was phased out as a prison, and its inmates, including de Sade, were transferred to the Bastille. This was a more miserably uncomfortable prison than Vincennes. He had a stove, but the fumes from it choked him. He was supposed to sweep out his cell; the idea infuriated him. But the loyal Renée visited him and brought him clothing and goodies when she was allowed. In spite of poor light, which made his eyes sore, he wrote like crazy.

In thirty days in 1785 he wrote *The 120 Days of Sodom,* a kind of anthology of human sexual behavior. (It was published years later.) He also wrote violent, hateful letters to his wife and her mother, and, when Renée came to visit him, he shouted abuse at her. He worked on a novel, *Justine,* which he later revised and enlarged. His disposition and behavior became so bad that Renée wasn't allowed to see him for ten months. He calmed down a little early in 1789, so Renée's visits became more frequent.

The unrest that became the Revolution was boiling up that spring. One day de Sade shouted through his bars for the people of Paris to assault the Bastille. They did it on July 14, but ten days earlier he had been moved to the insane asylum at Charenton—so fast that his manuscripts were left in his cell. The mob that surged in to destroy the Bastille scattered them, and for this he blamed poor Renée. She had delayed a few days in going to the prison to claim them. In those furious days anyone might well think twice before making such a journey.

One good thing the Revolution did was to abolish *lettres de cachet.* De Sade was released in the spring of 1790 by popular demand after twelve years in prison. After all, a man who hated the authorities couldn't be all bad, so he must be a friend of the people. Poor, put-upon Renée entered a convent and filed a formal petition of separation.

Another accomplishment of the Revolution was to abolish censorship, which had been rigidly enforced by the royal regime. The resulting freedom was just right for the publication of the marquis's books.

De Sade was well along in years now, shabby, poor, and enormously fat, but he lost no time in finding a girlfriend, an actress named Marie Constance Quesnet, whose husband had abandoned her. He set up house with her and hired several servants whom he really couldn't afford. The Revolution accepted him as a "citizen," which was a safer thing to be than a nobleman, and he worked at various jobs for the Revolutionary government.

In 1791 his novel *Justine* was first published. His heroine was a nice girl, one of twins. Her sister Juliette (about whom he wrote another novel) was a sinner from way back. The virtuous heroine of *Justine, or, Good Conduct Well Chastised* gets nowhere in a wicked world. Vice and evil win every round. But for Juliette, the depraved heroine of *Juliette, or, The Fortunes of Vice,* everything goes beautifully, in obscene detail with all possible perversions. During de Sade's imprisonment, when he couldn't get out to do any personal sinning, he had had plenty of time to think about what he could have been doing.

In his work for the revolutionary government, Citizen de Sade became a kind of judge. And in 1793 he saw the name Montreuil on a list of possible enemies of the people. Now he had power over that witch of a mother-in-law (and her harmless husband). De Sade could have plunged them into fatal trouble, but he saved them by simply keeping still. This seems out of character, but his father-in-law, after all, wasn't a bad sort.

De Sade's own name came to light on another list, with the comment, "His abominable sins surpass perhaps all those of the nobles of his time. . . . This evil man lives among civilized men and dares with impunity to count himself among the ranks of citizens."

Any accusation was dangerous in the climate of suspicion during the Revolution. On December 8, 1793, Citizen de Sade was arrested and condemned to the guillotine. For the second time he was under sentence of death. This time he didn't know why. Nobody needed a reason in those bloody years. He was locked up in a prison that had been a refuge for lepers but was now the last stopping place on the way to the guillotine. In two months, while he waited, more than 1200 men and women lost their heads.

The sheer confusion of the Terror saved him. He was temporarily in a makeshift hospital when his name was one of twenty-eight read off for execution. Nobody bothered to hunt for him. Just outside his hospital room was a vast, stinking pit filled with bodies, severed heads, and blood—but he wasn't in it.

On the ninth of Thermidor—July 27, 1794, by the calendar used outside France—the fanatical Revolutionary leader Robespierre was overthrown. Next day he lost his head to the guillotine. In a sudden about-face of government, the prisons were opened. Citizen de Sade was released after ten months on the equivalent of Death Row. He returned to his government job and his girlfriend.

Even revolution and the danger of death couldn't keep de Sade's mind off sex. He wrote another book, *Philosophy in the Boudoir*, a textbook of vice telling how to demoralize a young girl. Vice should, he said, be made an integral part of the habits of young people.

In 1797 *The New Justine* was published, a more elaborate version of the earlier novel. One critic wrote:

Justine could have been conceived only in the most barbarous and bloody convulsions; it is the true fruit of the Revolution. There are works that appear to have been inspired by the Graces; *Justine* must have been inspired by the Furies. It is written with blood and stinks of blood.

A literary magazine raged: "The most depraved nature, the most degraded spirit, the most bizarre and obscene imagination could not invent a work which could more outrage reason, decency, and humanity." The attack scared the author so badly that he proclaimed it wasn't his book. Two years later his new book, *The Crimes of Love,* was bitterly criticized, and police broke into the shop of his printer and seized some of his manuscripts. They also searched his house and picked up some filthy pictures.

De Sade had thus survived, though not without effort, the governments of Louis XV, Louis XVI, and the Revolution. In 1803, under that of Napoleon Bonaparte, he went to prison again. He had had the gall to address a copy of *Juliette* to Napoleon himself. Back to the asylum at Charenton he went, never to be free again. He wrote another book, but the police burned it.

A doctor at the asylum tried unsuccessfully to get him moved to some other institution, maintaining, "The unfortunates who are in daily contact with this abominable man receive continuously the impression of his profound corruption; and the mere idea of his presence in the house is sufficient to unbalance the imagination of those who do not come into actual contact with him."

His wife Renée died in a château in Normandy in July 1810. Bonaparte abdicated in 1814 and Louis XVIII took the throne. On December 2 of the same year the obese, sick old Marquis de Sade died in Charenton.

De Sade spent his life praising and justifying crime, especially cruelty. One of his heroes was Gilles de Rais; he mentioned this monster over and over in *Justine, Juliette,* and *Philosophy in the Boudoir.* His monument is not, however, the body of his writing but one word "sadism," which means delight in cruelty. He didn't invent the idea, but he became its notorious promoter.

29
Micajah
and Wiley Harpe

Ca. 1768–July 1799; ca. 1770–February
18, 1804

Does your daughter want to marry a
fellow who seems to you utterly unsuit-
able and perhaps downright villainous?
Nobody even tried to stop the girls
who married the murderous Harpes.

Micajah Harpe and his brother Wiley, known as Big Harpe and
Little Harpe, died in their early thirties, but even so they lived
too long. They ended their earthly careers violently, at the hands
of angry men, and both lost their heads. This was, however, less
nasty than what the brothers had done to their string of murder
victims. They developed a trademark: they eviscerated the body,
filled the abdominal cavity with stones, and dumped the corpse
in the nearest river.

The Harpes infested the wilds of Kentucky and Tennessee;
they roamed the Natchez Trace, the Wilderness Road, and along
the beautiful Ohio. They first came to public attention when they
held up William Lambuth on the Wilderness Road. He protested;
he was a Methodist circuit rider, and who ever heard of a
preacher who had any money?

But they took his pistol and the contents of his pockets and
searched his Bible to see whether any currency was concealed
in it. Now two frowsy women appeared out of the forest. The
highwaymen wrapped up their booty and, leading Lambuth's
horse, made off in the company of the two ragged women. They
turned and yelled, "We are the Harpes!" before they disappeared.

That was in April 1797. Before long the very thought of the
name Harpe made travelers' hair stand on end. Their female
companions were peculiar girls. The Harpes were madmen, prof-

iting little in hard cash by their murders but getting some kind
of awful satisfaction. The two women—who presently were
joined by a third—lived the harsh life of forest refugees when
they would certainly have been safer and more comfortable
somewhere else. They were sisters, Susan and Betsey Roberts.
Susan, tall, dark, rawboned, claimed to be married to Micajah,
"Big" Harpe. Betsey was blond and good-natured; the brothers
took turns with her.

After robbing the indignant Lambuth—who didn't realize how
lucky he was to be alive after that encounter—the four set up
as honest farmers near Knoxville. Little Harpe fell in love, after
his fashion, with a blond girl named Sally Rice. Her father, a
backwoods preacher, married them.

The Harpes raised hogs on their little farm. It occurred to
other farmers, however, that the Harpes sold more pork than
they produced. Some barns caught fire and burned down—
strangely, they belonged to the farmers who had expressed suspicion. A good team of horses was stolen from a man named
Edward Tiel, who didn't take the matter kindly. He gathered a
posse to visit the Harpes, but the Harpes had fled. Tiel and his
posse pursued and captured them, but shortly afterwards the
brothers simply melted into the forest. The same night, they
killed a man named Johnson in a tavern for reasons known only
to themselves, ripped the body open, and weighted the corpse
with stones. The Harpes, however, were inefficient at almost
everything but the actual business of slaughter. Even filled with
stones, Johnson's carcass floated.

The Harpes and their harpies moved on. An old peddler was
found dead, hacked with a tomahawk. A few items of women's
clothing had been taken from his pack. What seems especially
shocking is that the Harpes killed so casually for so little loot—
or is this a cynical idea, that murder isn't worthwhile unless it
pays off well? Two more victims were found; their names were
Paca and Bates. Then came the notorious case of Stephen Langford. For this killing, the Harpes were arrested and jailed.

In December 1798, Langford arrived at a tavern in the Wilderness, in so dangerous an area that nobody dared travel alone.
He stayed overnight, waiting for travel companions. In the
morning five persons straggled in; two armed men and three
women with two packhorses. They had no money, they said, so
Langford generously paid for their breakfast, and they got a

look at his wallet. The travelers departed together. A week later some cattle being driven along the trail spooked at the smell of blood, and Langford's hacked, stripped body was found in a ravine.

The Harpe group was captured with amazingly little trouble. They all gave their last names as Roberts, except Betsey, who claimed she was Betsey Walker. There was no doubt about their guilt; they had with them clothing recognized as Langford's and a notebook with his name in it. Off they went to the Danville jail to await trial.

The jailer took all sorts of precautions to make his jail escape-proof. He must have lost some sleep about arrangements for his female prisoners, because all three were pregnant and nearing their term. He lined up a midwife and even provided (at the taxpayers' expense) such delicacies as hyson tea and sugar.

Betsey's baby was a boy, born February 8. Susan had a girl March 7. Sally produced a daughter April 9. But between the second and third births the Harpe brothers escaped, in spite of all the jailer's efforts. They knocked a hole in the wall March 16 and took off for parts unknown.

In May, after the escape of the horrible Harpes, Governor James Garrard of Kentucky put a price of $300 each on their heads. Before news of this had time to spread very far, the brothers killed two more men, named Dooly and Stump. The killing of Stump was especially reprehensible, because when he saw them he took them for new settlers, and he crossed a river to make them a welcome-wagon present: a string of fish and a turkey.

Sally, Susan, and Betsey were tried May 17 for the murder of Langford. They all went free. And when next heard of the women and their babies were at Cave-in-Rock on the Ohio River (now in Hardin County, Illinois), waiting for the Harpes.

All through the forests angry men were now searching for the fearsome Harpes. John Trabue, age thirteen, was sent to borrow some flour and beans from a neighbor. His father, Colonel Daniel Trabue, was out in the yard discussing with Henry Scaggs a plan to trap Big and Little when the family dog limped in, badly wounded. The dog had been with Johnnie—but where was the boy? Two weeks later his body was found by accident, hacked to pieces. The killers had taken the flour but left the beans.

Big and Little Harpe joined their family at Cave-in-Rock. This is a big cavern, at that time much used by river pirates. A villain named Samuel Mason, alias Wilson, had been using the cave as headquarters since 1797. He enticed flatboat crews and passengers to stop there by displaying a sign: Wilson's Liquor Vault & House for Entertainment. Entertainment could mean literally anything! So people stopped for the fun. The fun often turned out to be murder and robbery.

Even the river pirates gagged at some of the Harpes' fun. A man and a girl from a flatboat were sitting on the cliff above the cave when Big and Little came up behind them and pushed them over the edge. They fell forty feet to the sandy beach. They weren't hurt, but they were scared silly.

Big and Little dreamed up something even more dramatic. They tied a naked man on a blindfolded horse and drove the animal off a 100-foot cliff. Both man and horse landed as a bloody, shattered mess. The river pirates told the Harpes to get the hell out. And they left, probably in May 1799.

They killed a boy named Coffey, who was out hunting strayed cows. They smeared a tree trunk with his brains. Two days later they murdered William Ballard. Then they caught up with James and Robert Brassel and killed James. Robert escaped, to report the Harpes' new trick: they had pretended that they, like dozens of honest men, were pursuing the awful Harpes. They killed John Tully, whose body was found under a log. John Graves and his son, thirteen, were found with their heads split open with an ax.

Then the Harpes and their women and babies took a holiday from crime and paid a visit to old man Roberts, father of Susan and Betsey, no doubt to show him the kids. Strange as Micajah and Wiley were, their women must have been even more peculiar. The women went in constant fear for their babies, because the infants' crying annoyed the fathers. In fact, the mothers, with their children, usually spent the night at some distance from camp. Surely they could have asked old Roberts' protection if they weren't happy with their pillar-to-post existence. But off they went again into the woods. The bloody-handed Harpe brothers must have had some very potent charms.

After leaving Grandpa Roberts, they killed a little girl and a Negro boy. They caught up with a fairly large party camping by the trail—two brothers named Trisword, their wives, children and black servants—and wiped out the lot, except for one man who escaped.

The Harpes had left their women behind somewhere when, on July 20, decently dressed and posing as Methodist preachers, the fearsome pair stopped at the cabin of James Tompkins, who invited them to stay for noon dinner. Big Harpe even asked the blessing, as a man of the cloth naturally would. Tompkins remarked that, for a couple of preachers, they were heavily armed. The Harpes explained solemnly that it was safer that way, because the Harpes might be around. Their host fretted a little because he was almost out of gunpowder. Whereupon Big Harpe pulled out his powder horn and gave Tompkins a supply so he could load his rifle.

The two murderous "ministers" rode on to the cabin of Moses Stegall, whom they knew. Moses was away, but his wife let them in. Major William Love, a surveyor, was there, too. During the night the Harpes killed Love because he snored! Then they took after Mrs. Stegall and the baby and set the house on fire.

Right after they left the Stegall place, the Harpes had the gall to accuse two men they met, Hudgens and Gilmore, of committing their own crimes at the Stegalls'. After some argument, the two innocent travelers agreed to appear before the nearest representative of the law and prove they hadn't done it. On the way, Big Harpe shot Gilmore dead and Little Harpe beat the brains out of Hudgens. (How anybody knew about the Harpes' accusation and the other men's sense of justice is open to question, because neither Hudgens nor Gilmore survived. But everybody for miles and miles told wild tales about the Harpes, some of them true. This one, true or not, fits their *modus operandi*.)

Stegall came home that night to find his baby dead, his wife dying, and his house on fire. In a cold rage, he recruited a posse from the neighbors who had seen the flames, and after long hard pursuit they caught up with the Harpes and their families. The two men leaped on their horses and galloped off while the three women stood around looking stupid. The man in the lead of the posse fired but his gun jammed. The next shot struck Big Harpe in the spine. It was fired with the powder that Harpe himself had provided to Tompkins two days earlier.

Little Harpe galloped off into the forest. Big Harpe, although paralyzed from his wound, rode a little farther before his pursuers yanked him down from his saddle. The furious Stegall kicked him and wanted to kill him then and there but his companions preferred to have Harpe tried for murder if he lasted long enough. He didn't. He took a long time dying, and he did some talking. He was not at all contrite about the murders he and his brother committed. In fact, he felt God had told him to scourge humanity. There was one killing he did regret, however, and it was one that his captors knew nothing about. He told of losing his temper because Sally's baby cried. He had grabbed the baby by the feet, swung it, and knocked out its brains against a tree. A baby killed for crying, a stranger killed for snoring—Big Harpe was obviously a man easily disturbed by noise.

Stegall, tired of waiting around for Big Harpe to cash in his chips, shot him in the side as he lay on the ground and then cut his head off. One of the women was required to carry the bloody head as they were herded along. Grasping it by the hair, she kept grumbling, "Damn the head!" At Robertson's Lick, Stegall wedged the head in the fork of a tree for a permanent exhibit. The place is still called Harpe's Head.

The three women were questioned September 4, 1799, as parties to the murders of William Love and Mary Stegall and her infant child James. Then Susan, Betsey, and Sally—all listed in the official records as "spinsters"—were jailed for trial September 28. They were found not guilty. Apparently they hadn't been at the Stegall place at all.

Little Harpe not only escaped, he changed his name and disappeared as far as pursuit was concerned. The Carolina *Gazette*, published in Charleston, South Carolina, ran this interesting news item October 24, 1799—a couple of months after the demise of Big Harpe, but frontiersmen didn't expect to read last night's news this morning:

> Lexington [Kentucky]
> September 10
> The two murderers by the name of Harpe, who killed Mr. Langford laft winter in the wildernefs, and were arrefted and broke the Danville gaol, killed a family on Pond River, by the name of Staple, on the 22d day of Auguft, and burnt the houfe; a party of men purfued and overtook them and their women; the Harpes parted. Micajah Harpe took two of the women off with him; the men purfued him, and in riding about 10 or 12 miles, caught him, having previ-

oufly fhot him. He confeffed the killing of Mr. Stump on Big Barren; he alfo confeffed of their killing 17 or 18 befides; they killed two men near Robertfon's Lick, the day before they burnt Staple's houfe. They had with them eight horfes and a confiderable quantity of plunder, feven pair of faddle bags, &c. They cut off his head. The women were taken to the Red banks. The above took place on Pond River in the county of Muhlenberg.

Little Harpe lasted almost five years longer than his brother. During this time Little Harpe joined the murderous gang of portly, pompous Samuel Mason, who was a grandfather before he made his mark as an outlaw leader on the Natchez Trace and the Mississippi River. Prospering, as the wicked sometimes do, Mason took time out for a visit to Natchez, pretending to be a planter from upriver. He loafed around pleasantly—until he was recognized. With his son he was thrown into jail. They were sentenced to thirty-nine lashes and twelve hours in the pillory—a light punishment for the crimes they had committed—and both of them squalled that they were innocent.

After that they disappeared for a while. A traveler's mutilated body was found with a gloating sign: Done by Mason of the Woods. Mason's organization prospered. The governor of Mississippi Territory exchanged diplomatic notes about him with the Spanish governor general of the Province of Louisiana, which was having trouble with thugs from the United States. Nothing much came of this, but the word got around that one Wiley Harpe was a member of Mason's gang. Little Harpe hadn't been missed by decent people.

At some time or other, Little Harpe married again. The unlucky bride was a Tennessee girl. A few days after they left on their honeymoon, Wiley returned in sorrow to her home and told a melancholy tale: her horse had run away and thrown her. She died, so he buried her. But later when people got suspicious, someone dug up her grave and found she had been beaten to death and mutilated.

Mason and his gang, including Little Harpe, continued to harass the Mississippi River Road until January 1803. Then Mason, his family, and a man who called himself John Taylor were captured near New Madrid, Missouri. At their trial by the Spanish government Mason kept hollering "Persecution!" as was his custom. A little matter of $7000 that he had with him he explained away: he had found it hanging on a bush in the woods. Money didn't grow on bushes then any more than it does now, although travelers occasionally did hide their money in trees when they camped for the night. But who in the world would trudge off the next morning and forget that much of it? Nobody, that's who.

John Taylor testified. He confessed that his real name was Setton—which it wasn't. He told a woeful tale about how he had constantly tried to get away from the villainous Mason, who wouldn't let him go. He accused Mason of dozens of crimes.

Now it was Mason's turn to squeal. Setton, not he, had done all those dreadful things, he insisted, and that was why he had kept Setton a captive, just waiting to turn him in. Setton and the Masons were sent down to New Orleans, where their case was held up because of international complications; their crimes had been committed on U.S. soil, so the Spanish court shipped them back upriver toward Natchez. On the way, the sloop that carried them was wrecked, and they got away on March 26.

Mason went back to highway robbery, this time with a price on his head: $1000 dead or alive. Naturally, everybody searched everywhere for the valuable Mason. In the fall, John Setton, who had called himself John Taylor, and a man named May turned up in Natchez with a great big lump of dried clay. Before a magistrate they broke open the clay ball and proved they had hit the jackpot. There was Mason's head: where was the $1000 reward? (Clay is the perfect medium for carrying somebody's head a long distance without its stinking.)

May and Setton didn't collect their money. An angry man strode in, reporting that he had just recognized, among the horses outside, two stolen from him some time back. Now the magistrate had two matters to straighten out, and a third one was added—another stranger gave Setton a hard look and proclaimed, "Why, that man's Wiley Harpe!"

He was thoroughly identified. A boatman announced that Wiley Harpe had two toes grown together and a mole on his neck. Sure enough, Setton did. Another man recognized him and said, "If you are Harpe, you have a scar under your left nipple where I cut you in a difficulty we had in Knoxville." And when he tore open Setton's shirt there was the scar.

James May and Little Harpe were tried separately—on a charge of robbery, not murder—at Greenville, some twenty miles from Natchez, and sentenced to hang on February 8, 1804. Wiley Harpe kept his lip sullenly buttoned, but May complained quite bitterly. He maintained that he wasn't guilty of any crime, and anyway he had relieved society of the infamous Samuel Mason. Shouldn't he get credit for that? In this world he didn't.

After the hangings, both men's heads were cut off and displayed on poles for public edification. The bodies were buried in a new graveyard near the Greenville jail, where there had already been four or five interments. Various relatives of the respectable departed protested indignantly at the idea of inflicting such awful neighbors on good families. They did more than protest. They couldn't keep May and Harpe out, but they could, and did, dig up their own folks and move them to an even newer burial ground.

What became of the Harpes' harpies? Sally's father, a reputable man (although he certainly lacked judgment when he married her to Little Harpe) attended her trial and took her home to Knoxville. She married again. Betsey married too, and lived with her new husband and her little boy on a plantation where her husband was employed. Susan and her baby daughter lived on the same plantation, and Susan made a living by weaving. Her daughter, called Lovey, grew up pretty but with a bad temper, and both mother and child developed reputations so bad that they were finally driven away.

30
Ali Pasha

Ca. 1744–1822

You've never had to deal with so
dangerous and persistent a promiser as
Ali Pasha, even when he carried out his
mother's wishes.

I talk not of mercy, I talk not of fear,
He neither must know who would serve the Vizier;
Since the days of our Prophet the Crescent ne'er saw
A chief ever glorious like Ali Pashaw.
(Lord Byron, *Childe Harold*)

Nobody today knows much about Ali Pasha. But in his own day he was quite a character. Admiral Lord Nelson thought highly of him, and Byron wrote about him. Victor Hugo described him as the only man alive in the 1820s whom he could compare to Napoleon. Ali was to the emperor, he wrote, as the tiger is to the lion. Had any of these esteemed gentlemen taken the trouble to examine Ali's record, they might not have been so laudatory. Quite simply, Ali was a four-star monster.

He lived and ruled in what is now Albania and northern Greece, what then was part of the Ottoman empire. The Sublime Porte (as the Turkish government was often called) was Ali's boss. It ruled, not very well, over the Balkan countries we now call Rumania, Bulgaria, Yugoslavia (except for the Adriatic coast), Albania, and Greece. Maybe "ruled" is too strong a word. The Sublime Porte was happy as long as everybody paid tribute and recognized the sultan as lord paramount.

It was an extremely confused area. Many small villages (some Christian and some Moslem) virtually ruled themselves. Some were part of a larger district headed by a pasha and owed allegiance to him. These pashas often fought among themselves, each trying to take over somebody else's towns. The result was anarchy. Since Ali Pasha was a past master at murder, rape, looting, fighting, and betrayal, he became a sort of super-pasha ruling a lot of districts.

At the time of Ali's birth, his father, Veli, was a lesser pasha, a run-of-the-mill tyrant. He already had a couple of kids by an earlier wife by the time he married Khamco, Ali's mother; and after siring Ali's sister, Shainitza, he died and was soon forgotten. Khamco poisoned her two stepchildren, and Ali became Veli's sole heir.

It's safe to say that nobody—other than Ali and Shainitza— ever had a mother quite like Khamco. A greedy, mean-minded bitch, Khamco got into her worst trouble by demanding that the people of one of her Christian towns, Khormovo, pay more tribute. No dice, said the Khormovans. Khamco then got the idea that a little Christian village (near Khormovo and belonging to the Moslem town of Gardiki) was just what she wanted. She set out to conquer it and thus enraged the Gardikiots. They joined with the Khormovans and captured Khamco.

Poor Khamco! For weeks she was locked up during the day and brought out each night to be raped by men from both towns. Khamco didn't relax and enjoy it. Eventually a kindly Greek ransomed her for 23,000 piastres. The Khormovans and Gardikiots never made a worse deal in their lives. They should have killed her.

Khamco never forgot. Over and over again, she insisted to Ali and Shainitza that it was their duty to kill her enemies. Everyday she drummed into her kids' minds what the Khormovans, Gardikiots, and others had done to her.

Afflicted with cancer of the womb, Khamco was soon to die. She called for Ali, who was off in his pashalic, and summoned Shainitza to read her will, most of which was a tirade against the Khormovans and Gardikiots. Khamco demanded that her children avenge her and called down on their heads a dreadful curse if they didn't. She drew up a list of villages she wanted burned and people she wanted killed. She was dead when Ali arrived. But he and Shainitza clasped hands over their mother's body and swore to avenge the wrongs done her. It was a vow neither forgot.

At the time of his mother's death, Ali was in his late thirties.

He had already distinguished himself as a first-rate bastard. As a boy, he had shown signs of being irrational. Virtually ungovernable, he preferred to be out in the woods by himself. Khamco had to force him to learn to read and write. He preferred stealing goats, sheep, and anything else at hand from nearby villages. His father had been this kind of thief, and Ali was a model son.

Almost to the end of his life, Ali had luck on his side. He was cunning, vicious, courageous, and persistent. He could ride and shoot better than most of his "subjects." And he was a handsome dog, not very tall, slim and engaging. His eyes were blue and he had fair hair. A heavy beard hid much of his face, but he managed to give a smiling, contented, and honest appearance. It was a lamb's smile on a lion's face.

Ali was a smooth talker. He could persuade his enemies to trust him, his wife of the moment that he loved only her, the Turks that he hated Greeks, and Greeks that he hated Turks. It was no wonder that he fooled Lord Byron. He was always plausible.

The future pasha of Jannina had a limited education. Although he knew every blood feud and political relationship in his own area, he had only the haziest view of European politics. Once he thought he would have his own navy and talked about having a ship-of-the-line built in Paris. At the time, he was mad at the Austrians and wished the French fleet good sailing to Vienna.

Most of the time, Ali's health was good, although once a year—at the approach of the rainy season—he developed a fever (probably malaria) that his subjects called "the Lion's fever." As a patient he was terrible. He was scared of dying and usually worked out his frustration by killing more "enemies" than usual. It's no wonder that his people worriedly asked about pasha's health. Killing people acted like a tonic on Ali, and each year he got well on this prescription.

All his life, Ali was a man of extremes. His memory was incredible, and he could remember faces and facts for years. A slight never skipped his mind, so his vengeance was terrible. When he lost his temper—which was every time anybody crossed him—he was a monster without restraint. He was greedy to excess, and, although he worked up an income of perhaps a million dollars a year, he always wanted more.

One of Ali's more kindly biographers noted with regret that the pasha was "selfish and cruel on a gigantic scale, a thief and a liar, jealous, vindictive, miserly, and mad with ambition." These defects, he added, could "to some extent" be offset by his good qualities.

But Ali's good qualities were few and far between. It's true that he was an able leader, a fine conversationalist, and a firm administrator. And he had no patience with religious bigotry. With Moslems, he was always a Moslem, and with Christians always a Christian, and he slaughtered both groups with dispassionate equality. Nor was he a racist. He used both Turkish and Greek spies in Constantinople to keep one step ahead of the sultan.

In sex as in cruelty, Ali lived to excess. His harem—when he traveled, it was called his "hen-coop on wheels"—was always well stocked with beautiful girls brutally torn from their fathers, lovers, and husbands. Ali rarely paid any attention to the niceties of courtship. When he saw a woman he wanted, his soldiers carted her off to the palace, and that was that. If her family objected, he had their house burned down and its residents killed. On the other hand, Ali loved handsome boys, and had quite a stable of these Ganymedes.

But it was the violent spilling of blood—always with good reason, according to Ali—that distinguishes the pasha as superbastard. He was guilty at least weekly, sometimes daily, of common, garden variety crimes like rape, extortion, arson, theft, and torture. But murder was his real forte—either singly or en masse.

No one knows who was Ali's first victim. It was probably a shepherd whose sheep Ali was stealing. This killing was a simple and unemotional act of removing someone who got in the way. Ali first made the big time by disposing of a hated brother-in-law.

Ali's sister, Shainitza, married a fellow also named Ali who ruled a nearby district of Delvino. Our Ali couldn't abide Shainitza's Ali. For one thing, he wanted to annex the other Ali's towns, and so the other Ali had to go. He asked his sister to poison her husband, the father of her two children. Shainitza refused but was too loyal to her brother to tell her husband of Ali's proposal.

Our Ali said okay and promised to forget it. He didn't. He

told the other Ali's sixteen-year-old brother, a boy named Suleiman, that he could marry the beautiful Shainitza if he would kill Ali.

Everything worked fine. Suleiman shot his brother dead. Our Ali was with him. Hearing the shot, Shainitza rushed in only to be told to shut up or she would be killed too. Ali ordered Suleiman to wrap Shainitza in his cloak—a ceremony equivalent of marriage—which Suleiman was only too happy to do. He consummated the marriage on the spot, while his dead brother's body slowly cooled a few feet away. Our Ali sent out word that the other Ali had died of apoplexy, but nobody believed him.

Ali then spent several years with no spectacular atrocities to his credit. In 1787, his Turkish masters fought a war with Austria and Russia, and Ali joined the army. He did pretty well and was soon a general. The sultan made him pasha of Jannina (in northern Greece).

The war over, Ali returned home and devoted himself to family affairs. He had not forgotten his mother's curse, and he decided that the time was ripe to take care of the people of Khormovo. Ali began by writing soft letters to the Khormovans. The latter, who had heard of some of Ali's misdeeds, responded in kind. It wouldn't be wise, they thought, to antagonize the pasha. Ali then proposed a visit to Khormovo to show his good faith. He promised to bring only a few soldiers with him to avoid unnecessary expense on the Khormovans. That was fine, said the Khormovans.

Ali arrived with 1200 men. The Khormovans were a bit taken aback, but since Ali was so pleasant they said nothing about it. Ali, after quartering his 1200 men in Khormovan homes, began discussing a treaty of friendship. After a few days of this, the pasha apologized to his hosts for being such a burden. He would, he said, retire to a nearby monastery where the treaty could be signed in the monastery church. True to his word, Ali marched out of Khormovo and summoned about a hundred of the city's leading citizens to join him for the signing of the treaty of perpetual friendship.

It was the custom for people entering church to leave their guns and swords outside. As soon as the disarmed Khormovans entered the church, Ali ordered their arms seized. Ali's soldiers then captured the Khormovan leaders and sent them off to Ali's capital in Tebelini, where they were murdered. Other soldiers sacked Khormovo, killing all the men they could get their hands on and selling the women and children into slavery. Ali ordered that Khormovo be razed to the ground.

One Khormovan, a rascal by the name of Chaoush Prifti, had been particularly nasty to Ali's mother. As it happened, Ali had a foster-brother, a mulatto named Yusuf Arab, who was known as the "Blood Drinker." He gave Chaoush to Yusuf to put an end to. Yusuf loved it. He ran a spit through Chaoush's body and roasted him alive over a slow fire.

Having disposed of the Khormovans, Ali turned to other affairs. His family life was never dull. His sister, Shainitza, wanted to marry her daughter to a young lad called Murad Bey. Murad was decent enough, but Ali hated him on first sight. Murad, it seems, was a friend of a certain Ibrahim whom Ali also hated. It was an outrage, Ali argued, that Shainitza would marry his niece to a friend of his enemy.

But Shainitza was deaf to such complaints. Preparations for the marriage of her daughter to Murad Bey went ahead. Ali was fit to be tied. He devised a beautiful plan. First, he had it noised about that someone was trying to kill him. Consequently he couldn't attend the wedding. He retired to a small house on a nearby lake. The upper room, where Ali slept, could be reached only by a ladder through a trapdoor. Anybody who wanted to see the pasha had to climb up unarmed.

In due time Shainitza's daughter married Murad Bey. A few days later, Ali sent for his new nephew-in-law. Murad left his gun and dagger below and climbed the ladder. It was awfully dark. Ali's men downstairs heard a shot. A bullet hit Murad's arm. He fell to the floor, and Ali jumped him. Murad fought well but was no match for Ali, who in the course of the struggle grabbed a glowing log from the fireplace and jabbed it repeatedly in Murad's face. Ali had obviously never heard of the Marquess of Queensberry's rules.

The pasha finally dispatched Murad with several knife thrusts. After smearing the boy's blood all over him, he cried for help. He told his would-be rescuers that he had killed his would-be assassin. After ordering a religious service to celebrate his "escape," Ali sent his soldiers to confiscate his late nephew's estates.

Ali desperately wanted a nearby Christian town called Suli. He wanted it, by Allah, and in 1790 he attacked it for the first time. No luck. The Suliots were too much for him, and they had help from neighboring towns like Khimara. He tried again in

1792 and still no luck. By this time, Ali was furious. He decided that if he couldn't get Suli he would try for Khimara, another town.

On Easter night the pasha sent 2000 men under the command of the Blood Drinker, Yusuf Arab, his foster brother. Many Khimarans were in church celebrating the Resurrection. As the priest intoned "Christ is risen," Yusuf and his men stormed into church. When they left, they had massacred the entire congregation. The blood-letting spread to the entire town, where the Blood Drinker murdered over 6000 Khimarans. Those left alive converted to Mohammedanism to save their lives. For this act of missionary piety, Ali received the title "Arslan" (Lion) from his master the sultan.

From time to time, Ali sent expeditions against Suli. Still no luck. And every now and then Ali got himself obliquely involved in the greater affairs of Napoleonic Europe. After one of his defeats of Austria, Napoleon annexed the Adriatic coast of what is now Yugoslavia and called it the Illyrian Provinces. In the process, the French occupied the town of Preveza, which Ali claimed for himself.

Ali announced to all and sundry that he meant to take Preveza and kill everybody in it. General Lascalcette, who commanded the French garrison, had 400 French and about 300 Prevezans to withstand Ali's 6000 to 7000 men. The issue was never in doubt, and Ali's son, Mukhtar, carried the day. His men carried off the women and children as slaves and massacred most of the Prevezans. That was October 12, 1798.

About 200 Frenchmen and 160 Prevezan soldiers surrendered. A huge Negro executioner, one of Ali's men, began the cutting, but his wrists swelled from all the work, and he had to stop. He said he was tired and nauseated from the smell of blood. The next morning, Ali's men had fun building a pyramid of the heads of decapitated prisoners.

Some 155 French prisoners were left. Ali stopped the executions and ordered the Frenchmen to flay the heads of their dead comrades, salt the skins, and stow them in sacks. He then had them load the sacks of human skins on their shoulders and march through the winter snows to Jannina. Many died of exertion, cold, and hunger. Those who reached Ali's capital were locked up in miserable conditions.

The Preveza affair made Ali a celebrity in Europe. Admiral

Nelson, who was sailing in the vicinity and who was spending most of his time trying to beat the French, sent one of his men to compliment "the hero"—Ali, of course. The sultan made Ali a Pasha of Three Tails—a kind of super-pasha. Ali was front-page news from London to Vienna.

Ali enjoyed his new-found fame. But he hadn't forgotten the Suliots. He launched a final attack, to win this time. His son, Veli, who commanded his troops at Suli, starved the city into submission. He signed a solemn treaty with the remaining Suliots, promising them safe passage to Parga, in nearby Albania. Veli sent 4000 troops to destroy the traveling refugees, but the Suliots were no pushover. They defended themselves well and reached Parga and safety.

Other groups of Suliots fared less well. Ali's troops killed many of them. It had taken him fifteen years, but he had finally won. To the end of his days, he regretted that so many Suliots escaped his vengeance.

From time to time, the pasha (now of the Three Tails) had trouble with his Greek subjects. Revolution was abroad in the land, and many Greeks dreamed of ultimate independence. They realized, however, that they would have to get rid of Ali first. Evthymio Vlachavas was such a Greek. He organized a small army and headed for Jannina. A traitor gave away his plans, and he was captured alive by Ali's forces under Mukhtar, who sent Ali the heads of sixty-eight of Vlachavas' friends and Vlachavas bound alive.

Ali had a field day. He ordered a public execution. He had Vlachavas tied to a stake and horribly tortured for hours. It was a sickening performance, but Vlachavas at last died. His torturers cut the body into pieces, and Ali had these ghastly remains positioned about Jannina for the edification of potential traitors.

The pasha also got his hands on Dimitrios, a Christian monk who had been one of Vlachavas' good friends. Ali always felt that Vlachavas had died too quickly, that the job had been bungled. It was going to be different with Dimitrios, and Ali first ordered that sharp bits of wood be driven under Dimitrios' fingernails and a strand of knucklebones be drawn tightly around his head. He then had Dimitrios hung upside down over a slow fire and roasted for a few hours. Since Dimitrios was still alive, to Ali's delight, the pasha had the victim cut down, laid on the ground, and covered with a large board. Various of Ali's guards then

jumped on the board for several hours to break as many of
Dimitrios' bones as possible. The pasha was pleased. Dimitrios
still lived, so Ali had him cemented in a container with only his
head in sight. Dimitrios was a tough old bird. He lived for ten
more days.

By now it was 1812. While most of Europe stood transfixed by
Napoleon's invasion of Russia, Ali was thinking of other matters.
The time was at hand, he said, to wreak vengeance on Gardiki,
that dreadful town whose citizens had so mistreated his mother.
His mother's curses were still fresh in his mind, and he determined to exact revenge for what the Gardikiots had done to the
sainted lady.

Ali gathered together a small army and laid siege to Gardiki.
It was a Mohammedan town, and many people (including the
sultan) thought Ali should stick to killing Christians. But Ali
couldn't care less whether the Gardikiots served Allah or God.
They had done wrong to his mother, and, by God or by Allah,
they would pay for it.

Ali's siege lasted for a couple of months, and finally Gardiki
asked for terms of surrender. It was agreed that at least sixty
leading Gardikiots would leave for Jannina to place themselves
as hostages in Ali's hands. Ali promised them life and property,
and the poor fools believed him. And so Gardiki surrendered.

Never a man to be bothered with promises, Ali summoned most
of the male Gardikiots before him. He ordered his troops to fire.
But a strange thing occurred. His Mohammedan soldiers refused
to shoot unless the Gardikiots were given arms. Not about to
grant so stupid a demand, Ali ordered his Greek Christian soldiers to begin the massacre. They were only too happy to be
ordered by a Mohammedan pasha to kill Mohammedan civilians.

Actually, it was Ali in a characteristic act of bravura who
fired the first shot. Thereafter, his Greeks rounded up the Gardikiots in groups of fifteen, drove them outside the city to Ali's
feet and butchered them. Some Gardikiots fled to the local pub.
Ali's men set it on fire and burned them alive. In less than two
hours, Ali's men slaughtered over 700 Gardikiots. Their bodies
were left to rot on the ground.

Later that same day, Ali's troops turned their attention to
their victims' wives, daughters, and mothers. They were raped
for two straight days. At last, wearying of this sport, Ali had

about a thousand of them hauled off to a nearby town where his sister, Shainitza, wanted her share of the fun.

Ali's sister acted like a madwoman. She was hard to take in her calmer moods but now she lost all restraint. She first had her victim's hair cut off (that was a bad thing to do in those days) and while stomping on it yelled that she was going to use it to stuff her beds. After carrying on for some time in this manner, Shainitza ordered that the dresses of all the Gardikiot women be cut off at the waist. She then commanded that, so dressed or undressed, they be driven out of town. To top it all, some nitwit told her that one of her own ladies-in-waiting had slept with a Gardikiot man. Shainitza took a knife and ripped open her belly.

Some Gardikiots had served in Ali's army for a long time, one for seventeen years. Ali ordered them all slain and over their corpses announced: "At last my mother is avenged! Mother, here's the blood I promised you!" On a wall in Gardiki he put up a sign saying: "Thus perish all the enemies of the house of Ali." Rotting bodies of Gardikiots pointed up the moral.

From Gardiki, Ali went to Tebelini, where his mother lay buried and there had the throats of twelve Gardikiots sliced on his mother's grave. Dear old Khamco! How she would have loved this touching act of filial devotion.

The last act of Gardiki's agony was played out in Jannina. Ali held sixty-four Gardikiot prisoners there and ordered his son, Mukhtar, to dispose of them in some interesting way. Mukhtar was happy to oblige. It was another Easter Sunday, in 1812. Mukhtar chose Demir Dost as the first victim. His arms and legs were pulled apart, various bones were broken, and finally his head was crushed in a spiked iron helmet. On the first day of the slaughter, Mukhtar killed only seventeen. It was slow going, and the executioners kept bellyaching how tired they were.

In ensuing days, two Gardikiots (a father and twelve-year-old son) were hanged and twenty-two strangled. Mukhtar murdered all sixty-four Gardikiots and had their bodies thrown into a well—a distressing example of pollution.

Ali was happy. He had avenged his mother and built his own small empire. He was lord and master of the Pashalic of Jannina and ruled thousands of people as he chose. The ancient Greeks would have enjoyed the next act. Hubris, or overweening pride, proved Ali's undoing. It was okay for him to go around killing

Christian Greeks and Frenchmen, but the sultan in Constantinople could only regard with disfavor Ali's growing power.

So the sultan outlawed the pasha of Jannina. Ali became a rebel with a price on his head. Anybody who killed the pasha of Jannina, said the sultan, would be a patriot and well rewarded.

It was war to the death, but Ali was no pushover. While fighting the Turks from time to time, Ali reigned serenely in Jannina. His temper was certainly exasperated now and then, and he indulged in minor atrocities. One of his Albanian subjects annoyed him, and Ali had him thrown into a leopard's cage. To the Pasha's annoyance, the leopard stupidly went over and licked the Albanian's face! Ali was outraged. He had the Albanian dragged out and cut up into small chunks. These were fed to the leopard—who cooperated this time.

But by 1820 things began to go wrong for Ali. The Turks captured several of his sons, among them Mukhtar and Veli, and displayed their heads in Constantinople. Ali's turn came next. After severe fighting, the Turks invaded Jannina and slew Ali. It was 1822. The Turks carried the head of the Pasha of the Three Tails to the sultan, who put it on public display. Everybody who was anybody went to see it, and one enterprising speculator tried to buy the head to show in London. He was outbid, however, by one of Ali's friends who got the head and had it decently buried.

Ali died full of years and with a certain feeling of triumph. He knew how people hated him, and he reveled in it. Shortly before his death, he boasted to the Ottoman empire at large that he had had at least 30,000 people slaughtered.

31
Shaka

1787 (?)–1828

*This African empire builder knew how
to get even with those who had mistreated him in childhood.*

Shaka began with two strikes against him but grew to such power and majesty that his innumerable subjects called him by the most splendid title they could imagine: he was the Great Elephant. Nothing could stand in his way.

Shaka was a bastard in both senses of that word. First, he was the result of an accident. The Zulus—a small, unimportant Bantu tribe in Central Africa until he built them into a great nation—had some peculiar customs. When a warrior killed a man, he had to "wipe his ax" as soon as possible. That is, on the way home from a battle he could ask any maiden outside his own tribe for sexual congress. This was known as "the pleasure of the road." But the union had to be incomplete, and every girl's mother examined her every month to make sure she was still technically a virgin.

A young chief, Senzangakona, asked a girl named Nandi, and she was agreeable. But they lost control of the situation. Her pregnancy was doubly scandalous; she wasn't married to Senzangakona and according to the rules she couldn't be, because they belonged to the same tribe. At first her family maintained that she wasn't pregnant at all. They blamed her condition on a beetle called u-Shaka, which was held responsible for menstrual disorders. When the disorder turned out to be a male infant, he was named Shaka in derision.

Senzangakona sheepishly took Nandi as his third wife, but she was disgraced. Little Shaka had a lot to live down. With everybody downright nasty to him and to his mother, it is hardly surprising he turned out mean and bitter—and tremendously ambitious. He hated everybody but his mother and a few aunts who consoled him. When he came to power, he rewarded them richly with herds of cattle and made them reigning queens. He also rewarded, according to his lights, a lot of people who had made his boyhood miserable.

The scorned little beetle with his load of hatred grew to be an imposing young man, a muscular six foot three, physically powerful, mentally brilliant, and unbelievably cruel in a society that took cruelty pretty much for granted. He was no longer scorned. Success in battles moved him up the social scale and in army rank. The Zulus' chief weapon was a light throwing spear, the assegai. After a warrior threw all his spears—without doing much damage, because the opposing forces fended them off with shields—he had nothing left but a club.

Shaka saw no sense in this system. He tried using his assegai for stabbing at close quarters, but the shaft usually broke. So he made the shaft shorter and thicker and the blade broader and heavier. Thus he developed a formidable weapon for hand-to-hand combat. The Zulus knew how to smelt iron ore and work metal, so all the blacksmiths went to work with a will (by order of the chief) and the new slashing, stabbing assegai was soon issued to the entire army. Shaka also improved their hide-covered shields and the use thereof.

Naturally he moved right up in the tribal ladder until he became chief. He had an excellent memory, and forgiveness was not in him. Neither was mercy. One of his first undertakings after he got his big promotion was to take revenge on the kraal, or village, where he and his mother had been objects of derision during his early childhood.

He had all the men paraded before him, and he picked out those who had tormented him years before. A few others he rewarded because they could claim they had done some kindness to his mother, Nandi. He told them to stick around and watch while he took care of the rest.

Those he hated were impaled on the sharp stakes of their fences. At the end of the day, some still survived in agony. Shaka finally put them out of their torment by setting fire to the entire kraal. The poor wretches, twisting in the flames, were glad to go.

Shaka didn't fool around when he undertook to whip his little army into shape. He ordained that his 500 soldiers should no longer wear sandals because *he* didn't. He said shod feet slowed up a fighting man. His idea of going barefoot didn't catch on, so he had to show the army who was boss. He had several baskets of devil thorns brought in and scattered on the parade ground. These big three-pronged thorns always have one prong pointing up, no matter how they fall. He ordered his men to harden their feet by stamping these vicious things into the ground.

Shaka led the stamping. His feet were already hard. Men who flinched or seemed to lack enthusiasm for this bloody dance died then and there under the clubs of a squad of enforcers who accompanied Shaka everywhere to make sure everybody understood his wishes. After seeing what happened to half a dozen laggards, the rest of the army stamped like crazy until there wasn't a devil thorn in sight. There was no more opposition to the idea of going barefoot.

Shaka reorganized the army and the lives of his people in ways that are almost beyond belief. He even demoted about half his warriors in social status. These were the men with some military experience—usually in battles they had lost—who wore an identifying head ring to show that they were mature and ready to take a wife as soon as they could scrape together enough cattle to give her folks. Zulu men could not marry young—they had to work a long time to pay for those cattle.

Shaka deprived them of their head rings, thus relegating them to the status of boys again, and he refused to let any of them get married. This change in the normal scheme of things left a lot of nubile girls running around loose, so Shaka organized them into regiments, too. They didn't take part in battles but performed march formations on special occasions, carrying miniature shields and singing.

The bachelor troops hadn't opted for celibacy; it was forced upon them. When sexual tension became too severe, Shaka turned loose some of his ladies' drill team to mingle with the men—which they did with whoops and hollers of joy, from bass to soprano.

When soldiers grew too old to be entirely effective in battle, Shaka let them put on head rings, get married, and settle down to a delayed normal home life, but they were still on call as ready reserves for the army.

Shaka himself never married, although through the years he

built up a private harem of twelve hundred women. He was careful to call them his sisters, never his wives. None of these young, available, eager, demanding "sisters" became pregnant by their king and master. When some of them managed it without him (there was two-way traffic over the kraal fence), he casually had them killed. With his own hands he smashed the lives out of several babies. He knew very well they weren't his.

His mother longed for grandchildren and yammered about it constantly. His excuse was that he didn't want to have children because royal sons had been known to depose their royal fathers. He did indulge in the "pleasure of the road," but history strongly suspects that the reason he wouldn't father children was that he wasn't able to.

With his sharply honed army, Shaka smashed more than a thousand clans among his neighbors. He began with 500 untrained men, accustomed to fighting as an unruly mob, in a tiny kingdom surrounded by stronger peoples. His military genius brought more than 100,000 square miles of territory under his direct and terrible rule. His Zulus conquered and absorbed (or obliterated) so many other groups that all the survivors were called Zulus.

Knowledge of Shaka's grim deeds was not confined to the black people he held in total subjugation. A few bold adventurers from Europe, coming in by way of Fort Natal (now Durban, South Africa), visited him, traded with him, were horrified by what they saw, but escaped alive and whole. One such visitor, Nathaniel Isaacs, was present when the Great Elephant casually ordered 170 young men and girls slaughtered on suspicion of adultery.

Another adventurer, Henry Francis Fynn, was with him in October 1827 on an elephant hunt when word reached Shaka, via a panting runner, that his revered mother was sick. She was eighty miles away, but her anxious son reached her death bed on foot in less than twenty-four hours. He was with her when she breathed her last.

The mourning, according to Fynn, was ghastly. When Shaka began to yell, fifteen thousand people came running, came screaming; by noon of the next day there were four times as many, milling around, shrieking, not daring to stop even long enough to take a drink of water. To relieve his feelings a little, Shaka had several men killed without ceremony. The rest of the hysterical mob set about killing anybody they could lay hands on. Fynn estimated that seven thousand of Shaka's own people were slaughtered that day in the horrible mourning for Nandi. When the king grieved, everybody grieved.

Nandi was buried in state with ten girls to keep her company. Shaka had their arms and legs broken before they were buried alive in her grave.

Then he announced the official mourning rites. No crops could be planted for a year. No milk could be used, although milk curds were the staple diet. After the food supplies on hand were consumed, everybody could just starve. Every woman who became pregnant during the mourning year would be killed along with her husband. Fortunately for the Zulus, Shaka lost interest in these rigorous rites after a few months and decided to let the matter drop.

He had become chief in 1816. When Nandi died, eleven years later, he was the ruthless despot of a vast empire. There were no other chiefs to worry about any more. They were his subjects or they were dead. As he went about his business of governing and judging, he was surrounded by alert, obedient executioners. If he flicked a hand, they bashed in a skull or expertly twisted a neck. The victim might be guilty of nothing more than sneezing when the Great Elephant didn't want to hear a sneeze, or of making him laugh when he wasn't feeling funny. His people were cruel in their long-established customs, but Shaka went beyond cruelty. Human beings, to him, were bugs to be eradicated at will.

He began to look around for new amusements. He rounded up three hundred women and asked each of them if she owned a cat. Whether she did or not, he had her killed. He slashed open a hundred pregnant women just to see inside.

The year after his mother died, so did Shaka. His people no longer adored him, no longer obeyed without question. They were scared out of their wits. Men condemned to execution no longer accepted death meekly, or even proudly, as their predecessors had done. Sometimes they fought back. Some villages were left empty as their inhabitants quietly sneaked away, preferring to become fugitives rather than corpses.

One of Shaka's aunts began to spread a rumor that he had

poisoned his mother. All the way round, the time was right for overthrowing the government. A conspiracy grew. It had three members: Dingana and Mhlangana, who were his half brothers, and Mbopa, his trusted comrade for many years.

While Shaka was receiving a delegation of Zulus bearing gifts, Dingana and Mhlangana stabbed him with their assegais, those potent weapons that he himself had perfected. Mbopa helped kill him. The Great Elephant died shrieking for mercy after a reign of twelve ghastly years.

In the life of this strange man there was a peculiar sidelight, a love story. The girl was Pampata, five years his junior. From the time she obliged him in the custom of "wiping his ax" after one of his early battles, she loved him dearly. He valued her affection, honored her by bestowing presents of cattle, listened to her advice (not necessarily following it), and appreciated the nice things she did for his mother. Of course he didn't marry her—he didn't marry any woman—but Pampata was the best friend he had.

After Shaka was assassinated, everybody in the neighborhood took to the woods, yelling, "The mountain has collapsed! The lord of the world is dead!" The assassins prudently departed, too.

When Pampata got the word, she didn't head for cover. She went weeping to look for the body of her beloved. So did the local hyenas. Any time is dinnertime when hyenas smell blood.

All that night in the deserted kraal, Pampata kept the yelling hyenas away from Shaka's body, using a pole as a weapon, as they padded hopefully around the remains of the lord of the world. At dawn the disappointed scavengers slunk away, looking over their shoulders at the tasty meal they hadn't been able to get at.

The circle of their paw prints remained in the dirt, but Pampata carefully wiped out her own footprints. When the assassins returned in the morning, they were dumbstruck—there was the body, untouched by the hyenas that had circled it. Shaka was so great a king that even in death the scavengers feared him! The three killers hastened to have their victim's body buried in a grain pit with scant ceremony.

Pampata sped through the forest to take word to another of Shaka's half-brothers, a chief named Ngwadi, a hundred miles away. At first a boy went with her. When he fell back, exhausted, she went on alone.

Troops led by one of the assassins were hot on her trail. When they attacked Ngwadi's kraal, the chief himself killed eight men in furious battle. When he fell, Pampata stabbed herself fatally with a toy spear that had belonged to Shaka. She had carried it all the way.

32
Henry Plummer

1837 (?)–January 10, 1864

*Do you suspect that your local law-
enforcement officers are corrupt?
They're probably shining saints compared with Sheriff Plummer. He didn't
even die game.*

Henry Plummer was an ambitious young fellow who wanted only to get rich. He was clever; he had a smart idea about how to get rich by taking gold away from other men who were foolish enough to slave for it by digging it out of the gravel in the Montana gold fields. Henry was the executive type; facing the fact that a lot of robbers could work more effectively than one robber, he organized a secret band and became its leader. He consolidated his position by getting elected sheriff. It was a job that virtually nobody else wanted.

His qualifications were impressive. He was the fastest draw in the Rockies and could fire five shots in three seconds; he had been town marshal someplace in California; he had killed an old friend right in public, but that was no drawback. He had pretty good connections with other fast-shooters and appointed several of them as his deputies. They were also members of his gang of bandits, commonly known as road agents.

Plummer's road agents called themselves the Innocents, wore the same kind of kerchief for a tie, had their whiskers cut the same way and even had a password: "I am innocent." This didn't do them much good in the long run, although several of them roared "I am innocent!" just before they swung at the end of a rope.

Plummer was almost six feet tall, slim, straight, and quiet. He was a rather handsome man with a poker face and gray eyes that looked right through you. He was about twenty-seven when he died in 1864.

Although he was an urbane and mannerly villain, he seldom removed his hat, and after he was dead and gone somebody figured out why: he feared that the shape of his head gave away the fact that he had the instincts of a murderer. Phrenology was becoming a fairly reputable science in the 1860s.

Sheriff Plummer and his merry men (between seventy-five and a hundred of them) robbed often, killed without compunction, lived well, and drank deep. He *was* the law in the gold diggings in western Montana. But he wasn't the only smart man in the gold gulches. A few of the others were becoming suspicious. And he found, to his dismay, that one of his deputies, D. H. Dillingham, was an honest man. This wouldn't do. One non-road agent could upset his whole rotten-apple cart. So one day in the summer of 1863, at Alder Gulch, three of Henry's henchmen (including two deputies) managed to get into a scuffle, kill the honest Dillingham, and toss pistols around so cleverly that nobody could prove exactly who fired the shot. The three were tried immediately in a riotous miners' court and all went scot free.

No shadow of suspicion fell on Sheriff Plummer for that fracas. He was far away, up at Sun River near the Great Falls of the Missouri, getting married to a nice girl named Electa Bryan. Nice girls were scarce, and there was considerable demand for them (and for not-nice girls, for that matter). Electa thought she was making a good match. The bridegroom was a man of substance, actually the most important public official in the unruly part of Idaho that became Montana Territory a year later. Nobody knows what discovery shattered Electa's dream of bliss, but the June bride left her husband before Thanksgiving, ostensibly to spend the winter back in the United States somewhere, and she never came back. Indeed, she had no reason to return, because Henry was hanged only a couple of months after her departure.

The killers of Dillingham went free, laughing all the way to the next holdup, and the Innocents throve like the green bay tree. They rode and robbed over two or three hundred miles of rocky road through densely forested mountains. But in December 1863 the roof began to fall on them.

The collapse began with the accidental discovery of the frozen body of a well-liked young man, Nick Tbalt (or Tibalt or Thibault), who had disappeared with a team of mules and was naturally suspected of stealing them. Nick had obviously been dragged, while still living, with a lariat loop around his neck, and then shot in the head.

The horrified grouse-hunter who found him hastened to the nearest cabin, where he asked help with loading the body into his wagon. The men in the cabin sneered at the idea that one more dead body was worth fussing about. The hunter loaded the body himself and drove angrily off to the nearest gold camp, Nevada City, to report.

A lot of men got mad about the cruel demise of young Nick and the off-hand manner of the men at the cabin, so they formed an unofficial posse and rode out there. They found one of Nick's missing mules and arrested the tenants of the cabin—handsome, blond George Ives and two other men—on suspicion of murder. This time a trial for murder had a happier ending, at least from the point of view of the more law-biding citizens. Although two of the men went free, the roistering, devil-may-care George Ives was sentenced to hang. And the community didn't fool around. He was strung up then and there. He dangled from a stout rope in the moonlight on the night of December 21, 1863. The other road agents in the crowd couldn't believe their own eyes. Henry Plummer wasn't there to witness it; he had business over at Bannack, in the Grasshopper Diggings, seventy miles away. If he had guessed how short his life span was going to be, he might have hastened back to California.

Leaving George Ives at the end of his rope, to be buried anon, a bunch of solid citizens began to mutter to one another that something should be done. Two nights after the hanging, twenty-four of them followed the Innocents' example and held a secret meeting. They organized a Committee of Vigilance, signed an oath to track down road agents, jumped on their horses, and set out through the snow for the Deer Lodge Valley. They had in mind, as first choice, three villains including two of those who had evaded punishment for the killing of Dillingham.

But once more evil triumphed over virtue. Their birds had flown, having been warned of impending doom. But they found out who had done the warning. Riding home, cold and hungry and very, very mad, they picked up two other men: a ruffian named George Brown, who had written a warning note ("Get up and dust, and lie low for black ducks"), and Erastus "Red" Yager, who had worn out a couple of horses in delivering it.

These two men constituted a real prize, especially Yager. Brown was only sullen, but Yager, to the surprise and gratification of his captors, talked his red head off. He told the Vigilantes everything they wanted to know, including some things they hadn't even suspected. He named Sheriff Plummer as head of the organized gang. He named twenty-two members of the Innocents and told what each one's specialty was—spy, message carrier, or holdup man. Yager talked and talked, without any promise of reprieve; he knew he was going to swing. Finally this most remarkable bean-spiller shook hands all around, and just before they knocked the support out from under his feet he said, "Good-bye, boys, you're on a good undertaking. God bless you." Brown was also hanged. Before they rode back to town, his executioners wrote a couple of signs and pinned them on the backs of their victims' coats. One said, "Red! Road agent and Messenger." The other read, "Brown! Corresponding secretary."

Now the non–road agent population stopped being afraid to open their mouths about having been robbed or pistol-whipped or knowing men who had been killed by road agents easily recognizable by their clothing or their horses. All of a sudden they could safely deplore lawlessness. Another Vigilance Committee sprang up over at Bannack, where Sheriff Plummer usually could be found.

Plummer began to worry a little. His carefully built empire was being undermined. He prepared to leave for safer regions with two villainous friends, Buck Stinson and Ned Ray. They didn't make it. On January 10, 1864, the Bannack Vigilantes struck. They arrested all three and held a quick trial while somebody went to get rope, since everybody knew the trial's outcome. All three were hanged on a gallows that Plummer had had built a few months before for the more or less legal execution of another evil-doer.

Most bad men, when it came to the crunch of standing on a packing box with a rope around their neck, toughed it out and at least made a good ending, either cursing their executioners roundly or expressing repentance. That is, they died game and got due credit for it when the stories of their deaths were told afterward. But Henry Plummer was a disgrace to the road-agent profession. He wept, he yelled, he pleaded for mercy. On his knees he wailed, "I am too wicked to die! Spare me and I'll leave this country forever!"

His grim, bearded executioners sniffed disdainfully and strung him up. Everybody was awfully embarrassed. Stinson and Ray died game—they yelled and cursed as badmen were expected to do.

Now the Vigilante Committee had got the hang of hanging, they swept through the road agents like avenging furies. The same day as the triple hanging, the Bannack group got two more men. Meanwhile, over at Alder Gulch, the Vigilantes made plans for a big roundup. Most of Plummer's merry men had lit out, but six bold ones were still there. On January 14, the Vigilantes (grown now to a committee of hundreds) got five of them, gave them a quick trial, and hanged them all in a row from a crossbeam in an unfinished building. Their last words were duly noted by witnesses, including what Boone Helm said as he watched Jack Gallagher's dying convulsions: "Kick away, old fellow, I'll be in hell with you in a minute." That was much more satisfactory to tell about than the cowardly wailing of the late Henry Plummer.

The Vigilantes rode far and fast and, by February 3, had executed twenty-two of Plummer's Innocents and scared the rest out of the county.

33
Henry Wirz

November 25, 1823–November 10, 1865

Injustice there has always been and always will be. Deciding for yourself where the injustice lay in this case should take your mind off your problems.

O nly one man was tried for war crimes after the War of the Rebellion ended. He was hanged. He was Captain Henry Wirz, commander of the infamous Andersonville Prison in Georgia from March 27, 1864, to the end of the war in April 1865. A total of 49,500 Union prisoners suffered at his hands. The largest number packed into the filthy stockade at one time, with inadequate food and water and only such shelter as they could make from their own ragged blankets and coats, was 33,000. In thirteen months, more than 13,700 men died there.

The emaciated survivors looked on Captain Wirz as the main author of their deprivations and suffering. But after he was executed the South saw him as a martyr, almost a saint. Bitterness resulting from his trial has not yet died down, after more than a century. In the years 1895–1910, thirteen northern states erected monuments in the prison area, commemorating their dead. In 1908, the Georgia Division of the United Daughters of the Confederacy erected a monument in the nearby town of Andersonville honoring the memory of Captain Wirz, with inscriptions calculated to make Northern visitors' blood boil. Women are long haters.

The trial of Captain Wirz opened August 23, 1865, in Washington, D.C. President of the ten-man military commission that tried him was Major General Lew Wallace, who a few years later, while Governor of New Mexico, wrote a bestseller called

Ben-Hur. Colonel N. P. Chipman was Judge Advocate, or prosecutor. Wirz had two defense attorneys, O. S. Baker and Louis Schade. Baker did most of the talking.

Henry Wirz—born in Switzerland, naturalized citizen of the United States—was on trial accused of conspiracy to destroy the lives and health of thousands of Federal prisoners and charged with thirteen individual counts of murder by his own hand or by his order. Wirz was lucky to have reached Washington alive. To keep him from being torn to pieces on the way from Macon, he had to be disguised. The escorting officer was credited by some people with having risked his own life to protect the hated prisoner.

Of the 146 witnesses sworn in, nearly 100 had been prisoners. The defense subpoenaed 106 witnesses; sixty-eight of them came, and Wirz's two defending attorneys discharged thirty-nine of these for reasons of their own. As the trial dragged on, the same questions were asked over and over by the prosecution, getting at the facts about conditions in the stockade and the hospital, about water supplies, lack of food, shelter and fuel; about crowding and filth, about the "deadline" beyond which a prisoner dared not reach even his hand; about cruel and inhuman punishments, about compulsory smallpox vaccination that caused gangrene, about packs of dogs used to track and tear men trying to escape, about which hand Captain Wirz used to shoot with because his right arm had been severely injured in battle in 1861, about Confederate guards who said they got a furlough as a reward for killing prisoners for minor infractions.

Captain W. S. Winder, son of General John W. Winder, planned the prison for 10,000 men. A heavily wooded area of eighteen acres near the village of Americus, Georgia, was cleared, down to the last tree and bush. When someone suggested that some shelter be left for the prisoners, Captain Winder replied: "That is just what I am not going to do. I will make a pen here for the damned Yankees where they will rot faster than they can be sent." Logs twenty feet long were set upright in the earth for the main stockade, which was surrounded by two somewhat lower ones. Fuel was provided so scantily that the prisoners dug out tree stumps and then the roots. (On alternate days their inadequate rations were doled out raw, and the men cooked them any way they could.)

A. W. Persons, a lieutenant colonel in the Confederate army, was the first commandant of Camp Sumter, camp of the soldiers assigned as guards, and of Andersonville prison. He testified that in June 1864, the year it was established, he enlarged the stockade; at its greatest, it enclosed twenty-three and one-half acres. But the thousands of prisoners kept pouring in until it was far too crowded. With great difficulty he collected lumber to build barracks, but his successor, General Winder, used the lumber to build houses—not for prisoners—outside the stockade.

Henry Wirz assumed command of the prison March 27, 1864, and set up the infamous "deadline," a railing about twenty feet inside the stockade. This further diminished the prisoners' living space. Reaching past the railing for a cup of water from the foul stream that flowed through the prison area was punishable by death. The small stream, filthy with drainage from the cookhouse, from the sinks (open latrines), and from the Confederate camp above, provided the only water for washing. There were many tiny "wells" with small amounts of water in them, scooped out by prisoners who guarded them against their fellows.

The prisoners who survived testified in these words:

George W. Gray: "When new prisoners came into the stockade, we were not permitted to warn them of their danger in regard to the deadline. They would immediately run to the brook for fresh water, would probably get over the deadline, and be fired upon by sentries. I have seen as high as six or seven men killed or wounded at that place."

James Clancy: "I saw a man shot by the guard at the stockade, down at the creek. I was going down to get some water in an old piece of boot leg that I had. A man was reaching in after some water; it was so muddy and full of grease and dirt that he was reaching over to get some cleaner water. Somebody stumbled against him so that a part of his body was over the deadline. The guard raised his gun and shot him dead. The next case was near nightfall, and a man was reaching over the deadline to get some pine burrs to cook his victuals with. The guard fired; he missed that man but struck another who was asleep. The brains and blood flew around. I got into conversation with a guard. I asked, 'What does Captain Wirz give you for shooting us?' He answered that they were promised thirty days' furlough."

Of the brook that ran through the camp and the swamp bordering it, Boston Corbett said: "It was a living mass of putrefaction and filth; there were maggots there a foot deep. Any time we turned over the soil we could see the maggots in a living mass. I have seen the soldiers wading through it, digging for roots to use as fuel. I have seen, around the swamp, the sick in great numbers, lying pretty much as soldiers lie when they are down to rest in line after a march.

"In the morning I could see those who had died during the night, and in the daytime I could see them exposed to the heat of the sun, with their feet swelled to an enormous size; in many cases large gangrene sores filled with maggots and flies which they were unable to keep off. I have seen men lying there not able to help themselves, lying in their own filth. They generally chose that place [near the swamp], those who were most offensive, because others would drive them away, not wanting to be near those who had such bad sores. They chose it because of its being so near to the sinks. In one case a man died there, I am satisfied, from the effects of lice. When the clothes were taken off his body, the lice seemed as thick as the garment—a living mass."

John H. Goldsmith, a prisoner assigned to clerical work for Captain Wirz: "I made out a furlough once for a man who had killed one of our own men; he received a furlough for thirty days. The soldier came there and claimed his furlough, saying he had earned it by killing a man." There were 30,000 prisoners at Andersonville when Goldsmith was there.

Over and over, former prisoners testified that Captain Wirz had stopped *all* rations on July 3 and 4, 1864, because of the huge influx of new men whom he could not get sorted out fast enough to please him. At various times he deprived the men in squads of ninety because one or two men were too sick and weak to line up for roll call.

Oliver B. Fairbanks: "The rations of all the prisoners were stopped while I was there. The reason he [Captain Wirz] gave for it was that he could not find the exact number of prisoners in camp. The rations were stopped for twenty-four hours twice inside of three days.

"His manner at roll call was very overbearing and abusive. He generally saluted the prisoners by calling them 'damned Yankee sons-of-bitches.' He often abused the prisoners. I know a person whom he kicked. He was my father. He was lying in a helpless condition, affected with scurvy. His legs and arms were drawn up so he could not straighten them. Captain Wirz told him to fall in at roll call or he would kick him. He did kick him. He said,

'You God-damned Yankee son-of-a-bitch, if you don't fall in at roll call I will not give you anything to eat for a week.' He stopped my father's rations. My father died, about a month after this. He made a verbal statement to me before he died. He said he died from sheer starvation and asked me not to tell my mother, his wife, the awful condition in which he was compelled to die."

Prisoners brought in from Richmond in early spring carried smallpox with them. In a laudable effort to keep it from spreading, the prison doctors vaccinated more than two thousand men. But a very large number of them were already suffering from scurvy; vaccination caused ulcers, and gangrene followed. Amputation of the arm was necessary, and many deaths resulted. The surviving prisoners believed their captors were using poison vaccine with malicious intent. (Confederate prisoners in northern camps made the same accusation.)

Fairbanks testified: "I saw several hundred cases of vaccination. I have seen holes eaten under the arms where I could put my fist in."

Fairbanks refused to be vaccinated, even when Wirz pointed his pistol at his head. Wirz had a ball and chain put on him until he consented two weeks later. After the vaccination, Fairbanks hurried to wash his arm and squeeze the wound. He suffered no ill effects and told his friends how to save themselves.

James K. Davidson: "I have seen men who were starved to death, thousands of them, inside the stockade. I saw men eating food that they took from the ground. I have seen men pick up and eat undigested food that had passed through other men. It came from men who were not able to go to the slough. I heard Captain Wirz say that he was killing more damn Yankees there than Lee was at Richmond."

Benjamin F. Dilley, a witness for the defense, contradicted just about everything the prosecution witnesses said, but even he agreed that the vaccine was dangerous. While assigned to sorting out men with smallpox, he asked Dr. Isaiah White to vaccinate him:

"Dr. White did not say that the vaccine matter was bad, but he shook his head as to say, 'Don't be vaccinated.' He told me he would get a scab from a child in the country and vaccinate me with that. It was sure death for a man to be vaccinated there if it took. His arm would have to be amputated, and I know of only one successful case of amputation." That involved a surgeon who had a bet that he could save a patient's life, so he took personal care of him for three or four weeks and won the bet.

Frank Maddox, on the burial detail, saw Captain Wirz at the burying ground with some other officers, heard him say he had given the God-damned Yankee sons-of-bitches the land they came to fight for—six feet of it. Maddox testified: "I saw Captain Wirz in the graveyard with the surgeons; they were laughing over the effects of the vaccinations one day. The doctor had been examining and had cut some bodies open and sawed some heads open. In some cases a green streak from the arm had extended into the body. They were laughing about it killing the men so."

The hospital (outside the stockade) consisted of tents without sides. Only the worst cases were admitted; care was minimal and conditions still awful. Many sick prisoners, desperate for whatever comfort was there, were turned back at the gate and died trying to return through the crowd to the filthy spot from which they came. Those in the hospital at least had a roof over them when they died—unless it was too crowded—and perhaps a board to lie on.

Joseph Alder: "I was a prisoner at Andersonville from about the middle of March to the eighth of September 1864. When I was captured there were seventy-one of us, including a young Negro boy. All that is left is about a dozen. About fifty of them died at Andersonville. I was part of the time in the hospital in the capacity of nurse. The majority of the sick men had to lie on the bare ground. Most of them had nothing to lie on and nothing to cover themselves with. It rained twenty days in succession in June. At that time there were about 200 men [hospital patients] lying out under the open sky without any shelter, bedding, or blankets. They had only a little water, and all they had to eat was a little corn bread and rice soup that I would not give a dog."

The bread was made of meal with the husks ground in it and unsifted. If men weakened by diarrhea ate it, their condition became noticeably worsened.

Many prisoners, as long as their strength lasted, kept the idea of escape uppermost in their minds. Captain Wirz had a man with a pack of dogs to track them down. He lost few prisoners except the thousands who escaped by dying. Joseph Adler testified.

"I saw a man lying on the ground; his clothes were all torn to pieces and you could see the marks of the teeth of the dogs right

in his throat. I heard Captain Wirz make the remark that it
served the damned dog right, meaning the man on the ground.
The man died the next day, right on the spot."

Dr. John C. Bates, Confederate surgeon at the prison from
September 19, 1864, to March 26, 1865, said of the hospital: "The
men were lying partially nude and dying and lousy, a portion of
them in the sand and others upon boards which had been stuck
up on little props, pretty well crowded together, a majority of
them in small tents, not very serviceable at best. The clamor all
the while was for something to eat."

Bates was a compassionate man, as some of the doctors there
were not. When he could, he smuggled in raw potatoes in his
pockets for the scurvy sufferers. He especially remembered a
boy of fifteen, with scurvy and gangrene, who kept asking for
food. Dr. Bates couldn't get him enough raw potato. "He became
bed-ridden upon the hips and back [sic], lying upon the ground.
We afterwards got him some straw. Those bed-ridden sores had
become gangrenous. He became more and more emaciated until
he died."

Because of gangrene, amputations were performed almost daily;
sometimes successive amputations were necessary. Dr. Bates
remembered that two or three of these were successful. Most
patients died. When he left Andersonville late in March 1865, he
was told that 12,878 men had died. He believed that seventy-five
percent of them could have been saved with proper food, clothing,
and bedding. The lack of these things was not entirely Captain
Wirz's fault. The Confederacy was short of almost everything
for its own armies.

Starving, sick, with untended wounds, penned but not sheltered, humanity was tested too far. Sometimes it snapped. Dr.
Bates testified:

"I would have expected that such abject circumstances would
have produced deep humiliation and resignation, but the effect
was otherwise. The moral feeling of the prisoners gradually
evaporated. Men seemed to abandon themselves. It seemed to me
at times that no man interested himself further than 'I'; a well
man would sometimes steal from a sick man. It seemed to me
that all lived for themselves, having no regard for anybody else.
I judged this to be superinduced by the paucity of the rations—
the starving condition of the men."

The prisoners were so crowded that they fought their comrades for the little space they had. Thomas H. Horne testified:

"When I was first put into the stockade I tried to find a place to lie down; I went to two or three places, but it was no use. One man said I could not lie down there. Pretty soon I had to fight for a place to lie down on. There was no room there, and they said we had no business there. Of course I got a place after a while.

"The men were perfect skeletons where I lay. They were half naked, filthy, lousy, too sick to get up. I lay on the ground many a night when I couldn't sleep, sometimes on account of men around me groaning in agony. When I would wake up in the morning I would see men dead all around me. One man died and lay there so long that he could not be taken out, and they had to bury him where he died."

Prisoners who refused other prisoners water from tiny, oozing wells, or bare lying-down space because they could not spare it, were not so bad as the group of comparatively healthy bullies that developed because of the breakdown of all human conditions in the stockade. These men, known as Raiders, robbed and assaulted weaker men. Everything—a ragged blanket, a worn-out pair of boots, a tattered jacket—had value. Over 100 sergeants of the squads of ninety in the stockade got permission from Captain Wirz to take action. From his own hat they drew twelve names for jurors. They held a trial for the worst of the Raiders, hanged six of them, and made six others run the gauntlet. The punishment organization was known as the Regulators. They became bullies, too.

Frederick Roth, in the U.S. Army since 1861 when he was fifteen, was pushed around by older, stronger men when he tried to buy from the prisoners who had little shops set up through the camp. He was shoved aside if someone else offered a trader more money than he could.

"After the Regulators were got up," he testified, "these traders put on airs a good deal. Some of the Regulators were looked down upon as distasteful as the Raiders. The biggest part of the camp were down on them." They drew six or eight rations of meat, and, when he got half a pound of bread, they drew four times as much.

Some astonishing testimony for the defense came from George W. Fechtner, age twenty-three, a Union prisoner also known as Charles W. Ross. He painted a rosy picture of Andersonville. As a prisoner, he had a very nice war. He ate well, with plenty of fruit and vegetables, and made money.

Fechtner was prison sutler part of the time, a lucrative job for a man brutal enough to handle it. He was chief of the Regulators and magistrate for part of the camp, inflicting such penalties as flogging on men caught stealing. He estimated that there were a thousand little storekeepers in the prison. They bought from the rebel sutler and got many stores from the hospital. They bribed the guards to let them go out into the country and buy.

Fechtner made it clear that he felt that when rations were stopped it was the men's own fault because they hadn't lined up for roll call—never mind that they were too weak to stand. Nobody *had* to be vaccinated, and he never saw a sore arm. He never even *heard* of Captain Wirz mistreating individual prisoners.

Fechtner was a self-made man. He started with nothing and sold his ration of corn bread for ten cents a day. He bought thirteen dozen eggs on tick at $3.60 a dozen. Business boomed. He bought sorghum at $1300 a barrel, Confederate money. At one time he had $5000.

As Fechtner described the camp, it was a busy, contented place where everybody with any git-up-and-go to him had a little business and made money; it hummed with trade, and all it took to get a good steak dinner was enough money. He said the prison abounded in tiny restaurants, but he never ate in them. He had a Frenchman for a cook. He considered his trading activities perfectly legitimate; he didn't rob anybody. He just knew the right guards to bribe.

In answer to a sharp question by the Judge Advocate, he replied, "I was regarded as a man of honor, and am wherever I go."

Realizing that members of the court were glaring at him with shocked distaste, he began to remember how kind he had been to other prisoners. He prated of his "charity." He had given money away every day. He began to weasel-word his testimony, having to explain that what he had said was not exactly what he meant. He looked to his image and remembered giving to needy soldiers. He obviously felt that, if any prisoner suffered, it was his own fault for not having the spunk to set up a trading business.

The milk of human kindness was not in George W. Fechtner. His testimony so shocked the court that one Frederick W. Hille was called upon to impeach his credibility. Hille said:

"Everyone in the whole camp complained of his cruelty. He would not give anybody a cent there." Asked about Fechtner's reputation as a man of honor, Hille replied: "Everybody called him mean, and when a man is what I call mean, he cannot have any honor."

Hille continued: "I once went down [to Fechtner's shop] with fifty cents to get some cakes with butter on them for a dying man. He said the charge was seventy-five cents. I said it was too hard to take money from a man in that way, that it was robbery. He said, 'Well, let the man die.' They were small cakes, such as we buy here for a penny. A single one there sold for twenty-five cents.

"One day a man lay right behind the shanty and Fechtner was looking out the window. Some person asked Fechtner to give that man a drink of water or whiskey as he was in a dying condition. He said, 'Oh, let him die, what do I care.' The man died about an hour afterward. He was broken down with hunger."

The long, terrible account of deprivation and cruelty went on day after day. Hear Thomas N. Way: "I was in the stocks eight days. I was bucked and gagged a day and a half. I was tied up by the thumbs for fifteen minutes because I was sick and not able to fall into roll-call. All this was done by order of Captain Wirz. I heard him give the order. I could not use my hands for two months afterward.

"The effect of the stocks was very severe. I was laid on my back with my feet and arms in the stocks, and my face was right upward in the sun. When a man is bucked and gagged, he is set down on the ground with his legs drawn up and his arms around his knees. The pole is put through under the knees and above the arms at the elbows; a stick is put in the mouth as far back as they can ram it. I have seen a hundred men or more punished in that way.

"The hounds caught me three times. I remember about a soldier being torn to pieces by hounds."

William Henry Jennings, a member of a Black regiment, was ordered to dig a ditch while a wound in his left thigh was still bleeding. One morning he could not go to work; he had caught a heavy cold, and his wound had never been treated. He testified that Captain Wirz ordered him whipped thirty lashes on his bare back. Then he spent a day and a night in the stocks with neither food nor water. When he was taken out and returned to the stockade, he could not walk.

George W. Gray told of a wounded man who asked at a sutler's shanty for something to wrap his wound. The sutler was willing, but Captain Wirz, who happened to be there, said, "No, he cannot have it unless he pays me a dollar." The wounded man produced his last money, a ten-dollar bill, and asked for change. Wirz kicked him out the door.

Martin E. Hogan, who had worked in the hospital, saw Captain Wirz take a sick prisoner by the collar because he could not walk faster. Wirz jerked him back and stamped on him with his boot. The man was carried past Hogan, bleeding from the nose or mouth. He died soon.

A defense witness told of mail handling; it was carefully sorted and passed out to the prisoners. But Lewis Dyer, a Black, for the prosecution, had no such tale to tell. While a prisoner he had been a servant in Dr. White's house, where he had seen about 3000 letters delivered. An officer's wife took out the enclosures—pictures, writing paper, needles and thread, postage stamps. She read the letters, made fun of them, and ordered Dyer to burn them, which he did.

Many witnesses told of private property being taken from them. Hear L. S. Pond: "The prisoners were ordered to be searched. I saw Captain Wirz take the daguerreotype of a lady and two children. The man seemed to be trying to hide the picture. Captain Wirz ordered him to give it up. Captain Wirz looked at it, threw it on the ground, and stamped his heel on it. I afterwards learned that the man's wife was dead, and the picture was all he had to remember her by."

Abner A. Kellogg: "Some blankets were taken from some of the boys, and canteens, pocketbooks, and watches. They were taken into Captain Wirz's quarters. The men never got them back. After standing four or five hours in the sun we were put in the stockade.

"I saw a sick man carried up to the gate. He had a sore on his back about the size of the crown of my hat. It was full of maggots. The sergeant asked to have the man removed to the hospital. Captain Wirz said, 'It isn't worthwhile, let him die there,' and he died, lying there by the gate."

Thomas H. Horne: "The rebel sergeants took what they wanted

from us, blankets, coats, and everything else. They took money and watches. I saw the rebel sergeants give the money and watches to Captain Wirz. I had five shirts on which they did not take, and I had two ten-dollar bills in my mouth. There was some one hundred dollars taken from a young man standing close by me."

Ambrose Spencer, a lawyer-turned-farmer who lived nine miles from the prison pen, visited the place once a month. He had seen the stockade after rain when the prisoners waded in mud a foot deep. "The condition of the stockade perhaps can be expressed most aptly by saying that . . . if the wind was favorable, the odor from the stockade could be detected at least two miles."

There was plenty of timber, he testified; there were sawmills and gristmills nearby. The land after all was fruitful. "Last year a very large supply of vegetables was raised, as I understood, for the purpose of being disposed of at Andersonville."

He remembered the winter of '64–'65, the coldest he had experienced in twenty-five years in Georgia; the temperature sometimes reached ten degrees below freezing. Once, in June, his thermometer showed one-hundred-thirty degrees in the sun. The prisoners were exposed to both cold and blazing sun.

The ladies of the county tried to relieve the men in the hospital. They collected clothing and provisions, three or four wagonloads. But the provost marshal refused them a pass to the hospital, and General Winder also flatly refused.

"I had a conversation with General Winder three days afterward," Spencer said. "General Winder stated, accompanied with an oath, that he believed the whole country was becoming Yankee, and that he would be damned if he would not put a stop to it. I remarked that I did not think it was any evidence of Yankee or Union feeling to exhibit humanity. He said there was no humanity about it; that it was intended as a slur on the Confederate government and as a covert attack on him. . . . He said he would as lief the damned Yankees would die there as anywhere else; that, upon the whole, he did not know that it was not better for them."

The day after the ladies' committee failed, Spencer was present at a conversation at the Andersonville depot; Captain Wirz, R. B. Winder, and Captain Reed, the provost marshal, were there with others. Reed said that if General Winder had approved they might have "made a good speculation out of the provisions and clothing." Reed had urged that the supplies be confiscated. "Wirz remarked that if he had his way he would have a house built there, and all the ladies [of the relief committee] be put in it for certain purposes. That was a most scandalous, infamous purpose, which I do not wish to repeat."

When the prison stockade was being built, Spencer had asked Captain W. S. Winder whether he was going to erect barracks or shelter of any kind. Winder said the damned Yankees wouldn't need shelter. Spencer asked why he was cutting down all the trees, which would be a shelter from the sun. He replied, "I am going to build a pen here that will kill more damned Yankees than can be destroyed at the front."

The ghastly tale went on, day after day. There were some sharp challenges from Defense Attorney Baker; almost always the judge overruled his objections. Once there was an exchange that sounds suspiciously like a challenge to a duel. The Judge Advocate (prosecutor) and Defense Counsel Baker snapped at each other during the questioning of one witness. The President, General Lew Wallace, vainly endeavored to quiet them:

THE PRESIDENT: Proceed with the examination of the witness.

MR. BAKER: Then I will have to correct the matter outside if I am not allowed to do so here.

THE JUDGE ADVOCATE: I will meet you on any occasion, and in any place.

MR. BAKER: I don't want to meet you; I simply want to correct your assertion.

THE PRESIDENT: If this does not cease instantly, I shall move to expel the counsel.

When the time came for summing up, Baker asked for more time to prepare the defense statement than Wallace would allow. The prosecuting attorney, Chipman, said he could prepare *his* statement in the time allotted. Thereupon both the defense attorneys withdrew from the case and Wirz had to prepare his own defense summation. He had the help of one of the court reporters, Henry G. Hayes, who read the statement aloud for him on October 18.

Wirz insisted that nobody had proved that any conspiracy existed. Furthermore, he was a mere captain, not responsible for the acts of his superiors. "A poor subaltern officer," he said, "should not have had the ordinary performance of his routine duties treated and characterized as proof of his being a conspirator, nor should he have been called upon to bear upon his overburdened shoulders the faults or misdeeds of others." As for the individual counts of murder, he didn't commit them or it wasn't his fault or it didn't happen that way.

The Judge Advocate presented his argument October 20 and 21. He repeated that Wirz, with other persons named and unnamed, was accused of having "maliciously, traitorously, and in violation of the laws of war, conspired to impair and injure the health and to destroy the lives, by subjecting to torture and great suffering, by confinement in unhealthy and unwholesome quarters, by exposing to the inclemency of winter and to the dews and burning sun of summer, by compelling the use of impure water, and by furnishing insufficient and unwholesome food, of large numbers of soldiers in the military service of the United States held as prisoners of war at Andersonville, Georgia, by the so-called Confederate States of America, to the end that the armies of the United States might be weakened and impaired, and the insurgents engaged in armed rebellion against the United States might be aided and comforted."

He conceded that much evidence brought forth by both sides had been prejudiced. Former prisoners testified remembering the injuries inflicted on them, and those who were from the rebel forces had been brought to court forcibly and testified in the hope of pardon or the fear of punishment. "And yet," he said, "there is a most striking concurrence in all this testimony, all agreeing that history has never presented a scene of such gigantic human suffering."

Throughout the trial, Baker had tried to prove that Wirz, because of unhealed broken bones in his right arm from a wound received early in the war, could not have performed the acts of violence with which he was charged. After Wirz had presented his defense and Judge Advocate Chipman had summed up for the prosecution, two doctors examined the prisoner right there in court. They agreed that he couldn't hurt anyone much with that arm.

Immediately after the doctors testified, the military commission considered the evidence and found unanimously that Henry Wirz (with others not present, including Jefferson Davis) was guilty of conspiring to injure the health and destroy the lives of

about 45,000 prisoners of war. He was found guilty on ten of
the thirteen counts of killing individual prisoners. An additional
finding was that he had caused the deaths of three men by means
of dogs.

He had only one life to pay with. He died by hanging, on
November 10—fast and neatly, not by long starvation, not crip-
pled by scurvy, racked with diarrhea, rotted with gangrene.

The record of his trial has some peculiarities. The testimony
of some witnesses flatly contradicts that of other witnesses, although all of them were under oath to tell the truth. Almost
every defense objection was overruled by the judge, who was not
without prejudice. It is impossible to study the 815 printed pages
of the record without feeling that the trial was rigged. There
had to be a trial, but there was never any doubt about what
the verdict would be, or the sentence.

Wirz's major defense was that he was simply doing his duty.
He was a mere captain who carried out the orders of his superiors. This was true. But if he inflicted even a fraction of the
heartless personal cruelties of which he was accused, even a few
of the deaths that were attributed to him, he went beyond his
duty.

Some witnesses, as well as official records of the Confederacy,
testified that Wirz had tried hard to remedy the awful conditions
in the prison pen. He had tried to get axes, wheelbarrows, buck-
ets to carry rations (eight thousand men had no containers),
cornmeal with the indigestible ground-up husks and cobs sifted
out. But the Confederacy, fighting with its back to the wall,
could not provide such things. Money was scarce, manpower was
scarce, mills were overburdened, transportation was very bad.

After the war, hundreds or perhaps thousands of veterans,
realizing that they had lived through a catastrophe of great historical significance, sat down to write their memoirs. Some of
them actually finished and published what they wrote. For years
there was a spate of "I was there" books about Andersonville and
other horrors.

One of the writers who could be sure of an audience was Jefferson Davis, first and only President of the Confederate States
of America. He was captured May 10, 1865, and kept a prisoner
for two years. Accused of treason and participation in the plot
to assassinate Abraham Lincoln, he was indicted twice but never
tried. He neither asked for nor received a pardon but was re-

leased on a writ of *habeas corpus* and freed on $100,000 bail. Horace Greeley was one of the ten men who signed his bond.

In December 1888, a year before his death, Davis finished writing "Andersonville and Other War-Prisons," which was published in *Belford's Magazine* and reprinted as a booklet in 1890. In discussing Andersonville, Davis defended the South by attacking the North. Southern prisoners suffered worse in Northern camps—particularly at Elmira, New York—than the men at Andersonville, he maintained, because the weather was colder. Andersonville was overcrowded because the North had abrogated a cartel covering the exchange of prisoners. (The Confederacy had refused to exchange their Black prisoners, considering them property rather than men.) Davis said the charge of cruelty against General Winder was unjust. Prison hospitals had little to work with because the North had declared medicine contraband. It wasn't starvation that killed Union prisoners, he said; they had plenty to eat but couldn't get used to bread made of cornmeal. Despondency helped kill them.

A chain reaction of recriminations followed publication of Davis's article. When N. P. Chipman, who had prosecuted Wirz, read what Davis had said, he seethed. He wrote *The Horrors of Andersonville Rebel Prison*, which was published in 1891. The year before, twenty-five years after the war ended, some of the Northern states had begun to erect monuments to their dead in the immense graveyard at the prison.

Those monuments infuriated some Southerners. In 1908, Sarah W. Ashe published a ringing defense in *The Trial and Death of Henry Wirz*, insisting,

"The South has nothing to reproach herself with in regard to the action of the Confederate authorities towards unfortunate prisoners." Mrs. Ashe took refuge behind the passive voice when she wrote, "Many wells were dug. Sheds and temporary shelters of planks were erected, and, as far as means permitted, every provision that human forethought could suggest was made for the health of the prisoners." Wells were indeed dug and shelters erected—but by the prisoners themselves.

Three years before Mrs. Ashe's book, the Georgia Division of the United Daughters of the Confederacy, simmering about all those Northern monuments, had set up their monument honoring Captain Henry Wirz. When retired General Chipman got wind of this, he wrote another book, *The Tragedy of Andersonville*,

Trial of Captain Henry Wirz, which he published in 1911. The War of the Rebellion had been over for forty-six years when the record was set straight once more. And it had been over for *fifty-six* years when the United Daughters of the Confederacy published a small book, *Henry Wirz and the Andersonville Prison,* subtitled *Facts and Figures vs. Myths and Misrepresentations,* by Mildred Lewis Rutherford of Athens, Georgia. She wrote with breathless indignation, unquenched by the passage of time: "There was never a trial more unjust in profane history, unless it was that of Thomas Cromwell, in English history, or of Mrs. Surratt, accused of complicity in the assassination of Abraham Lincoln."

The nation had been through two more wars when Henry Wirz was in the news again, in 1919. Three soldiers from a military encampment had defaced the Wirz monument by painting it with the German colors. One soldier was punished by the military; the other two were out of reach, having been discharged before they could be accused.

Various newspapers and magazines in the United States and France, in discussing how defeated Germany should be punished for war crimes, had dug up the case of Henry Wirz, in his grave for fifty-four years. There was talk at the Peace Conference of extraditing former Kaiser William for punishment. The French legal brief, justifying such action, cited the war crimes case of Henry Wirz. Leon Bourgeois, a former prime minister of France and first president of the League of Nations Council (and in 1920 winner of the Nobel Peace Prize), had quite a lot to say about Wirz and Andersonville. So did *Collier's, Frank Leslie's Magazine, The New York Times,* and other periodicals.

Mrs. Rutherford asked, "Is it any wonder that those boys of the North reading in France such vilifications of the South should attempt to desecrate that Wirz monument when they returned to America?"

The monument to Wirz was in the news again in 1956, when the Georgia legislature was asked for money to repair it. The legislature refused. These inscriptions are on the monument:

[ON THE FRONT:]

In Memory of Captain Henry Wirz, C.S.A. Born Zurich, Switzerland, 1822. Sentenced to death and executed at Washington, D.C., Nov. 10, 1865.

To rescue his name from the stigma attached to it by embittered prejudice, this shaft is erected by the Georgia Division, United Daughters of the Confederacy.

[SECOND SIDE:]

Discharging his duty with such humanity as the harsh circumstances of the times, and the policy of the foe permitted, Captain Wirz became at last the victim of misdirected popular clamor.

He was arrested in time of peace, while under the protection of a parole, tried by a military commission of a service to which he did not belong and condemned to ignominious death on charges of excessive cruelty to Federal prisoners. He indignantly spurned a pardon, proffered on condition that he would incriminate President Davis and thus exonerate himself from charges of which both were innocent.

[THIRD SIDE:]

"It is hard on our men held in Southern prisons not to exchange them, but it is humanity to those left in the ranks to fight our battles. At this particular time to release all rebel prisoners North, would insure Sherman's defeat and would compromise our safety here."

Aug. 18, 1864   ULYSSES S. GRANT

[FOURTH SIDE:]

"When time shall have softened passion and prejudice, when reason shall have stripped the mask of misrepresentation, then justice holding even her scales, will require much of past censure and praise to change places."

December, 1888   JEFFERSON DAVIS

34
Mariano Melgarejo

1818–1871

Are you frustrated in your efforts to achieve power? One man wanted to be president of Bolivia, so he "elected" himself.

Poor Bolivia! It has had a pretty rough time since liberation from Spanish rule in 1825. Home misrule has probably been more nationally satisfying than foreign misrule, but it hasn't meant much peace and tranquility for the peon. In its first hundred years, Bolivia had more than forty presidents (six of them assassinated in office) and 187 armed revolts. And nine different constitutions between 1828 (when the liberator of Bolivia, Sucre, left office) and 1871 (when Melgarejo fell).

More Bolivian presidents were proclaimed by the army than were elected by the voters, and an incumbent was more likely to be deposed and exiled than to finish his term in peace. Everybody seems to have his own list of presidents, since often two or three claimed to be top dog at the same time. It must be awfully trying for Bolivian kids to memorize the names of their illustrious chief executives.

Some presidents were civilians and some were soldiers, and historians have given the name *caudillo* to some from each group who were tyrants. *Caudillo* (as in Caudillo Franco) means a leader or chief with a charismatic character. And Bolivia, under the rule of "bullet and bayonet," has had more than its share. Some were pretty good, but most were awful, and the worst of the awful was a "barbarian *caudillo*" named Mariano Melgarejo.

Mariano was born on April 13, 1818, an unlucky day for his country. His father was a ne'er-do-well Spaniard and his mother a Quechua Indian. He was thus a *mestizo*, although his enemies said he was a *cholo* bastard, which was an impolite way of calling him a half-breed.

Some historians, even those who admit that Melgarejo was a bad hombre, have tried to explain away his barbarities by suggesting that with his delicate and sensitive nature he overreacted to being a real bastard. And some go so far as to justify his later murders, rapes, and general bad conduct on too much mother-love. That he was a spoiled brat may be true, but it is hard to understand why he ran away from home at age nine if he was so fond of his mother.

Anyway, young Mariano was nine years old when he joined the army as a packboy. Apparently he got his only schooling in the barracks. Although somewhere along the line he learned to read and write, most of what he picked up in the barracks was not the stuff of which good presidents are made. But he was brave, audacious, strong as an ox, and popular with the common soldiers and less cultured officers. His was a career of rapid promotions, and he soon became a general.

After running around as a minor revolutionary for some years, learning the ropes as it were, Melgarejo emerged as an important man in 1861 when he and an acquaintance named Manuel Belzú helped install Dr. José de Achá as president. But in 1865, both Melgarejo and Belzú threw out Achá. Each claimed the presidency, and Melgarejo let his troops loot the palace in Cochabamba to earn their gratitude, but even that gesture wasn't enough to persuade his men to attack Belzú. Melgarejo thought of killing himself, but a friend grabbed his pistol and said, "Let's try again!"

That was all he needed, and in a few days he rode into La Paz with only six soldiers as a guard. In the palace Belzú was celebrating the beginning of what he was sure would be a glorious era in the life of Bolivia. Outside, crowds were cheering the new president. Then someone spotted Melgarejo, and in silence the crowd opened a lane for Melgarejo to ride to the palace. Had he come, they said, to ask forgiveness?

Melgarejo jumped off his horse and entered the palace alone. Belzú, who by now had heard the news, came down the great stairway with one of his aides. The latter pulled a pistol on Melgarejo, who knocked it aside with one hand and shot the officer with the other. He then went up to Belzú and shot him dead with one bullet. With calm self-assurance, he stepped over Belzú's body, crossed the hall, and went out on the balcony to speak to the people below in the plaza. He shouted: "Belzú is dead! Now who are you shouting for?" The crowd was somewhat fickle; soon the capital and country rang with cheers of "Viva Melgarejo!" He was president of Bolivia.

What kind of a man was this Bolivian war lord with his own army? Aside from *"cholo* bastard" and "barbarian *caudillo"* he has been called the "Dictator of Dictators" and the "Scourge of God." With a bulky, squat body and small head, a sinister appearance, and a loud voice, he was a man who stood for no nonsense. That he was no coward was true, but some said it was the bravery and self-assurance from too much liquor. He hit the bottle pretty hard. Moreover, he was a mean drunk and acted in the most shameless fashion, turning the presidential palace into little more than a brothel, carrying on the wildest sexual orgies, shooting up the furnishings, and abusing his soldiers and women. One historian called him "generous, compassionate, sympathetic, and chivalrous to a fault" when he was sober, but the trouble was he was almost never sober.

Undoubtedly he had an animal magnetism that made him popular with soldiers and attractive to women. Early in life, he married Rosa Rojas, a girl of good family, but he soon got tired of her and left. "She was much too good for him," wrote one contemporary. He had two daughters by a mistress named Ignacia Beizaga, one of whom he married to a crony named José Aurelio Sánchez, the brother of the woman who was to become the love of his life.

Juana Sánchez was a raven beauty, and Melgarejo fell head over heels in love with her. Some said that she was a Jezebel, and it was true that she persuaded Melgarejo from time to time to get rid of people who crossed her. Others said that she was the only moderating influence in the brute's life and that when Melgarejo was unexpectedly merciful to some rebel it was all Juana's doing. There is the other theory, though, that he did sober up occasionally.

His barrack-room education had not left him much opportunity for scholarship, but it had left some peculiar ideas about people and events. He always admired Napoleon and argued how much better a general Napoleon was than Bonaparte! When the Franco-Prussian War broke out in 1870, it took some argument to prevent him from entering Bolivia in the lists as a French ally. But, finally convinced that Napoleon III was not the Napoleon he admired (who had died in 1821), he formally proclaimed Bolivia's neutrality. It was also a bit unnerving for his more educated associates to hear him discourse on Cicero, that "second-rate general of antiquity."

Melgarejo was president from 1865 to 1871. His captive press called him "the first citizen of the century" and the "first citizen of the Americas," but he was careful to go out only with four *rifleros* around him, armed to the teeth. He saturated the country with an army of spies. And he traveled around putting down revolts and dispensing his peculiar form of justice. Wherever Melgarejo was, said he, was the capital of Bolivia. In 1865, he moved the capital with him eleven times, and ten times in 1866. There weren't any revolts in 1867, so he stayed home, but there were six in 1868 and three in 1869. 1870 was another good year, and he was thrown out of office by a successful revolt in January, 1871. He had become a little more tyrannical, if that were possible, after each disturbance.

He was a military dictator and made no bones about it. On one occasion (before he got rid of Congress) he made a formal appearance to reply to one deputy's hope that constitutional rule would be restored. Melgarejo announced that he had just put the Constitution of 1861 in his left trouser pocket and the Constitution of 1868 in his right trouser pocket and that nobody was going to rule Bolivia but himself. So there.

On another occasion, while drunk, he proclaimed a constitution that he had never read. Usually, too, his ideas about constitutional government were directly expressed. He once shouted from the palace (drunk again) : "I'll rule in Bolivia as long as I feel like it, and anybody who tries to stop me will find himself strung-up in the nearest plaza."

As his term of office went on, he got noticeably worse, both politically and personally. He did away with councils, congresses, and constitutions right and left. He meddled with the church, confiscated the property of opponents, and finally proclaimed that all who opposed him were traitors to the country. Worst of all, he ordered the Indians to show proof of land ownership, and when they couldn't he confiscated their lands. He alienated parts of Bolivia to Brazil and Chile and introduced a worthless monetary system with the *"melgarejo"* (what else?) as the base unit.

On the international level, he got along well with United States agents, but not so with the British. Once, again drunk, he ordered the British Minister to Bolivia to be tied facing south on the back of a donkey heading north and led three times around the plaza in La Paz. News of this outrage reached London, and Queen Victoria demanded naval retaliation. But when it was pointed out that even the British navy couldn't get to Bolivia, the queen looked at a map of South America, crossed out the small landlocked country high in the Andes with two bold strokes, and announced: "Bolivia no longer exists." (Bolivian historians, at least, believe this story.)

Melgarejo was always broke. So was the country, and he had a devil of a time collecting taxes. In the palace, he had an old mattress thrown on the floor of one of the state rooms and received his ministers while seated on it. Drunk as usual, he once lamented to his finance minister: "A fine president I am. I haven't got any sheets. I'm going to Peru to get some." This Peru obsession was one of his hang-ups, and he was always being persuaded not to declare war on Peru. War was such a good reason, he said, for increasing taxes—which most people wouldn't pay anyway.

His treatment of the Indians became increasingly ferocious, and his land steals alienated most of the population. He also made another mistake that was to cost him dear: he alienated the army. The soldiers who had formerly idolized him found it harder and harder to stay loyal to this drunken bum. To visitors he would brag about his army's discipline and to prove it would order various aides and palace guards to jump out the windows. Those who obeyed broke legs and arms; those who didn't were shot. He had his own parlor games. He found it amusing to order soldiers to roll on the floor like dogs.

It was a wonder that even the long-suffering Bolivians put up with Melgarejo for so long. Finally, in January 1871, a military revolt gave him a bad conduct discharge from office, and he fled to Peru. His mistress Juana went with him, but they soon came to a parting of the ways. Broke as usual, he demanded back some of the gifts he had made her. She refused. He would show her, he said. Her brother José (Melgarejo's son-in-law) shot and killed him as he tried to break down the door to Juana's room.

35
Minnie Dean

1847–August 12, 1895

*Does it seem sometimes as if you can't
make a dollar without government
interference? Poor Minnie Dean, who
ran a baby farm, thought she could
get away with it.*

No powerful potentate was the lady
known as Minnie Dean, although
she arrogated to herself on several occasions the privilege of dispensing death. She was just a poor, weak woman who lived in
an obscure community at the far southern tip of New Zealand's
South Island. She lacked opportunity for villainy on a world-
renowned scale, but in her small corner she made the most of
such opportunity as she had. She specialized in adopting children
and then doing away with them.

Minnie—maiden name not recorded—was born in Edinburgh
in 1847, the daughter of a clergyman. At twenty-one she immi-
grated to New Zealand. At some time she contracted her first
marriage—she was known as Mrs. McCulloch—and at the end of
her life she expressed grief because she didn't know what had
become of her two daughters. That was typical of Minnie. During her career she mislaid several children belonging to other
people who didn't want them.

Then in 1872, when she was twenty-five, she married Charles
Dean, described as "an old settler." He might also be described
as remarkably inattentive to what went on in his own household.
The Deans had been married for fourteen years when they moved
to a twenty-two-acre place known as The Larches, at Winton,
nineteen miles from Invercargill. An estate with so elegant a
name should be pretty fine, but the Deans' house burned down
soon after they moved in, so Charles threw together a shack,

twelve by twenty-two feet, and added a lean-to. They had three rooms. These cramped quarters sheltered an astonishingly large number of persons, some of them very briefly.

For Minnie, devoted helpmeet of Charles, figured out a clever scheme that enabled her to contribute to the family exchequer. In those pre-Pill days, women were always having babies they didn't need. For a price that looks like a real bargain, Minnie Dean adopted them. Somehow there was quite a turnover of adopted children at her house. In 1893, even before the authorities became interested in Minnie's enterprises, Police Commissioner Hume called attention in an official report to a growing evil—baby farming. "It appears," said he, "that children, either by advertisement or otherwise, are placed in most unsuitable homes, where it is perfectly well understood that the sooner the child dies the better pleased all concerned will be." Children were taken off the mothers' hands for a premium of £6 to £20.

Minnie had already attracted the interest of the police on two occasions, but she went free both times. The first peculiar occurrence noted was in 1889 when a baby girl six months old, whom she adopted, became ill and died three days later. The officiating physician certified that the death of little May Irene was due to natural causes—convulsions.

Less than two years later, a baby girl six weeks old died. She was Bertha Currie. This time there was an inquest. The verdict was again death from natural causes, specifically inflammation of the lungs. Minnie testified that she did indeed take children into her home, in fact at the time she had ten of them, ranging from six weeks to eleven years of age. Three of them slept with her in one bed, four slept in boxes in her room, two slept in the lean-to with her husband, and one slept in the kitchen with Maggie Cameron, also identified as an adopted daughter. Maggie was a dressmaker who, in her fourteen years of residence with the Deans, remained as spectacularly ignorant of what was going on as Old Settler Charles himself.

The inquest on little Bertha Currie took place in 1891. Four years later, in April 1895, a detective named Livingstone interested himself in a classified advertisement in a newspaper: "A lady, country resident, wants infant to adopt. Comfortable home." It was a blind ad, with replies invited to "Mater" at the newspaper office. The detective checked and learned that a Miss Cameron, at The Larches, East Winton, had inserted the ad. But it wasn't really Miss Cameron; it was Minnie Dean using her lodger's name.

The next month a railroad guard noticed something queer: A lady passenger who had been carrying a baby got off the train with no baby in sight. He told the police, who discovered that a Mrs. Hornsby, embarrassed grandmother of a month-old girl baby born out of wedlock, had handed the child and some money over to Minnie Dean. On May 9 the police arranged a confrontation between Mrs. Hornsby, who exclaimed, "That's the woman I gave the baby to!" and Mrs. Dean, who sneered that she had never seen Mrs. Hornsby before in her life. One of the policemen present observed that Mrs. Dean seemed to be trying to hide something. It was a piece of baby clothing—and Mrs. Hornsby identified it as her grandchild's.

Mrs. Dean was arrested, and droves of policemen began to dig in the front-yard flower garden, which was stictly her province. She was especially proud of her dahlias and chrysanthemums. Her husband normally tended the vegetable plot out back, but Mrs. Dean always took care of the flowers. One of the searchers noticed that some cut flowers had been stuck into the ground. He started to remove the loose earth with his hands and found the bodies of *two* little girls buried side by side. The bigger one, about a year old, later identified as Dorothy Edith Carter, was wrapped in oilcloth. Eva Hornsby's tiny body was naked.

Charles Dean, who expressed utter horror at the discovery, was arrested too. The six children who at that time had been under the tender care of Minnie Dean were parceled out to more trustworthy foster parents.

The police hit the jackpot. They found a third small body, but this one was so bady decomposed that nobody could tell whether the child had been a boy or a girl.

Some very peculiar testimony developed at the inquest on little Dorothy Edith Carter in May, 1894. The child's grandmother had turned the baby over to a Mrs. Gray in April—and, lo, Mrs. Gray proved to be none other than Minnie Dean. A chemist testified that he had sold some laudanum to a woman who signed her name "M. Gray." Esther Wallis, age fifteen, who had lived with the Deans for five years (was *she* lucky to last so long!), had met Mrs. Dean off the train April 29, and helped carry a baby that that good-hearted lady had picked up the same day. This was Dorothy Edith. On May 2, Esther helped carry the baby to the railroad station. On May 4, Mrs. Dean returned, loaded down with things to carry: her handbag or suitcase, a tin hatbox that she had started out with, a brown paper parcel, some flowers and a parcel wrapped in a red shawl, but no baby. Esther carried the hatbox, which she noticed was a lot heavier than it had been. Mrs. Dean said it contained flower bulbs and dirt.

Other witnesses had seen Mrs. Dean on the train and had helped carry the heavy hatbox. One trainman had seen her get on carrying a baby and get off without a baby, but he was very busy and didn't check into the matter.

Eva Hornsby's inquest was held next. Mrs. Dean had accepted the child from the grandmother on May 2. The suspicion grew that toward the end of Minnie's train journey she had two dead babies with her, perhaps both in that tin hatbox, or maybe one was in one of the parcels.

The coroner's jury found that Eva Hornsby had been willfully murdered. Then the Carter baby's inquest was resumed. Traces of morphia—the right amount for the laudanum that "Mrs. Gray" had bought—were found in her kidneys. The verdict was that this baby had died of poison administered by Minnie Dean.

Both Charles and Minnie Dean were charged with murder, but Charles went free; all that could be found wrong with his actions was that he was married to his murderous wife and that he didn't keep track of the comings and goings of infant members of his own household.

An inquest was held on the long-buried and still unidentified third small body. Margaret Cameron, the dressmaker who had lived at the Deans' for fourteen years, testified that a boy named Cyril Scouller had lived there for three years but had vanished some five years earlier on a day when Mrs. Dean had sent her off to a neighbor's before breakfast with orders not to come back until after tea. Another child, called Henry, had disappeared one day while Margaret Cameron was away. And these weren't the only sudden, unquestioned disappearances. There had also been a William Phelan and a Sydney McKernan. The jury couldn't identify the skeleton but thought it might be William Phelan, although he had had fair, curly hair and the skeleton had fair, straight hair.

Minnie Dean was not tried for this killing. It wasn't necessary. On June 21 a jury found her guilty of the murder of little Dorothy Edith Carter. On August 12 of the same year, 1895,

Minnie Dean was hanged at Invercargill—the only woman ever hanged in New Zealand.

The grandmothers and other female relatives of the unwanted children who had been handed over to the tender mercies of Minnie Dean went scot free.

36
Liver-Eating Johnson

1823–January 21, 1900

Here's a man who figured out a spectacular revenge that left his enemies quite unable to take any retaliatory action.

John Johnston, who attained gory fame as Liver-Eating Johnson, was a sentimental fellow who treasured a keepsake as well as a grudge.

The keepsake was the first scalp he ever ripped off an Indian. That was in 1843, when young John was learning the fur-trapping trade and the bloody art of self-preservation up in the Rocky Mountains. His first teacher was a mountain man known as Old Hatcher. John was a sturdy young fellow in his early twenties then. He wasn't much of a talker, but he did show that scalp to somebody almost thirty years later. By that time he had taken hundreds more. He didn't save them all though.

John learned his business well, as is proved by the fact that he stayed alive long after it had deteriorated. The world had changed too by the time he died, in January 1900. The West had become downright civilized. In fact, it had turned so fancy that people whispered behind their hands, "Do you know what that man did once? He killed a Sioux Indian and pretended to eat his liver! That's why he's known as Liver-Eating Johnson."

That scare story was all wrong. It wasn't a single Sioux he killed; it was plural Crows. And there was no pretending about the quick lunch. He really ate their livers. Raw. You might say that he made eating the livers of assorted Crow Indians his hobby, as some people take up stamp collecting.

Another peculiarity was his method of fighting. Of course he used both knife and gun, like any proper frontiersman, but he also developed a fast, unexpected, and fatal kick. He normally wore two pairs of moccasins to protect his toes.

Young Johnson, having become prosperous in two or three seasons of trapping, took a wife, a comely Flathead girl whose name was Swan. He built a cabin for his bride, gave her a rifle and taught her to shoot it. She kept house (a couple of Ute scalps hanging on the wall helped make it homey) and taught him her language. He had done his courting—that is, his gift-giving to her father—in sign talk.

When winter came, he set off for a season of trapping—and he never saw his bride again. When he came home in the spring, he found her skull and scattered bones. He found another skull, a tiny one, all that was left of his child that had never been born.

The cabin had been ransacked and stripped of everything but a large hidden kettle with a hinged cover. John Johnson found an eagle feather with tribal decorations that gave him the clue he needed: The killers had been Crows.

He put the bones in the kettle which he hid in a crevice among rocks. He used to go back there sometimes to look at the bones and brood.

Within a few months, he was chillingly famous. He pursued Crow Indians, killed them, butchered them, and ate their livers. Even the boldest of his trapper friends never dared to march up to him and remark, "I was wondering, old hoss—how come you eat them there Injun livers?" As to his reason, your guess is as good as anyone's.

So the Crows called him Crow Killer, and the white population, such as it was, spoke of him as Liver-Eating Johnson. He dressed well in fringed buckskin garments supplied involuntarily by the same victims who provided his between-meal snacks. They didn't need clothes any more.

Sometimes the avenging Crows chased Liver-Eating Johnson; sometimes he chased them. Twenty of them were sent after him in revenge by the tribe. They lived long enough to regret it. One by one, over many years, he got all twenty, scalped them, and ate their livers—in a couple of instances, in plain view of other trappers who protested.

One day he made a mistake. On his way to visit the Flatheads, with a quantity of whiskey, he was captured by the Blackfeet. The Blackfeet were not bosom friends of the Crows—or of anybody except a couple of Canadian tribes—but they were especially not friendly to Flatheads. Therefore any friend of the Flatheads was no friend of theirs, and they thought it might be fun to turn this Flathead-lover over to the tender mercies of the Crows. Meanwhile, there was that captured load of whiskey that required immediate attention.

The Blackfeet tied Crow Killer's hands in front of him, after stripping him to the waist and taking away his weapons. They left him in a tepee with one young warrior to guard him while they took care of the whiskey.

Liver-Eating Johnson chewed the buckskin thong off his wrists. While his guard was refreshing himself with a cup of drinkin' liquor that someone had passed in from the noisy party outside, the captive kicked him. This incapacitated the young fellow. Johnson seized the guard's own knife, scalped him, and cut off one leg at the hip socket, while the unfortunate youth was still alive.

Johnson left quietly, without interrupting the drinking party, and set off into the snowy night. His camp and his partner were two hundred miles away. He had a knife, his flint and steel, his pants and moccasins, and a hindquarter of Blackfoot guard for rations. No blanket or shirt. Determination got him through.

One day he walked into the cabin where his partner was cozy by the fire, tossed down the leg—considerably hacked and gnawed by that time—and inquired, "How you fixed for meat?"

In February 1864, aged forty-one, John Johnston joined the Union Army in St. Louis. His fighting included the killing of various Indians, some of whom were, unfortunately, on the same side he was. He was reprimanded and had to give up his scalps. He was honorably discharged September 23, 1865. After he got back home to the West, he finished off his twentieth Crow, almost fourteen years after he began his vendetta.

After that, he buried the hatchet and became quite friendly with the Crows. They no doubt heaved a tribal sigh of relief. It was much better to have Liver-Eating Johnson for them than against them. He killed a considerable number of other Indians as the years went by, but not with the verve that had marked his bloody youth.

Ripples of the westward tide of emigration began to lap around his moccasins. He drifted from one mining camp to another. He became a deputy sheriff of Custer County, Montana, with headquarters at Coulson, forerunner of the city of Billings. He traveled some more, then was unanimously elected marshal of Red Lodge, a coal-mining town in Montana. Small boys adored him, with his tales of Indians, and he loved them.

In spite of his youthful diet of nourishing liver, his health failed when he was past seventy, and he spent his last few years in the Old Soldiers Home in Los Angeles. Liver-Eating Johnson, Crow Killer, died January 21, 1900, and is buried in the Veterans Cemetery there.

Nominations for Infamy

The blank space on this page, gentle reader, is for your own use. List below the people you know whom you consider eligible for the tag of bastard—"an obnoxious or nasty person." You'll feel better. You may wish to send the list to your "friends," but we advise you to tear out the page and burn it—with appropriate invocations and black magic—to avoid trouble. (You have enough trouble already, haven't you?) If, however, you borrowed this book, do not write in it, tear out pages, bend, staple, or mutilate. You'd better buy your own copy.

Bibliography

Parysatis

Durant, Will, *Our Oriental Heritage*, Vol. 1 in *The Story of Civilization*, 10 vols. New York: Simon and Schuster, 1942.

Herodotus, *The Persian Wars*. (tr. by George Rawlinson), in Modern Library Series. New York: Random House, 1942.

Plutarch's Lives, 11 vols. (tr. by Bernadotte Perrin). London: Heinemann, 1927.

Xenophon, *Anabasis* (tr. by C. L. Brownson). London: Heinemann, 1932.

Xenophon, *Cyropaedia*, 2 vols. (tr. by Walter Miller). London: Heinemann, 1914.

Shih Huang-Ti

Bashford, James W., *China, an Interpretation*. New York: The Abingdon Press, 1916.

Bodde, Derk, *China's First Unifier*. Leiden, Holland: E. J. Brill, 1938.

Cottrell, Leonard, *The Tiger of Ch'in*. New York: Rinehart and Winston, 1962.

Eberhard, Wolfram, *A History of China*. Berkeley: University of California Press, 1966.

Grousset, René, *The Rise and Splendour of the Chinese Empire*. Berkeley and Los Angeles: University of California Press, 1953.

Latourette, Kenneth Scott, *The Chinese*, 2 vols. New York: The Macmillan Company, 1934.

MacNair, Harley Farnsworth, *China*. Berkeley: University of California Press, 1946.

Seeger, Elizabeth, *The Pageant of Chinese History*. New York: Longmans, Green and Company, 1944.

Sulla

Appian, *Roman History* (tr. by Horace White), 4 vols. London: Heinemann, 1913.

Cicero, *The Speeches* (tr. by J. H. Freece). London: Heinemann, 1930.

Durant, Will, *Caesar and Christ*, Vol. III in *The Story of Civilization*, 10 vols. New York: Simon and Schuster, 1944.

Heitland, W. E., *The Roman Republic*, 3 vols. Cambridge: University Press, 1923.

Holmes, T. R. E., *The Roman Republic*, 3 vols. Oxford: The Clarendon Press, 1923.

Lintott, A. W., *Violence in Republican Rome*. Oxford: Clarendon Press, 1968.

Plutarch, *The Lives of the Noble Grecians and Romans* (tr. by Dryden and revised by A. H. Clough). Chicago: Encyclopaedia Britannica, 1952.

Sallust, *The Conspiracy of Catiline and the War of Jugurtha* (tr. by T. Haywood). New York: AMS Press, 1967.

Smith, R. E., *The Failure of the Roman Republic*. Cambridge: University Press, 1955.

Syme, Ronald, *Sallust*. Berkeley: University of California Press, 1964.

Mithridates

Duggan, Alfred, *He Died Old: Mithradates Eupator, King of Pontus*. London: Faber and Faber, 1958. (American ed.: *King of Pontus*. New York: Coward-McCann, 1959.)

The Cambridge Ancient History, Vol. IX, Chapters V and VIII. Cambridge, 1932.

Gaius, called Caligula

Baring-Gould, S., *The Tragedy of the Caesars*. London: Methuen & Co., Ltd., 8th ed., 1923.

Cassius Dio Cocceianus, *Dio's Roman History*, Vol. 7 (translated by Earnest Cary). New York: G. P. Putnam's Sons, The Loeb Classical Library, 1924. (Harvard University Press.)

Ferrero, Guglielmo, *The Women of the Caesars*, New York: The Century Co., 1911.

Josephus, Flavius, "The Antiquities of the Jews," in *The Works of Flavius Josephus* (translated by William Whiston). Philadelphia: Henry T. Coates & Co., no date.

Lissner, Ivar, *The Caesars: Might and Madness*. New York: G. P. Putnam's Sons, 1958.

Suetonius Tranquillus, Gaius, *The Twelve Caesars* (translated by Robert Graves). Baltimore: Penguin Books, 1957.

Tacitus, Cornelius, *The Complete Works of Tacitus* (translated by Alfred John Church and William Jackson Brodribb). New York: The Modern Library, 1942.

Nero

Cassius Dio Cocceianus, *Dio's Roman History*, Vol. 8 (translated by Earnest Cary). New York: G. P. Putnam's Sons, The Loeb Classical Library, 1924. (Harvard University Press.)

Plinius Secundus, Gaius (Pliny the Elder), *Natural History*, Book XI (translated by H. Packham). Cambridge: Harvard University, The Loeb Classical Library, 1940.

Suetonius Tranquillus, Gaius, *The Twelve Caesars* (translated by Robert Graves). Baltimore: Penguin Books, 1957.

Tacitus, Cornelius, *The Complete Works of Tacitus* (translated by Alfred John Church and William Jackson Brodribb). New York: The Modern Library, 1942.

Weigall, Arthur, *Nero, the Singing Emperor of Rome.* New York: G. P. Putnam's Sons, 1930.

Commodus

Balsdon, J. P. V. D., *Life and Leisure in Ancient Rome.* New York: McGraw-Hill Book Company, 1969.

Cassius Dio Cocceianus, *Dio's Roman History,* Vol. 9 (translated by Earnest Cary). New York: G. P. Putnam's Sons, The Loeb Classical Library, 1924. (Harvard University Press.)

Lissner, Ivar, *The Caesars: Might and Madness.* New York: G. P. Putnam's Sons, New York, 1958.

Attila the Hun

Bury, J. B., *The Invasion of Europe by the Barbarians.* London: The Macmillan Company, 1928.

———, *History of the Later Roman Empire,* 2 vols. London: The Macmillan Company, 1923.

Gibbon, Edward, *The Decline and Fall of the Roman Empire,* 2 vols. New York: The Modern Library, 1932.

McGovern, William M., *The Early Empires of Central Asia.* Chapel Hill, North Carolina: University of North Carolina Press, 1939.

Mierow, Charles Christopher, *The Gothic History of Jordanes.* Cambridge, England: Speculum Historiale, 1966.

Owen, Francis, *The Germanic People.* New York: Bookman Associates, 1960.

Thompson, E. A., *History of Attila and the Huns.* Oxford University Press, 1948.

Vogt, Joseph, *The Decline of Rome.* London: Weidenfeld and Nicolson, 1967.

Webb, Robert N., *Attila, King of the Huns.* New York: F. Watts, 1965.

Fredegunda and Brunechildis

Fourth Book of the Chronicle of Fredegar (tr. by J. M. Wallace-Hadrill). New York: Thomas Nelson and Sons, Ltd., 1960.

Funck-Brentano, Fr., *The National History of France, the Earliest Times* (tr. by E. F. Buckley). New York: AMS Press, 1967.

Gregory, Bishop of Tours, *History of the Franks* (tr. by E. Brehaut). New York: W. W. Norton and Company, 1969.

Kitchin, G. W. *A History of France,* 3 vols. Oxford: Clarendon Press, 1899.

Latouche, Robert, *Caesar to Charlemagne* (tr. by J. Nicholson). London: Phoenix House; New York: Barnes and Noble, 1968.

Michelet, Jules, *History of France,* 2 vols. (tr. by G. H. Smith). New York: D. Appleton and Company, 1882.

Moreton, MacDonald, J. R., *A History of France,* 3 vols. New York: The Macmillan Company, 1915.

Wallace-Hadrill, J. M. *The Long-Haired Kings.* New York: Barnes and Noble, Inc., 1962.

Marozia the Pope-Maker

Barry, William, *The Papal Monarchy.* New York: G. P. Putnam's Sons, 1906.

Brusher, Joseph S., *Popes Through the Ages.* Princeton: D. Van Nostrand Company, Inc., 1964.

Chamberlin, E. R., *The Bad Popes.* New York: The Dial Press, 1969.

Cotterill, H. B., *Medieval Italy.* New York: Frederick A. Stokes Company, 1915.

John, Eric (ed.), *The Popes.* New York: Hawthorn Books, Inc., 1964.

Kühner, Hans, *Encyclopedia of the Papacy.* New York: Philosophical Library, 1958.

Basil II Bulgaroctonus

Byron, Robert, *The Byzantine Achievement, an Historical Perspective,* A.D. *330–1453.* New York: Alfred A. Knopf, 1929.

Diehl, Charles, *Byzantine Empresses.* New York: Alfred A. Knopf, 1963.

———, *Byzantium: Greatness and Decline.* New Brunswick, New Jersey: Rutgers University Press, 1957.

Eckstein-Diener, Bertha, *Imperial Byzantium* (tr. by Eden and Cedar Paul). Boston: Little, Brown and Company, 1938.

Finlay, George, *History of the Byzantine Empire.* Edinburgh: William Blackwood and Sons, 1856.

Jenkins, Romilly, *Byzantium: The Imperial Centuries.* New York: Random House, 1966.

Hussey, J. W., *Church and Learning in the Byzantine Empire.* New York: Russell and Russell, Inc., 1963.

Oman, C. W. C., *The Story of the Byzantine Empire.* London: G. P. Putnam's Sons, 1893.

Ostrogorski, George, *History of the Byzantine State.* New Brunswick, New Jersey: Rutgers University Press, 1957.

Runciman, Steven, *Byzantine Civilisation.* London: Edward Arnold and Company, 1936.

King William Rufus

Costain, Thomas B., *The Conquerors: The Pageant of England.* Garden City: Doubleday & Company, Inc., 1949.

Freeman, Edward A., *The Reign of William Rufus and the Accession of Henry the First,* 2 vols. Oxford: Clarendon Press, 1882.

Ross Williamson, Hugh, *The Arrow and the Sword.* London: Faber and Faber, Ltd., 1955.

King John of England

Appleby, John T., *John, King of England.* New York: Alfred A. Knopf, 1959.

Costain, Thomas B., *The Conquerors: The Pageant of England.* Garden City: Doubleday & Company, Inc., 1949.

D'Auvergne, Edmund B., *John, King of England.* London: Grayson & Grayson, 1954.

Kelly, Amy, *Eleanor of Aquitaine and the Four Kings*. Cambridge: Harvard University Press, 1951.

Norgate, Kate, *John Lackland*. London: Macmillan and Co., Ltd., 1902.

Percy, Thomas, *Reliques of Ancient English Poetry*, Vol. 2. New York: E. P. Dutton & Co., Inc., Everyman's Library, 1938.

Sir James Douglas

Brown, P. Hume, *History of Scotland to the Present Time*, 3 vols. Cambridge, England: The University Press, 1911.

Burton, John Hill, *The History of Scotland from Agricola's Invasion to the Extinction of the Last Jacobite Insurrection*, 2 vols. Edinburgh: William Blackwood and Sons, 1905.

Dickinson, William C., *Scotland from the Earliest Times to 1603*. London: Thomas Nelson and Sons, Ltd., 1961.

Froissart Chronicles, 6 vols. (tr. by Sir John Bourchier), Lord Berners annis 1523–25. New York: AMS Press, Inc., 1967.

Mackenzie, Agnes Mure, *Robert Bruce King of Scots*. New York: The Macmillan Company, 1935.

————, *The Kingdom of Scotland*. London: W. R. Chambers, Ltd., 1948.

Maxwell, Sir Herbert, *Robert the Bruce and the Struggle for Scottish Independence*. New York, London: G. P. Putnam's Sons, 1897.

Mitchison, Rosalind, *A History of Scotland*. London: Methuen and Co., Ltd., 1970.

Scott, Sir Walter, *Tales of a Grandfather from Scottish History*. New York: George Routledge and Sons, no date.

Skeat, Rev. Walter (ed.), *The Bruce by Master John Barbour*, 2 vols. London: N. Trubner and Company, 1874.

Terry, Charles S., *A History of Scotland*. Cambridge, England: The University Press, 1920.

The House of Visconti

Burckhardt, Jacob, *The Civilisation of the Renaissance in Italy*. London: Swan Sonnenschein, 1909.

Butler, W. F. T., *The Lombard Communes*. London: Unwin, 1906.

Collins, Ross William, *A History of Medieval Civilization in Europe*. Boston: Ginn and Company, 1936.

Collison-Morley, L., *The Story of the Sforzas*. New York: Dutton, 1934.

Duruy, Victor. *The History of the Middle Ages*. New York: Holt, 1904.

Hallam, Henry, *View of the State of Europe During the Middle Ages*. New York: American, 1871.

Lodge, Eleanor C., *The End of the Middle Ages, 1273–1453*. New York: Macmillan, 1910.

Prescott, Orville, *Princes of the Renaissance*. New York: Random House, 1959.

Schevill, Ferdinand, *History of Florence from the Founding of the City Through the Renaissance*. New York: Ungar, 1961.

Sedgwick, Henry D., *A Short History of Italy (476–1900)*. Boston: Houghton-Mifflin, 1905.

Sismondi, J. C. L., *History of the Italian Republics in the Middle Ages*. London: Routledge, 1906.

Thompson, James W., *Economic and Social History of Europe in the Later Middle Ages (1300–1530)*. New York: Century, 1931.

Gilles de Rais

Gabory, Émile, *Alias Bluebeard: The Life and Death of Gilles de Raiz* (tr. by Alvah C. Bessie). New York: Brewer & Warren, Inc., 1930.

Lewis, Dominic B. W., *The Soul of Marshal Gilles de Raiz*. London: Eyre and Spottiswoode, 1952.

Vizetelly, Ernest Alfred, *Bluebeard*. London: Chatto & Windus, 1902.

Wilson, Thomas, *Blue-Beard*. New York: G. P. Putnam's Sons, 1899.

Winwar, Frances, *The Saint and the Devil: Joan of Arc and Gilles de Rais*. New York: Harper & Bros., 1948.

Tomás de Torquemada

Birmingham, Stephen, *The Grandees*. New York: Harper & Row, 1971.

Burke, Ulick R., *A History of Spain from the Earliest Times to the Death of Ferdinand the Catholic*. London: Longmans, Green, and Co., 1900.

Kamen, Henry, *The Spanish Inquisition*. New York: The New American Library, 1965.

Sabatini, Rafael, *Torquemada and the Spanish Inquisition*. London: Stanley Paul and Co., 1913.

Smith, Charles Merrill, *When the Saints Go Marching Out*. Garden City: Doubleday & Company, Inc., 1969.

The Borgias

Beuf, Carlo, *Cesare Borgia, the Machiavellian Prince*. Toronto and New York: Oxford University Press, 1942.

Burchard, John, *The Diary of John Burchard of Strasbourg* (tr. by Arnold Harris Mathew). London: Francis Griffiths, 1910.

Burchardus, Johannes, *Pope Alexander VI and His Court*, edited by Dr. F. L. Glaser. New York: Nicholas L. Brown, 1921.

Chamberlin, E. R., *The Bad Popes*. New York: The Dial Press, Inc., 1969.

Collison-Morley, L., *The Story of the Borgias*. London: George Routledge & Sons, Ltd., 1932.

Garner, John Leslie, *Caesar Borgia, a Study of the Renaissance*. London: T. F. Unwin, Ltd., 1912.

Gregorovius, Ferdinand, *Lucretia Borgia* (tr. by John Leslie Garner). London: John Murray, 1904.

Machiavelli, Niccolò, *The Prince* (tr. by Luigi Ricci). New York: The New American Library, 1952.

——, *The Prince* (tr. by Ninian Hill Thompson). Oxford: University Press, 1913.

Portigliotti, Giuseppe, *The Borgias* (tr. by Bernard Miall). New York: Alfred A. Knopf, 1928.

Sabatini, Rafael, *The Life of Cesare Borgia*. New York: Brentano's, 1923.

Selim I, the Grim

Davey, Richard, *The Sultan and His Subjects*, 2 vols. London: Chapman and Hall, Ltd., 1897.

Davis, William S., *A Short History of the Near East*. New York: The Macmillan Company, 1923.

Downey, Fairfax, *The Grande Turke*. London: Stanley Paul and Company, 1928.

Eversley, Lord, *The Turkish Empire from 1288 to 1914*. London: T. F. Unwin, Ltd., 1924.

Lybyer, Albert H., *The Government of the Ottoman Empire in the Time of Suleiman the Magnificent*. Cambridge, Massachusetts: Harvard University Press, 1913.

Marriott, J. A. R., *The Eastern Question. An Historical Study in European Diplomacy*. Oxford: The Clarendon Press, 1918.

Shotwell, James T., and Francis Deak, *Turkey at the Straits*. New York: The Macmillan Company, 1940.

Sawney Beane

Brown, John, *The Historical Gallery of Criminal Portraitures, Foreign and Domestic*. Manchester: J. Gleave, 1823.

Crockett, Samuel Rutherford, *The Gray Man* (fiction). New York: Harper & Bros., 1896.

The History of Sawney Beane and His Family, Robbers and Murderers. (Pamphlet, no author's name, place of publication not stated.) S. & T. Martin, 1810.

Roughead, William, *Rogues Walk Here*. London: Cassell and Company, Ltd., 1934.

Scottish Notes and Queries, 2nd series, Vol. 8, No. 9, March 1907.

The Duke of Alba

Cadoux, Cecil J., *Philip of Spain and the Netherlands*. London: Lutterworth Press, 1947.

Geyl, P., *The Revolt of the Netherlands*. London: Williams and Norgate, Ltd., 1932.

Grierson, Edward, *The Fatal Inheritance*. Garden City, New York: Doubleday and Company, Inc., 1969.

Hume, Martin A. S., *Spain: Its Greatness and Decay, 1497–1788*. Cambridge: University Press, 1898.

Lynch, John, *Spain Under the Habsburgs*, 2 vols. New York: Oxford University Press, 1964.

Mariejol, Jean H., *Philip II, the First Modern King*. New York: Harper and Brothers, 1933.

Motley, John L., *The Rise of the Dutch Republic*, 2 vols. New York: A. L. Burt Company, no date.

Oman, Sir Charles, *The Sixteenth Century*. New York: E. P. Dutton and Company, Inc., 1937.

Squire, Jack C., *William the Silent*. New York: The Baker and Taylor Company, 1912.

Wedgwood, C. V., *William the Silent*. New Haven: Yale University Press, 1944.

Ivan IV, the Terrible

Berry, Lloyd E., and Robert O. Crummey (eds.), *Rude and Barbarous Kingdom: Russia in the Accounts of Sixteenth Century English Voyages*. Madison, Wisconsin: University of Wisconsin Press, 1968.

Eckardt, Hans von, *Ivan the Terrible*. New York: Alfred A. Knopf, 1949.

Fletcher, Giles. *Of the Russe Commonwealth* (ed. by Albert J. Schmidt). Ithaca, New York: Cornell University Press, 1966.

Grey, Ian, *Ivan the Terrible*. Philadelphia: J. B. Lippincott Company, 1964.

Hingley, Ronald, *The Tsars 1533–1917*. New York: The Macmillan Company, 1968.

Kliuchevsky, V. O. *A History of Russia*, Vol. 2, 5 vols. (tr. by J. M. Hogarth). London: J. M. Dent and Company; New York: E. P. Dutton and Company, 1912.

Lamb, Harold, *The March of Muscovy*. Garden City, New York: Doubleday, 1948.

Waliszewski, K., *Ivan le Terrible*. Paris: Librairie Plon, 1904.

Lord Chief Justice George Jeffreys

Ashley, Maurice, *Charles II: The Man and the Statesman*. New York: Praeger Publishers, 1971.

Parry, Sir Edward Abbott, *The Bloody Assize*. New York: Dodd, Mead and Company, 1929.

Pearson, Hesketh, *Merry Monarch, The Life and Likeness of Charles II*. New York: Harper & Brothers, 1960.

Wheatley, Dennis, *"Old Rowley": A Private Life of Charles II*. New York: E. P. Dutton & Co., Inc., 1934.

Blackbeard the Pirate, Anne Bonny, and Mary Read

[Ellms, Charles,] *The Pirates Own Book*. Salem: The Marine Research Society, 1924. Reprint of 1837 edition.

Gosse, Philip, *The History of Piracy*. New York: Tudor Publishing Company, 1934.

The History of the Lives and Bloody Exploits of the Most Noted Pirates; Their Trials and Executions. (No author.) New York: Empire State Book Company, 1926 reprint.

Johnson, Captain Charles, *A General History of the Pirates* (ed. by Philip Gosse), 2 vols. Kensington: The Cayme Press, 1925. Reprint of *A General History of the Robberies & Murders of the Most Notorious Pyrates*, 1724.

Rankin, Hugh F., *The Golden Age of Piracy*. Williamsburg: Colonial Williamsburg, Inc., 1969.

Henry Bouquet

Eckert, Allan W., *The Conquerors*. Boston: Little-Brown and Company, 1970.

Flexner, James T., *Mohawk Baronet—Sir William Johnson of New York.* New York: Harper and Brothers, 1959.

Hagan, William T., *American Indians.* Chicago: University of Chicago Press, 1961.

Kent, Donald H., letter to Knollenberg, January 19, 1955, published in *Mississippi Valley Historical Review,* Vol. 41, No. 4, pp. 762–763.

Knollenberg, Bernhard, "General Amherst and Germ Warfare," in *Mississippi Valley Historical Review,* Vol. 41, No. 3, pp. 489–494.

The Mississippi Valley Historical Review, Volume 41, June 1954 to March 1955, Mississippi Valley Historical Society, published quarterly.

Pound, Arthur, *Johnson of the Mohawks.* New York: Macmillan, 1930.

Van Every, Dale, *Forth to the Wilderness, the First American Frontier 1754–1774.* New York: William Morrow and Company, 1961.

Webster, J. Clarence, *The Journal of Jeffrey Amherst.* Toronto, Canada: The Ryerson Press; Chicago: University of Chicago Press, 1931.

Jean Baptiste Carrier

Acton, John E., *Lectures on the French Revolution.* London: Macmillan and Company, 1920.

Carrier, E. H., *Correspondence of Jean Baptiste Carrier.* New York: John Lane Company, 1920.

Mathiez, Albert, *The French Revolution.* New York: Russell and Russell Inc., 1962.

————, *After Robespierre, the Thermidorean Reaction.* New York: Alfred A. Knopf, Inc., 1929.

Palmer, R. R., *Twelve Who Ruled.* London: Princeton University Press, 1941.

Sirich, John B., *The Revolutionary Committees in the Departments of France, 1793–1794.* Cambridge: Harvard University Press, 1943.

Taine, Hippolyte, *The French Revolution,* 3 vols. New York: Henry Holt and Company, 1878–1885.

Whitham, J. Mills, *A Biographical History of the French Revolution.* London: Routledge, 1930.

The Marquis de Sade

Bloch, Iwan, *Marquis de Sade: His Life and Works,* translated by James Bruce. New York: Brittany Press, 1948.

Gear, Norman, *The Divine Demon, a Portrait of the Marquis de Sade.* London: Frederick Muller Limited, 1963.

Summers, Montague, *The Marquis de Sade, a Study in Algolagnia.* London: British Society for the Study of Sex Psychology, 1920.

Micajah and Wiley Harpe

Coates, Robert M., *The Outlaw Years.* New York: Pennant Books, 1954.

Daniels, Jonathan, *The Devil's Backbone: The Story of the Natchez Trace.* New York: McGraw-Hill Book Company, 1962.

Rothert, Otto A., *The Outlaws of Cave-in-Rock.* Cleveland: The Arthur H. Clark Company, 1924.

Ali Pasha

Christowe, Stoyan, *The Lion of Yanina.* New York: Modern Age Books, 1941.

Plomer, William, *The Diamond of Jannina, Ali Pasha 1741–1832.* New York: Taplinger Publishing Company, 1970.

Shaka

Bryant, A. T., *A History of the Zulu and Neighbouring Tribes.* Cape Town: C. Struik, 1964.

Morris, Donald R., *The Washing of the Spears.* New York: Simon and Schuster, 1965.

Ritter, E. A., *Shaka Zulu, the Rise of the Zulu Empire.* London: Longmans Green and Co., Ltd., 1960.

Henry Plummer

Barsness, Larry, *Gold Camp.* New York: Hastings House, 1962.

Dimsdale, Professor Thomas J., *The Vigilantes of Montana, or Popular Justice in the Rocky Mountains.* (Various editions.)

Langford, Nathaniel Pitt, *Vigilante Days and Ways.* (Various editions.)

Henry Wirz

Ashe, S[arah] W., *The Trial and Death of Henry Wirz.* Raleigh: E. M. Uzzell & Co., Printers, 1908.

Chipman, General N. P., *The Horrors of Andersonville Rebel Prison: Trial of Henry Wirz.* San Francisco: The Bancroft Company, 1891.

———, *The Tragedy of Andersonville, Trial of Captain Henry Wirz.* San Francisco: The Blair-Murdock Company, 1911.

Confederate Veteran, Vol. 28, No. 6, Nashville, June 1919.

Davis, Jefferson, *Andersonville and Other War-Prisons.* New York: Belford Company, 1890.

Futch, Ovid L., *History of Andersonville Prison.* Gainesville: University of Florida Press, 1968.

Hesseltine, William Best, *Civil War Prisons: A Study in War Psychology.* Columbus: The Ohio State University Press, 1930.

McElroy, John, *This Was Andersonville,* edited by Roy Meredith. New York: Bonanza Books, 1957.

Rutherford, Mildred Lewis, *Facts and Figures vs. Myths and Misrepresentations: Henry Wirz and the Andersonville Prison.* Athens: published by the author, 1921.

Rutman, Darrett B., "The War Crimes and Trial of Henry Wirz," *Civil War History,* Iowa City, Vol. 6, 1960.

Stibbs, John Howard, *Andersonville and the Trial of Henry Wirz.* Iowa City: The Clio Press, 1911.

Strode, Hudson, *Jefferson Davis, Tragic Hero.* New York: Harcourt, Brace & World, 1964.

The Trial of Henry Wirz, Executive Document No. 23, Vol. 8, Second

Session 40th Congress, House of Representatives. Washington: Government Printing Office, 1868.

Mariano Melgarejo

Arciniegas, Germán, *Latin America: A Cultural History*. New York: Alfred A. Knopf, 1966.

Argüedas, Alcides, *Los Caudillos Bárbaros*. Barcelona: Luis Tasso, 1969.

————, *Historia General de Bolivia, 1809–1921*. La Paz: Futuro, 1967.

Crow, John A., *The Epic of Latin America*. New York: Doubleday and Company, 1946.

Dawson, Thomas C., *The South American Republics*, 2 vols. New York: G. P. Putnam's Sons, 1904.

Fagg, John Edwin, *Latin America, A General History*. 2nd ed., New York: The Macmillan Company, 1969.

Wilgus, A. Curtis (ed.), *South American Dictators*, Vol. 5 in *Studies in Hispanic American Affairs*, 5 vols. Washington, D.C.: The George Washington University Press, 1937.

Minnie Dean

Dyne, Dudley G., *Famous New Zealand Murders*. Auckland: Collins Bros. & Co., Ltd., 1969.

Hanlon, Alfred Charles, *Random Recollections: Notes on a Lifetime at the Bar*. Dunedin, N.Z.: Otago Daily Times and Witness Newspapers Co., Ltd., 1939.

Liver-Eating Johnson

Randall, L. W. "Gay," *Footprints Along the Yellowstone*. San Antonio: The Naylor Company, 1961.

Thorp, Raymond W., and Robert Bunker, *Crow Killer: The Saga of Liver-Eating Johnson*. Bloomington: Indiana University Press, 1958.